A Wideness in God's Mercy

A Wideness in God's Mercy

The Finality of Jesus Christ in a World of Religions

Clark H. Pinnock

Zondervan Publishing House
Academic and Professional Books
Grand Rapids, Michigan

A Division of HarperCollinsPublishers

A Wideness in God's Mercy
Copyright © 1992 by Clark H. Pinnock

Requests for information should be addressed to:
Zondervan Publishing House
Academic and Professional Books
Grand Rapids, Michigan 49530

Library of Congress Cataloging-in-Publication Data

Pinnock, Clark H., 1937-
    A wideness in God's mercy : the finality of Jesus Christ in a
world of religions / Clark H. Pinnock.
        p.   cm.
    Includes bibliographical references and index.
    ISBN 0-310-53591-3
    1. Christianity and other religions. 2. Jesus Christ—Person and
offices. 3. Religions. I. Title.
BR127.P56 1992
261.2—dc20   91-32906
                                                                  CIP

Edited by Leonard G. Goss
Designed by Bob Hudson and L. G. Goss
Cover designed by Art Jacobs

Printed in the United States of America

92 93 94 95 96 / **AM** / 10 9 8 7 6 5 4 3 2 1

Contents

85133

Introduction

*B*y *all accounts* the meaning of Christ's lordship in a religiously plural world is one of the hottest topics on the agenda of theology in the nineties. How will we communicate the gospel in a pluralist setting? The problem will become even more central if plans for a Parliament of World Religions, proposed for Chicago in 1993 to commemorate the 1893 gathering, go through. I believe this issue is second to none in importance for Christian theology.[1]

For two millennia the church has proclaimed the finality of Jesus Christ as the Savior of the world, but recently people have been asking exactly how this works. Does it mean that other religions lack significance? Does it mean we should ignore or seek to displace them? Should we see ourselves as fellow pilgrims on different paths to truth no mortal can fully grasp? A whole set of questions, new at least in the sense of urgency, have become of central importance to us in the nineties.[2]

NOTHING NEW UNDER THE SUN?

In one sense religious pluralism is not a new problem because there has always been a great diversity of paths claiming to lead to God. Prophets and sages have made a variety of divergent claims about ultimate reality and human destiny over the centuries. Often contradicting one other, they have spoken of truths thought to be decisive for human salvation. Millions, many noble and saintly among them, have ascribed to their various doctrines and behaviors.

Early Christians were aware of the existence of other claims in competition with their own. Given their small numbers, they must have felt overwhelmed at times by the cafeteria of religious options that confronted them in the Roman/Near Eastern world. But they were not intimidated or afraid to proclaim Jesus as Lord of the universe, even in the face of a bewildering confusion of conflicting truth claims often accompanied by violent persecution. On the contrary, belief in the finality of Jesus Christ was among their most precious beliefs. We need to discover again how they were able to do this.

Religious pluralism, it should be noted, is not just a problem for Christians. Other religions have to deal with pluralism as well. Any religion wanting to make an impact on the world outside its home territory will face many of the same pressures and anxieties we do. A religion in the modern world can scarcely avoid encountering other faiths or hide long from skeptical questions greeting their central beliefs. People will challenge not only the sole mediation of Jesus Christ, they will also wonder if Muhammad is the seal of the prophets, if the God of the East is really beyond good and evil, if Buddha-consciousness can actually address modern life and society. All religions have difficult questions to answer, not just Christianity. All of them have to explain how they view outsiders, people who have not heard, or do not accept their distinctive truth claims. The relationship between the universal and the particular is a puzzling problem for any world-class religion. If misery loves company, Christians can console themselves with the fact that they are not alone in facing up to this problem.[3]

THEN WHY DOES IT FEEL NEW?

Although the challenge of religious pluralism has been previously encountered in history, there are some factors in the modern situation that make the problem feel like a new one for Christians. One feature of Western experience which gives it a special twist is the phenomenon of the global village. Due to improved communications, the world has become smaller, so that we face a new reality in which we have moved closer together. In past centuries, one could not speak of world history as such. Each nation and civilization had its own story, living more or less unto itself, existing quite independently of the others. What outsiders may have believed and practiced was their business—it did not need to concern other groups, even if they happened to know about it.

This small world is fast disappearing. Increasingly all nations are inhabiting a single world they have to share in common. Living in isolation has become impossible. Countries are compelled, for example, to belong to trading blocks and to form strategic alliances. They are being impacted by people movements (often unwillingly), and the electronic media make it impossible to hide away in a corner. The twentieth century has seen a historic leap forward (not that the world was necessarily ready for it, spiritually or morally!) into what is fast becoming a single-world culture. Humanity is becoming one again and the situation is developing in which we will either learn how to get along with one another or simply perish.[4]

This means that religions, which represent an important dimension of world culture, are going to have to become genuinely global if they plan to compete or even survive. They will be forced to enter into new kinds of relationships with the other faiths, whether they want to or not. As Hans Küng says: "For the first time in world history it is impossible for any one religion to exist in splendid isolation and ignore the others."[5] Whether they choose to or not, religions will not be able to avoid contact with each other. It has become their destiny to live together in one world. Not a decision we were free to make, history and the providence of God have forced it upon us. Together we will have to face up to urgent issues of peace, justice, truth, and religious freedom. We will have to talk together, cooperate, and trust one another, whatever our inclinations may be. As Küng has also said: "Discussion with the other religions is actually essential to survival, necessary for the sake of peace in the world."[6]

Religious pluralism feels like a new challenge for many of us because we have been culturally sheltered in the West. Unlike fellow believers in the two-thirds world for whom pluralism is a fact of daily life, it is a new experience for us to be meeting Sikhs, Muslims, and Buddhists in our streets and shops. Globalization has come home to North America. We are experiencing it ourselves for the first time and we will have to become more global in our thinking.

There is another factor which makes religious pluralism feel newly challenging today, namely, the relativistic mindset of late modernity. A plurality of religions is not new—that has always existed. What is new is an ideology of pluralism which celebrates choice in and of itself and claims that choice is good no matter what is chosen. In this climate any diversity of choice is tolerable except one:

the mentality that believes that some choices are right and others wrong, some beliefs true and others false. That cannot be tolerated.

Relativism, then, is a new attitude pervading Western society that questions the nature of truth and makes one feel guilty for believing what our communities have believed for centuries. Instead of referring to reality, truth is now viewed as a function of where one is born. Choice is good in itself. Beliefs and customs of any culture are right ones for that culture, not necessarily valid for others. Religious beliefs are viewed as human constructions or useful fictions put into place to make life easier, but not to be accepted as objectively true or false hypotheses. It is a climate in which it is natural to think of religions as different but equally valid paths to salvation, equally valid responses to the Real. Religious claims are only true in the reduced sense of being existentially meaningful, not in the sense of making cognitive claims that might be worth examining. People are made to feel strange and a little guilty if they hold stronger convictions than that.[7]

Relativism is even more threatening in Canada where it is promoted by government policy and taxes under the name of multi-culturalism. Canadians are beginning to see that this mosaic madness is a good way to destroy a society, if a focus on unity is not maintained alongside diversity. We are at risk of seeing tolerance (which is good) become indifference to truth and morality (which is deadly error). The appeal is obvious; politicians will stoop to anything to buy votes, in this case the votes of minorities. But the social risk is becoming plain. It also trivializes the moral and religious foundations on which our society was constructed. At Christmas this year, a school principal in Toronto prohibited the singing of carols because he said they represented only one group of children in the school and were inappropriate for a pluralistic society. As a result the season was celebrated by the singing of "Frosty the Snowman," reducing one of the deepest expressions of hope and joy to triviality. Relativism is destroying the moral consensus and stripping us of ethical guidelines, leaving us with no instruments for evaluating behavior and measuring social life.[8]

There are reasons then why religious pluralism feels like a new problem even though it is not strictly new. Religious pluralism has always been present but not always in a context that leans towards relativism regarding truth claims. This situation along with the movement of peoples is putting a new spin on the old problem. There has always been a multiplicity of religions, but there has not always been a pluralistic mindset.[9]

THE THEOLOGICAL POT IS BOILING

The challenge of religious pluralism has gotten the theological pot boiling. The impact on modern theology has been tremendous. At one end of the spectrum, it has given radical theology the new lease on life it has not had since the sixties. The urgency of this problem is felt so strongly that certain theologians are prepared to make enormous doctrinal concessions to settle it. For example, the lordship of Christ, since it gets in the way of this ethical demand of late modernity that all religions be treated alike, has to be scaled down.[10]

A characteristic of contemporary theology is to be driven, not by Bible or tradition, but by practical or ethical issues of a progressive type such as those raised by pluralism, feminism, homosexuality, ecology, individual freedom, and the like. Practical issues drive theology today. This would be typical of the way people are now thinking: "Christ cannot be sole mediator between God and humanity, not because he did not claim it, not because the church has not confessed it, but because, in the present cultural mood, such a belief has become unthinkable and intolerable. Belief in Jesus Christ as the only Savior of sinners is not fair or equal treatment. It is prejudicial and promotes intolerance to believe in a God like that. It is not politically correct." The radical challenges to Christianity today are not coming from intellectual criticisms as previously, but rather from the realm of liberal ethics. People are saying in effect that if God is not in line with ethical liberalism, s/he will not receive our worship.[11]

Predictably, having produced such a radical proposal at one end of the spectrum, the challenge of religious pluralism has also created a conservative backlash at the other. Instead of opening them up to more generous attitudes, pluralism actually has produced a hardening of attitude among traditionalists. It has produced a refusal to rethink almost anything and a resistance to fresh ideas that might help resolve the problem, even ideas defended earlier by orthodox theologians.

The harshness characteristic of the relationship between Protestant theology with the other religions historically has not lessened but is actually growing in some quarters. Although there is indication of movement in the direction of rethinking this position of total rejection of the other religions among some evangelicals (for example, C. S. Lewis, J. N. D. Anderson, Colin Chapman, Charles Kraft, Stuart Hackett, John Sanders, and others), resistance to rethinking it is also very strong and may be getting stronger (James Borland, John Gerstner, Robert Morey, Robert H. Gundry, R. C. Sproul, Harry Buis, Dick Dowsett, Ajith Fernando).[12]

A majority of evangelicals today are hardline restrictivists in my estimation.[13] The only possibility for encountering God and receiving salvation in this view is to exercise explicit faith in Jesus Christ in this earthly life. General revelation is not sufficient; all must receive God's revelation in Christ. Outside of this special revelation, there is near-total darkness. Other religions are error and falsehood and non-Christians with few exceptions are on their way to hell. The main motivation for missions is to rescue people from this fate. It is likely that only a few will be saved but (if that should happen) God is not to be blamed for it. That is what God predestined to occur in any event. One reason for writing this book is to challenge this way of thinking.

Alongside radical theology and the conservative counterreaction, something else that is very significant is happening in contemporary theology. A middle path has been developing between the two extremes, a megashift in Christian thinking moving us in the direction of greater theological globalism. It can be seen in the Catholic church, in the Protestant mainline, and among a growing number of evangelicals. I refer to a greater appreciation of how wide God's mercy is and how far-reaching God's salvific purposes are. An optimism of salvation is replacing the older pessimism. Walls of separation are crumbling, the self-protective nervousness in the presence of competitors is diminishing, and one senses a greater willingness to acknowledge the positive ways in which religions contribute to human well-being. A good news orientation is prompting people to seek fresh answers to the old questions.

AN EVANGELICAL THEOLOGY OF RELIGIONS

Evangelicals are far behind in the discussion. Being behind is not necessarily a bad thing, if it means that we avoid foolish errors that jeopardize the gospel. Being behind is not good if it means we are failing to think things through, if we are not searching the Scriptures or seriously seeking the mind of the Lord in these matters. In any case, the time has come to catch up with the discussion and to put together an evangelical theology of religions. There is nothing like this at present, so it will be my aim to provide such a proposal. I hope it will fill the gap which now exists and find its niche. I also hope it will nudge fellow evangelicals who have so far been reluctant to speak out, owing to the intimidation they may feel from hardline restrictivists. I hope they will do so because there are those better equipped than myself to make the case.

The proposal I want to place on the table involves five components to be discussed in five chapters. The plan is first to set forth two parameters within which a theology of religions should operate, then develop a theology of religions in the remaining three chapters. Here is a sketch of the proposal.

First, the biblical and theological basis for an optimism of salvation grounded in the love of God for all humanity will be outlined. I oppose the fewness doctrine which accepts that only a small number will be saved, and I maintain that God's universal salvific will enables Christians to have deep hopefulness for the nations. This is an attitude we need if we are to deal with the challenge of other religions.

The second concern is Christological. Alongside the first axiom, I will place a second one, namely, that a high Christology must be a part of any truly Christian theology of religions. But I intend at the same time to argue vigorously that our belief in Jesus Christ as the one mediator between God and humanity does not by any means entail a negative attitude toward the rest of the world, nor does it specifically require Christians to be exclusivist or restrictivist in their interactions with world religions. In other words, while resisting current attempts to reduce the Incarnation to a myth and the Trinity to a unitarian model of theism, I will insist just as emphatically that a high Christology does not entail either a pessimism of salvation or an exclusivist attitude toward people of our faiths. The first two chapters together will lay down the fundamental axioms on which everything else rests.

Having put the parameters in place, I will approach the question of other religions directly. First, in chapter three I will answer the question how Christians should relate to people of other faiths, arguing that the Bible views religious activities on a spectrum which runs all the way from truth to error, from nobility to vileness. Religion according to the Bible is a profoundly ambiguous category about which it is inappropriate either to be naïvely optimistic or naïvely pessimistic. We must repudiate any a priori view of other faiths as either wholly good or wholly bad and learn to judge religion on its merits or demerits, case by case.

Second, in chapter four I will face the fact that religions in the objective sense (as cumulative traditions) are not static but constantly changing over time. This being the case, it is possible for Christ to impact them. To facilitate the impact, I will recommend truth-seeking dialogue as the mission activity we need to employ. These chapters investigate two phenomenological topics alongside the two theological parameters established before.

The last chapter takes up the question of access to salvation on the part of those who have not heard the gospel. What will be the eschatological destiny of the unevangelized? Eschatology, though much talked about, is not a well-developed topic in evangelical theology, and I will try to defend a wider hope suggesting how God judges people fairly on the basis of the light they receive in their own historical situations. In this connection, I must also speak about our theology of world mission and its motivations. If mission and evangelism is at the heart of what "evangelical" means, one cannot discuss the theology of religions in isolation from the Great Commission.

ROUNDING THINGS OFF

Let me explain some of the terminology. By "exclusivism" I mean the position that maintains Christ as the Savior of the world and other religions largely as zones of darkness. I will also speak of "restrictivism," which restricts hope to people who have put their faith in Jesus Christ in this earthly life. By "inclusivism" I refer to the view upholding Christ as the Savior of humanity but also affirming God's saving presence in the wider world and in other religions. By "pluralism" I mean the position that denies the finality of Jesus Christ and maintains that other religions are equally salvific paths to God.

Using such terms, one could say that my proposal is exclusivist in affirming a decisive redemption in Jesus Christ, although it does not deny the possible salvation of non-Christian people. Similarly, it could be called inclusivist in refusing to limit the grace of God to the confines of the church, although it hesitates to regard other religions as salvific vehicles in their own right. It might even be called pluralist insofar as it acknowledges God's gracious work in the lives of human beings everywhere and accepts real differences in what they believe, though not pluralist in the sense of eliminating the finality of Christ or falling into relativism.

Though I am trying to change evangelical thinking on this subject, I can hardly expect the book to solve all problems or answer all questions. I would hope that it might supply the kind of framework within which a better evangelical solution to the problem of other religions might be found. My study has many limits. The study of world religions is a gargantuan task, and sorting out historic Christian attitudes to other religions is not simple. Mastering the current theories is difficult. I think the value of this book will be its effort to find a framework within which neglected biblical themes can be retrieved and placed, and thus help advance the evangelical discussion. I hope it will open some doors to further research and more detailed studies of particulars, and that it might be a first step in a new direction for evangelicals. I hope it might place the issue of religious pluralism on the agenda of evangelical theology for the nineties, the way the Lausanne Covenant placed social concerns on the evangelical agenda for the seventies. The time is right.[14]

One

Optimism of Salvation

A *fundamental point* in this theology of religions is the conviction that God's redemptive work in Jesus Christ was intended to benefit the whole world. Hence the title—*A Wideness in God's Mercy*. The dimensions are deep and wide. God's grace is not niggardly or partial. To use a phrase of political columnist Ben Wattenberg's: The good news is that the bad news is not true. For according to the Gospel of Christ, the outcome of salvation will be large and generous.

Nineteenth-century Calvinist theologian William G. T. Shedd said there were two soteriological errors to avoid: "First, that all men are saved; secondly, that only a few men are saved."[1] My intention is to avoid both errors, and in this chapter specifically to refute the fewness doctrine and replace it with an optimism of salvation based in Scripture. It is important because the position one takes on this issue will influence and condition one's attitude to God and to non-Christian people. Another reason it is important is that to accept the fewness doctrine invites the pluralist theologies to come into play.[2]

The first two chapters belong together, spell out the two-sided truth claim at the heart of Christianity; and provide the parameters for soundly Christian thinking about a theology of other religions. The two components of this dialectical truth claim are *universality* (God's love for all humanity) and *particularity* (the reconciliation of sinners through Jesus' mediation). This two-sided truth is visible everywhere in the New Testament: "For God so loved the world that he gave his only begotten Son" (Jn 3:16). "This is how God showed his love among us: He sent his one and only Son into the world that

17

we might live through him" (1 Jn 4:9). "And we have seen and testify that the Father has sent his Son to be the Savior of the world" (1 Jn 4:14). ". . . God was reconciling the world to himself in Christ" (2 Co 5:19). In these central texts we are told that God gave a gift to the whole world in the person and work of Jesus Christ. No other foundation can be laid than this for Christian theology and mission (1 Co 3:11). It offers the two basic parameters for a theology of religions: God provides salvation for the world (the many) through the person of his Son (the one).[3]

This chapter focuses on the first axiom, the universality side of the equation, and inquires into the scope of God's salvific will and the extent of his graciousness. One really needs to know whether or not God is committed to the salvation of the race or only intends the rescue of a relatively small number from hell and judgment. Is God interested in human welfare on a large scale, or is he content to be involved with a fairly slender thread of history? The answer to these questions affects one's approach to the nations and their religions. It determines whether an optimism or a pessimism of salvation conditions our thinking and whether we are full of hope or are hopeless in respect to the multitudes of non-Christian people. Universality needs to be discussed first because it marks a major fork in the road.[4]

The foundation of my theology of religions is a belief in the unbounded generosity of God revealed in Jesus Christ. This topic, like many others, comes down to the question of God. Who or what is God and what does he want or intend? Is he the kind of God who would be capable of sitting by while large numbers perish, or the kind to seek them out patiently and tirelessly? Does God take pleasure and actually get glory from the damnation of sinners as some traditions maintain, or is God appalled and sadded by this prospect? My reading of the gospel of Jesus Christ and my control belief causes me to celebrate a wideness in God's mercy and a boundlessness in his generosity towards humanity as a whole. (When I use the term "control belief," I mean a large-scale conviction that affects many smaller issues.) The issue is summed up for me by what the apostle Peter says: "[God] is patient with you, not wanting anyone to perish, but everyone to come to repentance" (2 Pe 3:9). I cling to Paul's word too: "[God] wants all men to be saved and to come to a knowledge of the truth" (1 Ti 2:4). Paul also said: "For God has bound all men over to disobedience so that he may have mercy on them all" (Ro 11:32).[5]

There are different reasons why Christians have felt threatened by the existence of other religions in the past and have found it difficult to relate lovingly to them. These would include geographical isolation, awkwardness in the presence of conflicting truth claims, and competition between our mission and theirs. There is also a theological reason why we have felt uncomfortable with people of other faiths—a lack of confidence in God's generosity toward them. Dark thoughts have clouded our minds. For centuries, thanks largely to the Augustinian tradition that has so influenced evangelicals, we have been taught that God chooses a few who will be saved and has decided not to save the vast majority of humanity. God is planning (in his sovereign freedom) to send most of those outside the church to hell, and he is perfectly within his rights to do so. If as a result large numbers perish, theologians have assured us that God would feel no remorse and certainly deserve no blame. The result of such instruction is that many read the Bible with a pessimistic control belief and find it hard to relate humanly to other people. This is hardly surprising. We have to answer the question, Does God love sinners at large or not?

This negative control belief is what drives certain Christians straight into theological pluralism. They are led into extremes in their revising of Christian doctrine chiefly because they cannot accept God, as revealed by Jesus, as One who would consign most people to hell and deny them access to salvation. Theological liberalism reacts sharply and correctly to such a cruel and incoherent reading of the gospel that has all too often marred the orthodox tradition and assassinated God's character. Speaking boldly, pluralists are right on this point; insofar as certain of its representatives have presented God as a cruel and arbitrary deity, orthodox theology badly needs revision and correction. However, my belief is that trinitarian theism does not entail a cruel and arbitrary God at all, and changing it provides no solution.

The first move theologically is to establish an optimism of salvation, to make it perfectly clear that God is committed to a full racial salvation. The God we love and trust is not One to be satisfied until there is a healing of the nations and an innumerable host of redeemed people around his throne (Rev 7:9; 21:24–26; 22:2–6). I intend to make the case for salvation optimism, and for a hermeneutic of hopefulness that may assist us in negotiating a necessary paradigm shift away from our current pessimism. To put it out in the open, I want evangelicals to move away from the attitude of pessimism based upon bad news to the attitude of hopefulness based upon Good News, from restrictivism to openness, from exclusivism to generosity. If we could but recover the scope of God's love, our lives and not just our theology of religions could be transformed.[6]

A HERMENEUTIC OF HOPEFULNESS

The basis of an optimism of salvation is found in the earliest chapters of the Bible, in the global covenants established in those passages. There is a universal orientation there that we should not miss. The first major division of Genesis deserves an importance greater than is normally given to it. Genesis 1-11 depicts the beginning of history and places the calling of Abram in the context of God's concern for the whole world. These narratives are revolutionary even today. God's dealings with Abram are situated in the context of universal human history. The patriarch is called from Ur of the Chaldees, not for his own sake or his family's sake, but for the sake of the whole world. God called Abram so that all of the families of the earth might be blessed in and through him (Ge 12:3). This is the beginning of a pattern that will become familiar throughout the rest of Scripture, the pattern of God setting aside one person (Abram) to be the source of salvation for many (the human race). It seems to be God's way to choose a single representitive of the group to deal with the whole group, and this appears most singularly in Jesus being presented to us as the last Adam, the one who represents the race as its Redeemer (1 Co 15:22).

The early chapters of Genesis present God as maker of heaven and earth, creator and judge of all nations. This means that all the peoples belong to God, as a psalmist says when he writes: "Rise up, O God, judge the earth, for all the nations are your inheritance" (Ps 82:8). All are God's peoples. We can speak of a covenant of creation such that the whole world and its peoples belong to God who created humanity to relate to him. God made us for himself, to do us good and not to destroy us. The scope of God's concerns embraces the whole of humanity, not just Abram and his descendants. Any attempt to present God's saving plan on a small scale is on the wrong track and misses the point of early Genesis.

Alongside a creation covenant is also a Noahic covenant which precedes the call of Abram and illumines its meaning (Ge 9:8–17). After the flood, God establishes a covenant for all peoples in Noah. Pointing to the rainbow in the clouds, God says: "This is the sign of the covenant I have established between me and all life on the earth" (Ge 9:17). By this pledge we understand that God is concerned, not with a single strand of history, but with the entire historical tapestry, including all the earth's peoples. God announces in this covenant that his saving purposes are going to be working, not just among a single chosen nation but among all peoples sharing a common ancestry in Noah. The pattern of representation is visible again: Because of the obedience of the one (Noah), God extends his mercy to many (all humanity). In Noah, God establishes a global or cosmic covenant with all nations, with all Gentiles, a covenant with the whole human race prior to his dealings with Abram and the Jewish people.[7]

Unfortunately, it is common to interpret the Noahic covenant in a minimalist way and to see it as a covenant only of physical preservation and not of redemption. But surely this is a divine commitment and promise that transcends merely preserving the race from another flood. The promise to Noah prepares the way for the blessing of all nations through Abram a few chapters later. The call of Abram implements the promise to Noah. Both covenants are universal in scope. For a reader not to see this suggests a hermeneutical presupposition blocking truth out. Others do not miss the obvious point.[8]

The universal orientation of the biblical prologue continues in the genealogies of Genesis 10. Though brief and enigmatic, these lists of names give the impression that God is concerned with the welfare of all nations and watchful over their expansion in the earth. All peoples derive from Noah and are intended to live in harmony with one another, in spite of their racial and linguistic differences (Ge 10:5). The point is that God is not a tribal deity, not just the God of Jews or even Christians, but the Lord and judge of all the earth.[9]

Further glimpses into God's saving work among people at large, prior to the call of Abram, is given in anecdotes concerning such persons as Abel, Enoch, Noah, and Daniel. These were men of faith who lived before Abram's time and who are held up as examples of the life of faith by the New Testament (Heb 11). As the author of Hebrews says: "By faith Abel offered God a better sacrifice than Cain did. By faith he was commended as a righteous man, when God spoke well of his offerings" (Heb 11:4; cf. Mt 23:35). Augustine traced membership in the heavenly city back to him, though he thought such believers were rare (*City of God*, 15:1). Hebrews continues: "By faith Enoch was taken from this life, so that he did not experience death" (Heb 11:5). Enoch was also a believer, a pagan saint who walked with God. Apparently God dealt with him on the basis of the response he made to the light of revelation he had. Hebrews adds: "By faith Noah, when warned about things not yet seen, in holy fear built an ark to save his family" (Heb 11:7). Noah was a fearless preacher of God's word, a man who suffered derision because of his faithfulness, a man with whom God established a new beginning for humanity (2 Pe 2:4). Less well known, Daniel is mentioned by the prophet Ezekiel in a passage where the prophet labels Israel's sins so grievous that he thought God would not even listen to the prayers of Noah, Daniel, and Job, were they to intercede on its behalf (Eze 14:14). Daniel must have been a righteous and holy man, and another of the faithful souls who are part of the cloud of witnesses who encourage us to live by faith (Heb 12:1). All these men, being neither Jews nor Christians, pleased God because they sought him with the faith response which pleases him (Heb 11:6).

Somewhere we lost this biblical theme and need to retrieve it. The Bible says that there are true believers in the wider world who trust God and walk faithfully before him. The Apostolic Constitutions, a compilation of early Christian traditions, knew it: "From the beginning God raised up priests to take care of his people, Abel first, then Seth, Enoch, Noah, Melchizedek and Job" (8:3, 5). Even the Westminster Confession admits: "Although the work of redemption was not actually wrought by Christ til after his incarnation, yet the virtue, efficacy and benefits thereof were communicated unto the elect in all ages successively from the beginning of the world" (8:6). Is this not a remarkable admission, coming as it does from a rigorously

Augustinian document? It says that people are able to benefit from Christ's work without knowing or confessing his name but by responding to the light shining in the darkness and which the darkness did not put out (Jn 1:5). It confirms Paul's statement, that God has never left himself without witness even in ancient times (Ac 14:17).

From the earliest chapters of the Bible we learn a fundamental (if neglected) truth, that salvation history is coextensive with world history and its goal is the healing of all the nations. This is a testimony which stands as a corrective to so much Western theology, which has not been universal in its orientation but rather has narrowed God's saving purposes to a tiny thread of history and limited participation in salvation to the adherents of church and synagogue. These witnesses tell us that God has it in his heart to bless the whole race and does not want only to rescue a few brands plucked from the burning.

It is essential to grasp the meaning of the call of Abram in the context of the book of Genesis. Western theology has regularly considered his call and election in a way which stands in contradiction to the vision of early Genesis. This is a terrible mistake. God's call to Abram and to his seed after him to be a special nation makes sense in the context of God's concern for all the nations, when viewed in the context of the creation and Noahic covenants. Abram was chosen by God for the sake of the world, not for his own sake. His election was not a sign of God changing his mind about the other nations, wanting now to save only some and rejecting others. No, the decision to call Abram designates the path God has chosen to bring about the salvation of the many through the faith of the one, the principle of representation.

The election of Abram is evidence of God's desire to save the world. This is not Calvin's view of it though: "The decree is dreadful indeed, I confess" (*Institutes* , bk. 3, chap. 23, sec. 7). It is not an election in which God arbitrarily selects some to be saved while appointing others for damnation to his glory. The meaning of Abram's election does not tell us that God has suddenly changed his mind, that the God who made a covenant with all flesh in Noah has lost interest in humanity at large and decided instead to save only a single family, leaving the rest to perish. That makes absolutely no sense however you look at it, exegetically or theologically, morally or rationally. No, this election is for the sake of *all* peoples. After the call of Abram, God is still King, exalted above all peoples and acting with them in mind (Ps 99:2). The psalmists speak repeatedly of his rule over all the nations, just as the prophets do (Ps 8:1; 22:27–28; 46:10; 47:1; 49:1; 50:1; 66:1,8; 67:3; 82:8; 96:3,7,10; 97:9; 100:1). The covenant made with Abram has to be interpreted in the context of the covenant made with Noah and with Adam. It is not a startling reversal.

The Old Testament makes it clear that the election of Israel is a corporate election (not an election of individuals) and a call to service (not to privilege). Israel is summoned to be God's priestly people in the earth (Ex 19:6). Her election is not the selection of certain individual Jews to be saved as the Augustinian paradigm would have it, but the election of a people for service and witness. As Isaiah the prophet put it so eloquently: "I will also make you a light for the Gentiles, that you may bring my salvation to the ends of the earth" (Isa 49:6). This is the election of a people to a ministry of redemptive servanthood. Election does bring privileges, but primarily it carries responsibilities. God chose Israel because he had a special task for the Jews to perform, not because he loved them as opposed to loving others, or because they were better than the rest.[10] It is a calling which can succeed or fail. In fact, Paul speaks of the failure of this mission: "God's name is blasphemed among the Gentiles because of you" (Ro 2:24).

Few would deny that this corporate emphasis is the orientation of the Old Testament's doctrine of election. Election in the Hebrew Bible refers to God's calling of Israel as a corporate entity to service. But many would insist that the New Testament says something different, something in addition to that. They would contend that it introduces election in the sense of double predestination (where God by sovereign fiat decrees some to be saved and some to be condemned).[11] What a tragic and influential error. The Old Testament doctrine of election remains unchanged in the New Testament. The New Testament does not reinterpret election to mean the selection of certain individuals to be saved, leaving others aside. Christians are God's chosen people the same way that Israel was, chosen in Christ to be a servant community and witnesses to the kingdom of God. They have been called out of darkness to declare

God's praises (1 Pe 2:9). Their calling is to be the first fruits of the new creation, the anticipation of a much larger harvest to come (Jas 1:18).[12] Election invites us into the eschatological community of salvation, not so that we can revel in God's arbitrary choice of us instead of others, but so that we can serve God and issue the invitations to all peoples for God's endtime banquet.[13]

It was a disaster in the history of theology when Augustine reinterpreted the biblical doctrine of election along the lines of special redemptive privilege rather than unique vocation on behalf of the world.[14] What a mistake to have made vocational election into a soteriological category. Karl Barth had all the right instincts when he insisted that election is good news and not bad, even if the decision to speak of the election of the race in Christ was not the best alternative. I myself think it more biblical to speak of God loving rather than electing the world, and retaining the term "election" to refer to a choosing of some on behalf of the many. What is universal is God's love for the race; his election of Abram or of Israel or of the church is the way God implements his love for humanity. I would rather say that God loves the world and therefore elects a people, prophets, and apostles in order to implement his love for the entire human race.[15]

It is hard to exaggerate the importance of this point. Election has nothing to do with the eternal salvation of individuals but refers instead to God's way of saving the nations. It was a major mistake of the Reformation to have decided to follow Augustine in this matter, taking election to refer to grace and salvation. It manages to make bad news out of good news. It casts a deep shadow over the character of God. At its worst, it can lead to awful consequences in terms of pride, arrogance, superiority, and intolerance as the ideology of election takes hold. It causes the church to become, not a sign of the unity of humanity in the love of God, but the sign of favorites in the midst of the enemies of God.[16]

We have already encountered two serious errors in traditional theology, errors which greatly affect and condition our attitudes in the area of religious pluralism: the denial of God's universal salvific will and the understanding of election as a selection of certain individuals to privilege. These errors lead people to ignore the global covenant with Noah and to view their own election as a favored status. They help create the hermeneutic of pessimism and promote other equally unfortunate attitudes.

After the call of Abram, God is still presented in the Old Testament as active among nations beyond Israel's borders. God's concern for the world at large does not stop once Abram is called. He is still in dialogue with Gentiles. This neglected biblical theme reinforces the fact that in choosing Israel to be his servant, God is not playing favorites or turning his back on the rest of the world. This is important for us in a day when people are quite concerned about fairness. Many would find it difficult to believe that God would distribute his goods arbitrarily, or leave people out of his reckoning for no good reason. Fortunately, this is not the case.

First, one can observe his concern for the nations beyond Israel in the interaction which God has with the various non-Israelites mentioned on the margins of biblical story. In addition to the pagan believers we have mentioned already (Abel, Enoch, Daniel and Noah), there are others who lived during the period of Israel's ministry, yet outside her sphere and covenant. Job is an obvious example, a pagan held up as a model of righteousness and piety in both the Old and New Testaments. As James says, "You have heard of Job's perseverance" (Jas 5:11). Here was a believer outside the line of Abraham, a just and godly man of the covenant struck with Noah. Another was Melchizedek, a Canaanite priest of a god he called El Elyon, God Most High (Ge 14:17–24). It is quite remarkable to see Abraham receive a blessing from this pagan priest and pay a tithe to him in return. I think that the compiler of Genesis wants to tell us that, though Abram had a special calling from the Lord, he is not to think (and we are not to think) that there are no other believers among the nations and no positive contributions to be appreciated from non-Israelite religion and culture.

Another one of these pagan believers was Abimelech, king of Gerar, described as a man who acted with integrity and in the fear of God (Ge 20:1–18). On first encountering him, Abraham appears to have rushed to the conclusion that neither Abimelech nor anyone else in his house had any fear of God. But this proved to be mistaken. He was in fact another pagan who had a right relation with God outside the boundaries of Israel's covenant. Still another was Jethro, Moses' father-in-law, a priest of Midian (Ex 18:1–12). Jethro had known and worshiped God outside the covenant with Israel before he met Moses, and was delighted to learn how great God was to deliver Israel out of Egypt. He realized that the god he had served was better revealed as Yahweh, and therefore joined in the worship of him with Moses and Aaron. Baalam, the pagan soothsayer, is another interesting case. Though hardly a pagan saint, he had the name of Yahweh on his lips and he was enabled by the Spirit to convey insight into the will of God for Israel for that situation (Nu 22:8). Evidently, God was not unwilling to reveal his plans regarding Israel to a non-Israelite prophet.

Jesus referred to a pagan saint known as the queen of Sheba; he said, "The Queen of the South will rise at the judgment with this generation and condemn it; for she came from the ends of the earth to listen to Solomon's wisdom, and now one greater than Solomon is here" (Mt 12:42). The queen was a stranger to God's revelation to Israel, a pagan woman from Sheba (probably Yemen), and in search of God's wisdom (2 Ch 9:1–12). Obviously God did not leave her without witness, and she responded favorably to it. Sincere in her search for God, she prefigures the Magi, coming as she did from a pagan culture far away to worship God (Mt 2:1-12).[17]

It strikes me as very odd that evangelicals have not seriously considered this information and consequently have such difficulty accepting the possibility of pagan saints in the wider world. Is it any wonder why liberals throw up their hands at our claim to be biblical? How can we deny, based on this material, that God works outside so-called salvation history? These examples prove (*prove* is hardly too strong a word) that God is prepared to be the God of pagan peoples who believe and that he is also present in the religious sphere of their lives. It simply astonishes me when those who advocate biblical inerrancy so strongly show themselves unwilling to let the Bible speak to them in ways that contradict their traditional interpretation.

Second, there are teaching passages in the Old Testament which confirm the point that God is in dialogue with the nations. For example, consider the telling comment God makes through Amos in a moment of exasperation: "'Are not you Israelites the same to me as the Cushites?' declares the Lord. 'Did I not bring Israel up from Egypt, the Philistines from Caphtor and the Arameans from Kir?'" (Am 9:7). Though a rhetorical question, the prophecy of Israel's destruction and restoration suggests that God is concerned for other nations and even intervenes in their histories. It is reminiscent of Psalm 87:4: "I will record Rahab and Babylon among those who acknowledge me—Philistia too, and Tyre, along with Cush—and will say, 'This one was born in Zion.'" This helps us understand how another psalmist can say: "Clap your hands, all you nations; shout to God with cries of joy" (Ps 47:1). And these remarkable words: "God reigns over the nations; God is seated on his holy throne. The nobles of the nations assemble as the people of the God of Abraham. For the kings of the earth belong to God; he is highly exalted" (Ps 47:8–9). Although Israel is certainly central in the Old Testament narrative, we should not miss the frequent texts that remind us of God's interest in the wider world as well. This is no surprise since he chose Israel for the sake of the world, not for its own sake.

Along these lines, it is clear from the book of Jonah that God cares for the people of Nineveh and wants to save them too. Even though the Assyrians were fierce enemies of Israel and a cruel people, God is prepared to accept their acts of repentance. He does not even require them to visit the temple in Jerusalem, or to become Israelites, but is willing to accept them just as penitent Ninevites. Jonah, for his part, was less than enthusiastic about this, because he thought that God's election of Israel put Jews like himself on a rather higher plane than cruel and unclean Assyrians. But he was mistaken, and the book of Jonah stands in the canon to testify to the universal salvific will of God.

According to the prophet Malachi, Assyrians are not the only pagans God cares for. After telling the Jews that he will not accept their sacrifices, God adds this oracle (according to one possible translation of the verb): "From the rising of the sun to its setting, my name *is* great among the nations, and in every place incense *is* offered to my name and a pure offering; for my name *is* great among the nations, says the Lord of hosts" (Mal 1:11). Although it is possible that the verbs be rendered as future, and that the text is therefore a prediction of what it will be like in messianic times when all nations come to know the Lord, the context does suggest that the present tense would be more appropriate. Comparing the Jews' behaviour to present Gentiles would have greater force than comparing them to Gentiles in the messianic age. Perhaps I am drawn to that interpretation because of the flow of my argument, but the opposite might also be true. Perhaps others prefer the future tense in this verse owing to their resistance to the very point I am drawing from all these texts. Why are we so reluctant to accept that God is in dialogue with other nations, in spite of so many Scriptures that say he is? It seems to me that the restrictivist control belief prevents readers from considering a present tense in Malachi 1:11 or taking seriously the import of a dozen other texts like it.

Jeremiah too speaks about the universality of God's judgments. "If at any time I announce that a nation or kingdom is to be uprooted, torn down and destroyed, and if that nation I warned repents of its evil, then I will relent and not inflict on it the disaster I had planned" (Jer 18:7–8). There is no limitation here. Apparently any nation or kingdom on earth can turn from its wickedness and receive divine mercy.

The overall point is that according to the Old Testament God is in dialogue with all the peoples of earth. What he is doing in the call of Abram and the election of Israel is not in opposition to the salvation of the world but on behalf of it. The history beginning with Abram and world history at large are not two histories going in opposite directions. The idea is that world history becomes salvation history. Those who are chosen are called to be God's experimental garden in the midst of world history, moving things forward in the direction of the transfiguration. The elect are not a sign of damnation to the others but a sign of God's saving purposes for the world.[18]

The picture of God's global reach is confirmed again and again in the hope for the salvation of the nations that many of the Old Testament prophets articulate. They do not think only or chauvinistically of the salvation of Israel. Isaiah is particularly eloquent on this point, and in one of his visions he portrays the nations flowing to the mountain of the house of the Lord and learning to walk in the ways of the Lord. His hope was broad and expansive (Isa 2:1–4). The whole human race will be unified under the reign of God and experience his peace. In another oracle, the Lord declares that he will make himself known to the Egyptians and to the Assyrians, that they may be his peoples too, alongside Israel. Isaiah says: "The Lord Almighty will bless them, saying, 'Blessed be Egypt my people, and Assyria my handiwork, and Israel my inheritance'" (Isa 19:25). In another vision,

God lays a feast for all peoples of the world, removes the veil of blindness which presently covers them, and goes on to promise that he will swallow up death forever and wipe away the tears from all faces (Isa 25:6–8). What a perfect expression of the wideness in God's mercy!

The same optimism is echoed in many of the psalms as well: "The nations will fear the name of the Lord, all the kings of the earth will revere your glory" (Ps 102:15). Another psalmist looks forward to the day when men and women will declare God's praise in Jerusalem, "when the peoples and the kingdoms assemble to worship the Lord" (Ps 102:22). The protolog of early Genesis agrees with the eschatology of the prophets and psalmists in stimulating hope in us for the substantial redemption of the world.

The Old Testament paints a glorious picture of God's global reach of salvation, but evangelical theology often misses a number of its important features. Committed by tradition to the fewness doctrine, we have not been free to rejoice in God's global covenants. Bewitched by the alien doctrine of double predestination, we have overlooked the meaning of the call of Abram. With a guard up, we have ignored the tradition of holy pagans, which tells us that God is in dialogue with people beyond the borders of Israel and the church. Let us listen more diligently to the Old Testament, for it lays the foundations for Christian theology in this as well as in so many other matters.

If the universality of God's plan of salvation already is plain in the Old Testament, it is central to Jesus' proclamation of the kingdom of God. The quenched Spirit has returned and God is moving to establish his rule in a fallen creation (Mk 1:14–15). God as the Creator has sovereign rights over the world and intends to demonstrate his lordship through power informed by love. His rule will be reestablished, the world transfigured, and his will done on earth as it is in heaven (Mt 6:10). On that day, there will be joy in the presence of the Lord with his people at the banquet table. All flesh will see the glory of the Lord, and the powers of darkness will be overcome forever.[19]

Power and kingdom language alone would be oppressive if not qualified by other images. What characterised Jesus' preaching of the kingdom was not a pettiness on God's part regarding his divine rights, an insecurity in reestablishing them or the need to save face. On the contrary, the hallmark of the kingdom was God's boundless mercy to undeserving sinners. This is what distinguished Jesus' message from what other groups in Judaism were saying at the time. God forgives the publican who simply asks for mercy (Lk 18:9–14). God receives back the prodigal son who had forfeited any claim on his father's goodwill (Lk 15:11–32). There is joy in heaven when a sinner repents (Lk 15:6). We are told to invite the poor, the crippled, the lame, and the blind to our table because they are the ones God invites to his (Lk 14:13). Reflecting the Father's mercy, Jesus compares himself to a hen who wants to gather all the chicks under her protective wings (Mt 23:37). The decisive element in Jesus' teaching and acting was the communication of a sense of the boundlessness of God's grace to sinners.

This feature works itself out in themes of hope. God's grace will issue in the eschatological pilgrimage of the nations, a theme drawn from the prophets of the Old Testament. From all over the world, as the seers had announced, men and women will come to the messianic banquet of God. Despite the fact that Jesus was sent primarily to Israel, one should not confuse penultimate means with ultimate ends. Although God had a special arrangement with Israel which Jesus had to pursue, the overarching goal was the inclusion of Jew and Gentile alike in the kingdom of God (Mt 8:11). Jesus actually lists some of the unexpected ones who will be there: the Ninevites, the queen of Sheba, the inhabitants of Tyre and Sidon, and those of Sodom and Gomorrah (Mt 10:15; 11:22; 12:41–42). Jesus made it very clear that all nations will have a share in God's salvation and are being summoned to the epiphany of God. God does not want his house half empty; he wants it to be filled (Lk 14:23).[20]

Underlining his doctrine, Jesus practiced what he preached, shocking some people in the process. His behavior corresponded with his message, as he said that ours should (Mt 7:21). In choosing to have table fellowship with sinners, for example, Jesus underlined the point about God's great generosity to them (Lk 15:1–7). When he commended the faith of the Roman official, he was saying something about God's priorities (Mt 8:10). In talking with the woman from Samaria (Jn 4:1–26), in praising the Good Samaritan (Lk 10:33–37), in paying heed to the Syro-Phoenician woman

(Mt 15:22), Jesus was telling people about God's mercy. He proclaimed a God who loves the least and the lowest, and he confirmed the doctrine by his actions. God's care about the well-being of his creatures caused Jesus to act in a caring manner, and his doing so indicates a new way of living for us as well. This is a way of life which reflects God's mercy: practical love, abandoning selfishness, a willingness to serve, a love for neighbors, a love even for enemies, and a willingness to forgive as God forgives.[21]

This comes out strongly in Luke's Gospel, where the narrator takes pains to show that God loves everyone, Jew and Gentile, man and woman, slave and free, rich and poor. No one group or any certain territory holds a favored position in relation to salvation. God is bringing these blessings to all people on earth. Exclusivity and elitism are out of the question. The barriers that divided us before are coming down. God's love for humanity will be the solid basis for that unity of the human race that needs to be restored.

Luke's book of Acts reflects this same generous and inclusive attitude to outsiders. Peter declares after his change of heart: "I now realize how true it is that God does not show favoritism but accepts men from every nation who fear him and do what is right" (Ac 10:34–35). He had been guilty of harboring narrow attitudes, but God helped him to a broader vision and a more generous approach.[22]

Paul has the same attitude according to a speech he gave to people at Lystra: "In the past, he let all nations go their own way. Yet he has not left himself without testimony" (Ac 14:16–17). This represents a gracious and understanding appreciation of their past and their culture. In a later vignette, Paul is described in Athens as acknowledging the good intentions of the Greeks in worshipping the unknown God. The gist is recorded of a sermon in which the apostle builds positively upon truths the Athenians possessed in their own scriptures (Ac 17:22–31). Evidently Paul thought of these people as believers in a certain sense, in a way that could be and should be fulfilled in Jesus Christ. In this speech he recognizes the wider work of God in the world, in relation to which the Gospel can be proclaimed. This coheres with the principle Paul states in Philippians: ". . . whatever is true, whatever is noble, whatever is right, whatever is pure, whatever is lovely, whatever is admirable—if anything is excellent or praiseworthy—think about such things" (Php 4:8).

Apparently the apostle is open to whatever truth or goodness he happens to come across, whatever the context.[23]

Why in Acts does Paul sound more generous than he does in Romans? The assumption is that we are right in reading Romans in a pessimistic manner. It may be that Romans is more generous than we have assumed. In the epistle to the Romans Paul says that God has made known his power and deity to all human beings (Ro 1:19–20). He adds that God also has revealed his moral law to everyone and has written it on their hearts (Ro 2:14–16). His point is that Jews and Gentiles alike possess the light of divine revelation and are responsible for knowing it, because God will judge them on the basis of it. It is not a negative thing to say that everyone in the whole world has access to God's truth, whether they know about Jesus or not. Granted, Paul is stressing the failure of sinners to respond to God in order to show why Jesus had to come. He is insisting that humanity cannot save itself apart from the work of God in redemption. But it is wrong to read into his words in Romans the idea that he is denying that many Jews and Gentiles in the past have responded positively to God on the basis of this light, as Luke also intimates in the book of Acts.

Moving ahead into the epistles, we encounter much to confirm an optimism of salvation. Paul's whole doctrine of the person and work of Christ, for example, confirms it from several angles. First, from the point of view of the person of Christ, he identifies Jesus with the power of creation. Jesus is a cosmic Christ: "For by him all things were created: things in heaven and on earth, visible and invisible, whether thrones or powers or rulers or authorities; all things were created by him and for him. He is before all things, and in him all things hold together (Col 1:16–17). God's fullness dwelt in Jesus who embodies in his flesh the plan of God underlying the creation itself. This means that what is happening in salvation history is the heart and soul of world history. What has now been revealed through Christ has always been true, his work in history is the consequence and fulfilment of the purposes of God in the creation. What one sees in salvation history reveals God's aims for the whole world. Clearly, a high Christology does not entail a narrow but a broad attitude on our part. We will return to this in the next chapter.

Second, from the point of view of Christ's redemptive work, the dimension of universality is plain. Jesus is presented as the last Adam, representing the race as the first Adam had, except that in identifying with us Jesus Christ destroyed sin, defeated death, and won salvation through his obedience unto death and his glorious resurrection (Ro 5:18; 1 Co 15:20–28; Php 2:6–11). Truly, Jesus is the Savior of the world (1 Ti 4:10), the one Mediator between God and humanity (1 Ti 2:4–6), and the one through whom God has reconciled the whole world (2 Co 5:18–21). This is a most universal vision.

Third, because of the resurrection, Jesus was raised up by God to be life-giving spirit. His resurrection set in motion a chain of events that will result in our resurrection as well. "For as in Adam all die, so in Christ all will be made alive" (1 Co 15:22). Jesus was raised up on behalf of us all, to be the first fruits of the resurrection of all flesh. Jesus recapitulates the purpose of God for humankind and reverses the process which led to our downfall, opening up the way to new life. This was the heart of the Greek theology which became the classical consensus of creedal Christianity and the essence of orthodoxy.[24] I am not suggesting these are easy ideas to explain rationally, but I am suggesting that Paul had a great understanding of the global reach of God's salvation.

Finally, there is the breathtaking picture that the Revelation of John gives us of the consummation of history. Like Moses on Mount Nebo, John the Divine glimpses the promised land, a renewed and transformed world, the work of the God who makes all things new (Rev 21:5). The prophet sees the new Jerusalem coming down from heaven and observes the kings of earth bringing the glory and honor of their nations into it (Rev 21:24–26). He senses that nothing of the splendor of their cultures and civilizations—the art, music, languages, literature, artifacts, racial characteristics—is going to be lost or wasted. Drawing on the symbolism of Isaiah 60, the seer tells us that every human achievement, imperfect though it is, will find its place in the transfigured life of the world redeemed. He talks about trees, the leaves of which will be for the healing of the nations. The nations themselves, though smitten of God for their sins, can receive healing and restoration (Rev 22:2). G. B. Caird comments: "Nowhere in the New Testament do we find a more eloquent statement than this of the all-embracing scope of Christ's redemptive work."[25] According to John's vision, God is not even going to give up on the nations that fought and resisted him and persecuted his people so cruelly. God will finally win a victory over them, not through naked power, but through boundless love. It will not be a victory which will see them destroyed, but a victory in which they are healed. Though we are always tempted to doubt it, how could it be otherwise? How could the One who is "king of the ages," who created the whole world, and whose throne is surrounded by Noah's rainbow, not have a purpose for the whole creation or be content to rescue a pathetic remnant (Rev 15:3; 10:6; 4:3)? St. John is not pessimistic; he doesn't think God will let them perish. Victory was on his mind: "The kingdom of the world has become the kingdom of our Lord and of his Christ, and he shall reign for ever and ever" (Rev 11:15). Or again: "All nations will come and worship before you, for your righteous acts have been revealed" (Rev 15:4).

Christians are often too pessimistic about the scope of God's salvation in Christ. They have entertained dark thoughts that only a few will be saved and not many, that souls will be saved and not bodies, and that the new order has no continuity with the old. But Revelation corrects all such mistakes. Salvation is going to be extensive in number and comprehensive in scope. The Bible itself closes with an eloquently portrayed optimism of salvation, including the renewal of all things and the salvation of all peoples.

In view of such passages as these, John R. W. Stott admits, "I have never been able to conjure up (as some great evangelical missionaries have) the appalling vision of the millions who are not only perishing but who will inevitably perish. On the other hand, as I have said, I cannot be a universalist. Between these extremes I cherish the hope that the majority of the human race will be saved."[26]

How appealing all of this is from an apologetic standpoint as well. It resonates with a hope within the human breast. Experience itself demands that beneath our human lives exists a ground in reality for confidence in the final worth of our existence. If there is no such ground, what is the point of anything?[27]

A MEGASHIFT IN HISTORICAL THEOLOGY

The reader may be wondering whether I am not laboring the obvious. What Christian theologian, it might be asked, doubts the global reach of God's salvation? This is a natural but also a naïve question in the context of Western theology. Since Augustine, theology generally has not been informed by an optimism of salvation. Evangelicals are heirs to a tradition that has restricted the scope of salvation to the glory of God, as it supposed. This unhappy development needs to be given a brief historical review.

The problem of restrictivism was not created by the Greek theologians of the early church. Their theology began very positively with respect to the scope of salvation. Optimism of salvation was visible both in the broad motif of recapitulation, as well as in the wider hope they entertained. According to the former, the work of Christ as last Adam who represents all humanity was emphasized by Irenaeus. God came into the world in Jesus in order save humanity from sin and death, to restore and perfect the creation. This is indeed a broad concept of redemption. Alongside this conception and appropriate to it, there existed a wider hope eschatology as well. While holding fast to the finality of Jesus Christ, the Greek theologians also held that God gives revelation and the possibility of salvation to everyone in the world.

Access to salvation for all was realized by a "logos" doctrine which theologians like Justin Martyr, Clement of Alexandria, Origen, Theophilus of Antioch, and Athenagoras entertained. They all spoke of the seminal word or reason in which all humankind partakes, and they considered that persons who live by this word of God were in effect Christians, even though they had never heard of Jesus or were able to confess him.[28] Responding to the question which has become perennial concerning the people born before the time of Christ, Justin said: "We are taught that Christ is the first-born of God, and we have explained above that he is the Word of whom all mankind have a share, and those who lived according to reason are Christians, even though they were classed as atheists. For example, among Greeks, Socrates and Heraclitus" (*Apology*, 46).[29]

It is clear that Christian theology began with a conviction that God was concerned about all people and was at work among them all. George Lindbeck suggests that this might explain a certain behavior which he observes in the early Christians, namely, a subtle combination of relaxation and urgency in relation to non-Christians. On the one hand, they do not seem obsessed about the fate of the majority of pagans among whom they lived, yet on the other hand they still engaged in vigorous mission activity among them. Lindbeck suggests that if we entertained the sort of position visible in the theologians of the second century, the paradox would certainly be eased.[30] In any event, it is striking how Christians today are turning back to the broader perspectives and wider hope characteristic of the work of the Greek fathers.[31]

The Bible is a matrix of parable, narrative, and teaching, but it does not contain what we would call systematic theology, even though it contains abundant material for constructing it. Therefore, systematic visions like the one just mentioned arise in the history of doctrine as a result of reflection on the basic Christian story. Because these visions are human efforts to interpret a complex set of facts, there always tend to be rival versions of them. In the case of the early theologians, they took a more liberal point of view than the system of Augustine's (which we discuss next). They thought that God loved the world, that Christ died for the world, and that it was up to persons to choose redemption or to refuse it. They did not think that God predestined people in their choosing or their refusing, and they read the Bible with a certain leniency when it came to the application of redemption. But this was not to last.

Augustine, on the other hand, operated with control beliefs of much greater rigor and severity. With his theology, Christian attitudes toward outsiders begin to harden, and a pessimism of salvation takes over. The spirit of Cyprian's famous slogan, "outside the church, there is no salvation" (*extra ecclesiam nulla salus*), replaces the more generous approach in the Western church. We begin to hear a greater emphasis on the exclusiveness of salvation. Now, it is not so much the passion to include as many as possible, but keep the standards of entry into salvation high.[32]

In part this new attitude was due to a historical and not primarily a theological factor. As the church became a political power with the conversion of Constantine, the enemies of the state automatically became enemies of Christianity as well. Similarly, when the spectre of Islam appeared later at the doors of Europe, the paranoia would only increase. Such political developments do not encourage the sort of open, loving attitude proper to Christian missions.

There were theological factors at work too. There were features in Augustine's thinking which led him inexorably to a pessimism of salvation. In the bitter Pelagian controversy, for example, he was driven to emphasize the sheer gratuity of divine grace at the expense of any human contribution. Though this would not in itself require a fewness doctrine (Warfield and Shedd were Augustinian but did not hold it), Augustine took it in the direction of a pessimism of salvation. People are hopelessly lost in sin, can do nothing to save themselves, and deserve nothing from God as judge. One can only be saved by the sovereign decision of God and, should he not be inclined to save some sinners but choose rather to let them to perish in hell for their sins, God would in that case be as much glorified in their damnation as he would have been in their salvation. This is the way Augustine's mind worked. His ecclesiology was so restrictive that he actually was prepared to defend the view that unbaptized babies suffer everlastingly in hell. He thought that general revelation, though it exists, possesses no salvific value. As to the number of the elect, Augustine says: "Many more are left under punishment than are delivered from it, in order that it may thus be shown what was due to all" (*City of God*, bk. 21, chap. 12). He even speculates that Christ came so late in human time because there were so few likely to accept him in the millennia previous to his coming that it was no use coming any sooner just for a few (*Predestination of the Saints*, chap. 17). To follow Augustine's thinking requires a strong stomach theologically.[33]

I think that Karl Rahner's judgment on this is sound. "It can be said that Augustine inaugurated and taught to Christendom a view of world history according to which—in the incomprehensibility of God's providence—world history remained the history of the *massa damnata* from which in the last resort, by a rarely granted election of grace, only a few were saved. For him the world was dark and only weakly illuminated by the light of God's grace, a grace that can be seen by its rarity to be unmerited. Even though Augustine from time to time showed that he was aware of the presence in the church of many who seemed to be outside it and vice-versa, nevertheless for him the group of those who are saved and enter into glory is more or less identical with the communty of those who believe explicitly in Christianity and the church. As a result of an incomprehensibly just judgment of God, the rest remain in the *massa damnata* of humanity, and on the whole the outcome of world history is to be found in hell."[34]

With Augustine a new and severe paradigm in theology was born, a package of dismal beliefs which would eat its way into the consciousness of the Western churches and erode the positive biblical spirit in their thinking. The approach is well-known to practically every Christian and non-Christian alike. It views every person as totally depraved, guilty for the sin of Adam as well as their own sins, completely unable to do anything other than sin, and deserving of everlasting conscious punishment in hell. But Christ, as a kind of third party, bore the punishment for those sinners fortunate enough to have been predestined to be saved. Meanwhile, the Spirit exercises God's power to compel them to accept the message by irresistible grace. Those unlucky enough to leave this life without having exercised explicit faith in Jesus Christ are almost certain to suffer in hell forever. As James Packer puts it, "The New Testament perspective is one of wonder and praise that some are saved and there is no thought that God would let himself down did he not provide for most or all." In other words, were God to save only a small minority of humankind, he would be completely justified.[35]

It may strike some readers as extraordinary that Augustine could have come up with such a harsh attitude, considering the biblical material we have surveyed. And how could he also have ignored so completely what the theologians before him had said about these matters? Although he read no Greek and therefore would have lacked direct influence from the Greek fathers, he was certainly not ignorant of what they said. Therefore, he must have rejected it. One sees that, for example, in a letter to Bishop Evodius, in which Augustine refutes the idea of Clement of Alexandria that Christ's descent into hell might offer some hope for at least some of the wicked.[36] I have to suppose that it was the bitter controversy with Pelagius that drove him to place such a strong emphasis on divine sovereignty in grace and to accept the harsh notions which accompany it, including soteriological predestination, total depravity, everlasting conscious torment in hell, strict limitations on who can be saved, forbiddingly high ecclesiastical walls, the importance of living within the jurisdiction of the Catholic church, and pessimism for anyone living beyond its borders.[37]

As an orthodox theologian myself, I have no interest in making Augustine seem harsher than he was, or in putting the orthodoxy he helped to create in any more difficulty than it is already in. In so many other ways Augustine was a great Christian thinker to whom we are all indebted. Therefore, I note that Augustine spoke of true religion among the Gentiles before Christ came. He knew about godly pagans such as Job and Enoch, even though he thought them rare and exceptional. It should also be remembered that the formula, *"extra ecclesiam nulla salus,"* was originally directed at schismatics and heretics, not at the unevangelized, and therefore did not have as its purpose a denial of grace existing outside catholic Christianity. There were other ideas to come later within the tradition of Augustine, ideas such as the "baptism of desire" concept, which eases the problem of the unevangelized and even became official teaching at the Second Vatican Council. So it would not be right to exaggerate the harshness of the theology and tradition from Augustine, or pour more criticism on it than it deserves.

At the same time, it was a tragic development in many respects. For, however we explain it, something ugly entered Christian theology through Augustine. His kind of mentality would receive classic expression in this often-quoted statement from Fulgentius of Ruspe, a disciple of Augustine's, which became incorporated in the Council of Florence: "There is no doubt that not only all the heathens, but also all Jews and all heretics and schismatics who die outside the church will go into that everlasting fire prepared for the devil and his angels."

What makes this especially sad for Protestants is that even if one could rescue Augustine's reputation on this point it would not be possible to rescue the reputations of others in our tradition, such as Luther and Calvin and others who voiced opinions every bit as severe and harsh as Augustine's. Calvin, after praising the clarity of general revelation, concludes that, "It is impossible for any man to obtain even the minutest portion of right and sound doctrine without being a disciple of Scripture" (*Institutes of the Christian Religion,* I.6.2). Luther declared: "Those who remain outside Christianity, be they heathens, Turks, Jews or false Christians (Roman Catholics), although they believe on only one true God, yet remain in eternal wrath and perdition" (*Larger Catechism,* II.iii).[38]

What can be said about this development? First, remember that the attitude of harsh exclusion was once a novelty in the history of doctrine, being the view neither of Scripture nor the first theologians. We are free to deny that God is glorified by saving as few as possible, or by excluding the majority from salvation. Second, it is a little ironical that the term *evangelical* would come to refer to a theology that in certain expressions, looks more like an attack on the Good News of the New Testament. Third, never forget that this very harshness more than anything else propogates radical pluralism. It incites some to forsake orthodox traditions entirely, and to fall into vague unitarianism to escape them. The irony of this is that trinitarian orthodoxy was created, not by Augustine who inherited it, but by theologians like Irenaeus who rejected the sort of harsh views that were introduced later by the Bishop of Hippo.

What seems to have happened is that Christians have picked up the very exclusivism warned against in the gospel. Jesus himself rejected the notion that election confers privileged status and is the basis of superiority. God's kingdom is not the place for those who want to protect their own salvation in opposition to the salvation of others. There is no basis in the gospel for viewing outsiders suspiciously, holding them at arms length, or for being fearful lest the unclean be saved. Pharisaism is not exclusively Jewish, for there is the identical tendency in Christianity and other religions as well.

Fortunately, major rethinking on the global reach of God's salvation is now under way across the churches. The more lenient approach, seen in the Greek fathers, is fast coming back into favor, and the cloud which has darkened theology in the West for centuries is finally passing over. It is a time of opportunity (*kairos*) for the church to recover the gospel as Good News for the whole world, an opportunity not to be missed.

It has taken centuries to turn things around, for the change to be accepted. In recent times, it burst most dramatically upon the scene at the Second Vatican Council, where the whole tenor was positive in relation to the potential of the Christian message uniting a divided humanity in Jesus Christ. It would be fair to say that this has been the historic attitude of Greek Orthodoxy, has become the view of the Protestant mainline, and is being increasingly shared by conservative evangelicals as well.[39] Why is this happening? It seems to me that

God is correcting a mistake in historical theology by means of historical factors, combined with a fresh reading of Scripture. The new world situation, moving as it is in the direction of a global village, has impacted us and impelled us to read the Bible in some new ways. Believers everywhere are coming to appreciate more adequately the grand scope of God's generosity in Jesus Christ. It would seem that the moderation of Erasmus is winning out over the harshness of Luther and Calvin.[40]

Inevitably, a shift of major proportions causes some dislocation and division. Nevertheless, this can be minimized. Optimism of salvation enjoys such a broad biblical basis that it can be negotiated smoothly. Roman Catholics, Lutherans, Calvinists, Wesleyans, Pentecostals—all of them can make the shift to greater universality in their own way while dealing with the special challenges their tradition creates. For example, even strong Augustinians have been able to make the shift to an optimism of salvation. B. B. Warfield was able to make the shift and find a way to overcome the fewness doctrine by means of postmillennial eschatology, and by raising expectations in regard to the number of God's elect. (According to the logic of Augustinianism, God might sovereignly decide to save most or even all sinners, since nothing affects his decision. There is nothing to require that the number of the elect be few.) Warfield's way will not be the preferrred way for all others to follow, but it illustrates my point. If an Augustinian as tough as Warfield can make the shift to optimism of salvation, then anybody can.[41]

As I say, Warfield's solution will not work for everyone, although some can only be pleased to see him and others attempt it. It will leave others uncomfortable at points: first, because it still leaves large numbers eternally lost in absolute terms, even though the overall percentage is lowered; second, because in Warfield's view sinners are lost because God hates them and has decided to damn them; third, because the view holds that the saved are saved by divine coercion; fourth, because it does not question the assumption of a sovereignty by which God might have chosen to save none, though luckily he decided to save a lot; and fifth, because the solution does not recognize the work of God among the nations outside the church. Nevertheless, despite all of that, Warfield's efforts show that he wrestled with an error in the received traditions and tried to correct it.

Karl Barth took a different path. He chose to avoid the problem of fewness by rethinking what divine election in Christ means, taking it to refer to the whole of humanity chosen in our representitive. Neal Punt, on the other hand, made the same shift by presuming the election of persons rather than their reprobation, without having to alter the Reformed faith as radically. I think that any theological tradition can find a way to entertain an optimism of salvation on a scriptural basis. Catholics have already done so, and it is far easier for the Lutherans than for the Calvinists. It is not a question of relativism, approving whatever theory yields the desired practical results. It is more a matter of it being possible for a central biblical theme about God's love for the whole world to be restored in the various traditions of Christian reflection after a long period of its being obscured.

In making this shift away from the fewness doctrine, the challenge will be to affirm the universal salvific will of God without falling into one trap or another. There are three obvious pitfalls awaiting us when we move in this direction—*relativism, universalism,* and *unitarianism.* I will discuss each of these later in the book. Suffice it to say first that an optimism of salvation does *not* entail relativism. Recognizing how generous God is does not imply for a moment that all religious claims are equally valid. Second, an optimism of salvation does not entail universalism either, that is, in the sense of the final salvation of all. In the light of scriptural warnings, it would seem that, although the possibility of salvation exists for everyone, it is impossible to affirm the actuality of salvation for all. A decision has to be made. Salvation is not automatically conferred upon people. Third, an optimism of salvation does not in any way require a unitarian Christology. Far from denying the Incarnation, it focuses on the global reach of the triune God, including the Logos made flesh, and thus rests upon the orthodox doctrine of God. Far from helping us solve the problem of religious pluralism, denying the Incarnation undercuts any hope of the salvation of the nations since it is from the Gospel that people discover how loving God is. Our very ability to say that God loves the world derives from the fact that God gave his only Son. Let me say more about this last danger now.

KNOWING GOD IS LOVE

The main thrust of this first chapter stands in opposition to the fewness doctrine, a doctrine which is a heresy of orthodoxy more than religious liberalism. But it does have a bearing on theological pluralism as well. Pluralists delight in the doctrine of God's love for the whole world, but they are less forthcoming when it comes to explaining how we know this. How do we know God is love and desires the salvation of the world? After all, it is not something which original Buddhism or Islam or Hinduism clearly teach. To be fair, this type of theistic belief did not come to the fore in the history of ideas through a universal religious intuition, or natural theology. If it did, it would be more common. No, the idea of God as personal love is a notion which was mediated through a particular historical revelation, namely, through the experience of Israel and the ministry of Jesus of Nazareth.

There is a reason why we do not notice that right away. The word *God* in English is so associated in our minds with biblical revelation, and the image of a loving, personal deity, that it requires effort to realize how it received this meaning. God, we must remember, is not a word with much definite content cross-culturally. It gets a lot of its specific meaning from a standard outside itself. When, for example, it is understood to refer to personal, loving transcendence, it is almost certain to have been given this meaning by the Judeo-Christian tradition, which is distinctive at this point. God is not just a universal given in philosophy and religion, but he has the sense of loving personality because of Israel's traditions culminating in Jesus of Nazareth.

It is important to remember this, especially when pluralists like Paul Knitter and John Hick call for a theocentric rather than a Christocentric theology. The idea is that being God-centered would be less divisive among other faiths than being Christ-centered. They suppose that God unites us, while Jesus divides us. But there is a fallacy in this. It is not an easy thing to divide God as a loving person from Jesus of Nazareth. If one is to be theocentric in the sense that religious liberals desire us to be, that is, to believe in the personal God who loves all humankind, one would have to be Christocentric to do so. This is because the idea of worshiping God as a loving personality and the Savior of the world arises from Christology. It arises from a commitment to Jesus as the window into ultimate reality, and is based on Jesus as a self-characterization of God. Focusing on Christ is not different from being God-centered—it is a way of being God-centered.

Theocentricity, which places God at the center letting Christ revolve around it, has been called a Copernican revolution in theology. But it is less a revolution than it appears. It is a misleading and incoherent proposal. What happens is that liberals climb up the ladder of Christology to arrive at a God defined as loving personality, and then think they can kick the ladder away, hoping no one will notice and nothing will be affected. The sleight of hand involves retaining the word *God*, in the sense in which Jesus embodies him, and then dropping belief in the Incarnation while hoping that nobody would notice that the "theo" of theocentric was Christologically defined. But the term God, or deity, is not a free-floating category with a distinct meaning, except perhaps in the general sense of transcendence. If we are talking about God with a human face, about One who loves humanity, seeks the lost, and forgives our trespasses, then the God we are obviously talking about is the God and Father of Jesus Christ—not a generic deity. This God is defined by Jesus and normatively grounded in the person and work of Christ. The irony is that in not seeing this point clearly, much theological pluralism is covertly Ptolemaic.

Ironically, the proposal of theological pluralism, which would undercut the normativeness of Jesus Christ, removes (perhaps unwittingly) at the same time the very basis for knowing God as personal and gracious, loving and forgiving. The paradox lies in the fact that the universality of God's love is known through the particular event of the Incarnation. One can only be sure there exists a gracious and loving God if it is the case that Jesus Christ is Lord. What is theologically primary (the universal salvific will of God) turns out to be epistemologically secondary, because it is grounded in the Christ event. Gavin D'Costa puts the question this way to the Christian pluralists: "How credibly can Hick expound a doctrine of God's universal salvific will if he does not ground this crucial truth in the revelation of God in Christ, thereby bringing Christology back onto centerstage?"[42]

When this problem dawns on pluralists, as it seems to dawn on them a few years after they make their move, they are compelled to retreat into virtual agnosticism. Having replaced Jesus with God, they soon have to replace God with the Real, and soon after that they replace the Real with salvation. (They are not the people to be complaining about epicycles.) The fact is that God loses decisive meaning when the Incarnation is reduced to myth, and loses all content once God is required to be the center of religions, including those without any clear belief in God.

To clarify, I am not denying there is a knowledge of God apart from Jesus Christ. I accept the doctrine of general or cosmic revelation, and I believe that many people in the other religions worship God, even if in ways that fall conceptually short of the revelation of God's nature which Christ brings. The point I am making is that the distinctive profile of God as the lover and healer of the nations is surely a uniquely biblical one. It is a Christian belief, and not a Buddhist or Taoist or Islamic one. Because it does not hang conceptually in mid-air, one cannot drop Jesus Christ as normative and expect theocentrism to mean much. That God might be the loving Savior of the world has come to the attention of humanity through the traditions of Israel, and by way of Jesus accepted as normative. It is impossible to deny his normativeness and retain the image of the God he uniquely reveals. John is stating a plain fact: "No one has ever seen God, but God the One and Only, who is at the Father's side, has made him known" (Jn 1:18). It makes no sense to climb this ladder and accept the God at the top, and then kick the ladder away.

WHAT HAS THIS TO DO WITH OTHER RELIGIONS?

Optimism of salvation has much to contribute to our attitude regarding other religions in general, though only a little in the way of specific detail. In general, it creates a deep hopefulness in us for the salvation of humanity. It assures us that God is drawing the world to himself. It lets us thrill to God's command: "Turn to me and be saved, all you ends of the earth" (Isa 45:22). We know that all peoples of the world are called to be God's people, and we are encouraged to know that it is not a small salvific program that God is pursuing. God sent Jesus to be the Savior of the world, not the Savior of a select few. This fact empowers us to approach all persons in a spirit of openness and love. It fills us with optimism and expectation because we know what God is aiming at.

But it does not, as I said, yield a lot of specific details. It does not, for example, indicate the path that God is following in relation to other religions. In theory, God (if he were Barthian) could be very negative about the religious dimension of life, denouncing religions as human efforts at self-salvation. And he may have decided to save humanity by an act of unmerited generosity at the end of history, beyond the boundary of death. Or, God (if he were Rahnerian) might decide that religions (suitably re-arranged) could serve as pointers to the Christ. Or, God (if Hickian) might choose to treat all religions as valid responses to himself and oppose claims to uniqueness and finality.

God could take any of these routes and defend them. Merely having an optimism of salvation does not confirm or deny any of them. Unless there is further information, they remain no more than interesting speculations. Therefore, it is necessary for us to look further in Scripture, to see if any light is shed on the actual specifics of God's arrangements with the nations. These arrangements will be investigated in subsequent chapters after the second axiom is put in place.

Two

Jesus, Savior of the World

O_f *the two axioms* underlying the theology of religions, the first consists of the boundless mercy of God which makes possible an optimism of salvation; the second axiom consists of the finality of Jesus Christ as the decisive manifestation and ground of God's grace toward sinners. In this chapter we turn to this second axiom.

According to the New Testament, God provided salvation for the world through the work of one mediator, Jesus Christ. This means that universality (salvation for the world) is reached by way of particularity (salvation through Jesus) in Christianity. Our proclamation is that God is healing the nations through the mediation of his Son, rather than in some other way. In his wisdom, God is reconciling the world to himself, not through religious experience, not through natural revelation, not through prophets alone, not through all the religions of the world, but through Jesus Christ.[1]

In the present climate of opinion, this claim, central though it is to Christianity, causes embarrassment to those who believe that such claims cause hard feelings and create divisions in the context of religious pluralism. It is too heavy a burden to bear, and they long to find relief from it. Obviously, this is in sharp contrast to the attitude of the New Testament witnesses to the finality of Jesus Christ, whose response was one of gratitude for what God has done for the world through him. Their hearts were full of praise for the mighty works of God they had witnessed (Ac 2:11). Jesus was an asset, not a liability, as far as they were concerned. Jesus brought salvation for the whole world. More than a teacher, more than an example, they saw in him

49

the decisive manifestation of God in human flesh, the reversal of the ruin which sin had wrought, and the possibility of a new beginning for those who put their trust in him. Thus the finality of Jesus Christ was not something they wanted to apologize about.

But the claim concerning Jesus Christ does require some explanation in the present context. The apostle Paul said that the gospel would be foolishness to the Greeks and a scandal to the Jews, and it is so today. Although the truth of the finality of Jesus Christ may thrill Christian hearts, we would have to admit the claim is not instantly intelligible or problem free for the modern mind. Why, people ask, would the maker of heaven and earth deal with the whole race through a single mediator? That seems like an inefficient strategy, calculated to guarantee that large numbers of people would get left out. Besides, is it not parochial-sounding to be making such exalted claims for a first century Jew from Nazareth? Can we not play down traditional beliefs, such as the Incarnation, and put the emphasis instead on doctrines that would contribute better to global unity and cooperation among peoples? The pressure is there, even on traditional Christian believers. Is this not why the dialogues between Christians and other religionists conducted by the World Council of Churches sound weak and relativistic to evangelicals, even though the organization itself is founded on a high Christology? (Member churches must confess Jesus Christ as God and Savior.) Even where belief in the finality of Christ is upheld and not denied, there is a strong temptation to conceal it on account of the current climate of opinion.[2]

The second axiom is about Christology. Because the issue is so fundamental and because the objections to it are so strong, we have to get down to basic questions. Why, for example, do we require such a high Christology in the first place and how (if we must require it) can it fail to promote a narrowness of outlook toward those who worship God outside churches? The latter question is important because it is undeniable that a high Christology has more than occasionally in the past led people to adopt narrow and exclusive attitudes. It is easy to see why. If Jesus is the only way to the Father, then the pathway to salvation appears narrow and beyond the reach of most people. It is not far from there to the sort of typical belief expressed by Philip Melanchthon: "It is certainly true that outside the

Church, where there is no gospel, no sacrament, and no true invocation of God, there is no forgiveness of sins, grace, or salvation, as among the Turks, Jews, and heathen" (*On Christian Doctrine*).

Any theologian, therefore, who believes a high Christology is essential to sound doctrine is obliged to explain why it does not necessarily lead (if it does not) to sound doctrine. Otherwise, sensitive folk will succumb in large numbers to the views of seductive pluralists who claim a high Christology inevitably leads to harsh conclusions and must therefore be revised for that very reason. After all, religions tend to be naturally exclusivist and competitive. Perhaps Christianity fell into an unhappily exclusivist posture unwisely and needs to rethink its position?[3]

Here is the heart of the pluralist objection to church Christology: Unless it is revised downwards, it will be impossible to promote the kind of constructive and cooperative interreligious relationships that we need today. Religious peace will become unattainable, and ultimately world peace will also elude us. The question is urgent. Does the high Christology in the church's confession of faith permit openness to other faiths, or does it require harsh, restrictive responses? My argument will be that a high Christology does not entail a narrow outlook, if we learn to think in a trinitarian manner about these issues.

Before actually tackling this problem directly, we must face the prior question—is the high Christology of church tradition necessary? Since belief in Incarnation as a metaphysical claim obstructs (we are told) the path to interreligious dialogue, is there is any way to prevent this happening and being an obstacle? Can the case can be made, for example, on exegetical or other grounds that would enable one to interpret the New Testament fairly and yet not come up with such a problematically high Christology? After all, the tradition has erred before; maybe it erred here. Or, one might suggest, Incarnation was a good way to think of Christ in the early church, given the circumstances, but not such a good way for today. If it were only possible, some are saying, not to have to bear the burden of belief in the Incarnation, it would become possible to open up more positive relationships with other faiths.[4]

In our first chapter, the challenge came mostly from the conservative side, from restrictivist uses of orthodoxy which deny universality. In this chapter, the situation is reversed. The threat stems from forms of liberal theology which defend an optimism of salvation through bold revision of Christology. Therefore, we are confronted with a new challenge here: What can be said to those who defend the universality of God's love through a strategy of jettisoning the church's central claim for Jesus?

THE BASIS OF A HIGH CHRISTOLOGY

What evidence from the New Testament has led Christians for centuries to hold a high Christology? If the belief is not well-founded scripturally, but rather largely a result of later church traditions, then we ought to know about it and decide what to do. No one denies that Christology has a history of development over time. But what about its origins and historical foundations? Does church Christology originate from the biblical witness, or from later theological reflections? Is it or is it not firmly rooted in the New Testament?

Although I will not defend high Christology on the basis of tradition, as something central to Christian identity, tradition is never without significance. Belief in the Incarnation has been central to the grammar of the Christian community for a long time, and the prominent category of confession and worship for centuries. The church has always proclaimed the fact that God entered human history in Jesus Christ and made himself known in this utterly personal manner. She has confessed that God has spoken to humankind through his Son, whose life, death, and resurrection she took to be the experience of God in one mode of his eternal being. This constellation of beliefs about Jesus Christ is the chief reason why many like Augustine became Christians in the first place. We cannot pretend that Christianity has not been theologically trinitarian and incarnational throughout its history. Incarnation has been at the core of its distinctive belief system. It would be startling (to say the least) if Christians were to discard or minimize this emphasis now.[5]

Nevertheless, however historic the belief is, and however treasured are its associations, it ought to be—as every Christian belief ought to be—securely founded on the original New Testament witness. If it is not, we have a major problem and have to look at revision. Is the church's high Christology securely established from an exegetical point of view or not?

In approaching this question, it is important to begin at the beginning, that is, with God and not with Christ. The Bible is theocentric. "In the beginning God created the heavens and the earth" (Ge 1:1). It is about God first and foremost. But it is about a God who is very unique, a God very different from the gods of the nations round about Israel. The God of the Old Testament witness is not a pale, generic deity who can easily serve as the proposed center of the world's religions as the pluralists seem to suggest. This God with a strange name (*Yahweh*), a name to distinguish him from the other gods, is of such a nature and possesses such attributes as put him in sharp contrast to the quarrelling, warring deities of the Ancient Near East.[6] When considering the uniqueness of Jesus, one should not run ahead of the game and forget the uniqueness of Israel's God. Transcendence, as presented in the Bible, is not a pale and generic transcendence, but a sovereign, free, and surprising divinity.[7]

This is a key point. The religions of the world such as Judaism, Buddhism, Sikhism, and so on, present distinctive ideas about the nature and attributes of God. The gods are not carbon copies of each other. Gods and religions are not generic. Each makes distinctive claims. Biblical religion too has unique things to say, especially news of certain divine purposes and activities which, if valid, are marvelous and earth shaking. The distinctiveness of Jesus Christ has to be judged and examined in the context of the novelty of the biblical story as a whole, as well as of the biblical deity.

It would then be misleading to consider New Testament claims for Jesus in a vacuum when they are part and parcel of a larger claim to uniqueness on behalf of Israel's God. Biblical theism as a whole must be the context for assessing Christology. Uniqueness belongs first of all to the God of the Bible; and, if it should be said that Jesus is unique, it will only be because of the special relation to God he is thought to enjoy as God's Son. Uniqueness and finality belong to God. If they belong to Jesus, they belong to him only derivatively. He is not unique in his own right as an independent being, but as the Father's beloved Son. The major claim of uniqueness in the Bible is the claim made on behalf of Israel's God, and only afterward on behalf of Israel's Messiah. Yahweh, the God of Abraham, Isaac, and Jacob, is unique among the gods of the nations. It is neither more nor less offensive to worship Yahweh than it is to confess that Jesus is Lord. They are both highly distinctive claims and totally interrelated.

That Yahweh is not a generic deity is plain from the first commandment: "You shall have no other gods before me" (Ex 20:3). Israel is being told that there are other gods being worshiped in the ancient Near East, but the Lord is very different from them and not to be confused with them. He is a "one of a kind" deity, the incomparable, the only true and living God. The Old Testament constantly reminds its readers that God is not to be confused with other gods, whether Babylonian or Egyptian or Canaanite, and will occasionally mock the other gods to make the point. "Who is like you among the gods?" There is none like him. Yahweh is the God who created heaven and earth, who acts in human history, calls Abram to be the channel of his grace, and promises salvation to the nations. The God of the Bible is a unique divine agent, not a no-name pluralist God. He is unique, like no other, a personal God with special characteristics, the living God. This is where one must start when considering claims in the Bible to his uniqueness.[8]

The uniqueness of Jesus Christ arises from this soil and context. Christology is born of it. Should Jesus share the glory of God, as Christians believe? Then he will share in that same uniqueness. If the God of Israel in his freedom came into history in the Christ event (something which cannot be ruled out on the basis of the Old Testament and might be actuality), it comes as no surprise that Jesus was acclaimed and lifted up as someone decisive alongside that God.[9]

A bare possibility does not prove that the claim for Jesus' unique status is true, of course. However, it does establish that, were such a claim founded in historical fact, a high Christology would certainly follow and require little expansion from later traditions. If, for the sake of argument, Yahweh were thought to have come into human history in the person of Jesus of Nazareth, then Christ's uniqueness and normativity would be assured by that fact alone.

A second facet of Old Testament teaching that is relevant and germane as background to Christology should be seen before going to the New Testament. Not only is the God of Israel unique among deities, the coming Messiah is presented as unique and decisive for all peoples. I refer in particular to one such text, the depiction of the coming one in Daniel 7:9–14. In a passage so influential for the New Testament writers, we hear of a mysterious figure called "son of man," who comes to the Ancient of Days with the clouds of heaven. This imagery of clouds, used in the poetry of Ugarit for the movement of the god Baal, alerts us to the divine dimension of this Son of Man. The Messiah will combine in his person genuine humanity (son of man) together with divine honor (the clouds). Appropriately, a kingdom and dominion will be given to him along with worship. The text says: "He was given authority, glory and sovereign power; all peoples, nations and men of every language worshiped him. His dominion is an everlasting dominion that will not pass away, and his kingdom is one that will never be destroyed" (Da 7:14).[10]

Though scholars debate the details of the text and its original intention, it is clear that a kingdom is to be established and a messianic figure (whether an individual or group) is coming whom all the nations will bow down to and serve. The details of this vision do not all have to be clear to grasp the crucial issue. If the New Testament (not to say Jesus himself) actually associates Jesus Christ with the son of man figure from Daniel (as it certainly does: see Mark 14:62), we need look no further to understand how the language of uniqueness and finality came to be applied to Jesus Christ. There is no need to go outside Jewish presuppositions or to appeal to later hellenistic developments to understand where the heart of the high Christology comes from. The category of a unique and universally relevant Savior is already provided by Daniel in chapter 7, and is utilized by the New Testament for this very purpose. When Jesus came proclaiming the kingdom of God and presenting himself as the Son of Man, the only logical conclusion for anyone who responded to his preaching would be that Jesus was very special and requires every knee to bow to him.

A high Christology is not only unsurprising when we find it in the New Testament, but it is predictable and almost inevitable, given the identification of Jesus with the son of man of Daniel. There is no possibility that if Jesus saw himself as Son of Man he could have failed to see himself as a unique Savior figure. Or, if one takes a more critical posture toward the authenticity of these Son of Man sayings, there is no way that the church, seeing Jesus as Son of Man, could have failed to have drawn the logical conclusion that he is unique—a person of divine significance. If Jesus is this son of man of Daniel, he cannot possibly be merely one religious leader among others. He must be one of a kind. For the prophecy presents a figure who is human and possibly divine, whose work (not spelled out) merits universal obeisance. A person does not have to be a Christian to see that this is the only rational way to identify and assess his significance, if he is to be equated with the Son of Man figure.[11]

So it is clear, even without opening the New Testament, where the church's high Christology comes from and why it is hard to revise it downwards. This prophetic oracle by itself, and its use by New Testament writers to explicate the significance of Jesus, explains practically singlehandedly why the first Christians considered Jesus to be a unique and decisive person. It does not require a sophisticated argument. The confession of Jesus as Lord and Savior of the world rests on Jewish presuppositions, and does not derive in any essential way from later church tradition.

Moving into the New Testament, the striking fact underlying everything else is the devotion and reverence accorded the risen and exalted Jesus alongside God. However we explain it, this is an immutable fact. Jesus as God's agent of the kingdom has been awarded divine status and has become an object of worship in a monotheistic Jewish context where one would not expect such a thing to happen. Whatever happened to bring about such a mutation in the faith of Israel?[12]

First, there must have been something in the ministry of Jesus that had an impact upon his followers. Jesus must have made some sort of claim for himself and his mission. There is no need to exaggerate this. Some Christians give the impression that they think Jesus went around saying point blank that he was God. Obviously he did not; it does not do our cause any good to pretend otherwise. What can be fairly said?[13]

Jesus' message was centered on God and the kingdom; therefore, the claims he made for himself arose from this context. He did not go around like a madman calling attention to himself. He was consumed by the messsage of the coming reign of God, and it is in relation to this announcement of the long-awaited divine intervention that the claims he made for his person and work have meaning. Jesus himself featured the coming of the kingdom of God in his ministry to the poor and captive in his teaching on the power of the Holy Spirit. This event and its world-wide ramifications was the subject on which Jesus dwelled. He does not strike one as an egoist.[14]

At the same time, the foundations of Christology originate and are grounded in the proclamation of the kingdom and Jesus' unique role in its coming. Jesus proclaimed God's kingdom in such a way as to imply significant claims about his own importance. He believed that God's kingdom had drawn near in him, being evidenced by the action of the Spirit of the last days which was at work in him healing the sick and casting out demons (Mt 12:28). God's kingdom is central, but it is Jesus who champions, initiates, reveals, bears, and mediates the kingdom. The rule of God is present in the world through him, and operative in his words and deeds. It lies behind this kind of saying to his disciples: "Blessed are the eyes that see what you see. For I tell you that many prophets and kings wanted to see what you see but did not see it, and to hear what you hear but did not hear it" (Lk 10:23).[15] Paul Knitter, with the honesty typical of his work, admits (though it is not to his advantage in the argument) that Jesus saw his role as pivotal in the coming of the kingdom of God: "There are grounds, therefore, to conclude that Jesus understood himself as exercising a special, a unique, role in God's plan."[16] This admission does not of course favor the Christological reduction he is himself proposing.

In the public ministry, Jesus places himself in a strategic position as far as the relationship between God and humanity is concerned. He saw himself as central to what God was doing, as one can see in a hundred texts. People marvelled at the authority of his teaching, his authority to interpret the true intent of the divine law, and the audacity he assumed to forgive sins. His disciples noticed the special "abba" relationship which he enjoyed with his Father as Son of God. They heard him say to them and others, "Follow me!" and observed him compel people to decide about his mission and about himself. Jesus said that people's attitude to him would affect their own eternal destiny. He proclaimed that the kingdom of God was breaking into history, and that he himself was the Incarnation (at least) of the action of God. Jesus stood in the very place of God on earth. These facts about Jesus are plain. It is no great mystery why, afterward, the early church made normative claims for him. Jesus laid most of the groundwork for it.[17]

Much of Jesus' own Christology was implicit and indirect. He did not go around with the purpose of claiming great things for himself. His self-understanding surfaced rather in quiet ways; for example, in the seemingly innocent use of the term "amen" (verily, truly). He used this as a term to mark off his word on a subject. It was as if to say, "These sayings of mine are reliable and true." It was this unheard of sense of divine authority which amazed people, the pretension to stand in God's place and to say what God says. Heinrich Schlier says that in this simple usage "we have the whole of Christology in nuce."[18]

Another example would be Jesus' use of the term "abba" for God (Mk 14:36). He knew God in a way that only a Son could know him, and his claim to authority was grounded in this intimacy with God (Mt 11:27). The full meaning of this relationship was not immediately apparent, but it laid a firm foundation for the growing realization after the Resurrection of the divinity of Jesus.[19] While it is true that the fourth Gospel makes Jesus' divine sonship clearest, the claim itself is rooted in Jesus' own consciousness of sonship in all of the Gospels. John's Gospel is really only making more explicit what is historically original. James Dunn concludes correctly that, "Although John's Gospel is a well-developed portrayal of Jesus' claim to divine sonship, that claim is in fact well rooted in Jesus' own ministry, and particularly in his prayer address to God as 'abba'. Jesus, we may say with confidence, thought of himself as God's son and encouraged his disciples to share his own intimate relationship with God as his son."[20] Indeed, had Jesus not made claims of this kind, it would be puzzling why the early church worshiped him as Divine Lord later.

It would be an exaggeration to say that Jesus claimed to be the Incarnation of the Logos in these exact words. This was not his way of speaking about himself. It would only be self-defeating to inflate the evidence and be discredited in the eyes of critics who know what Jesus actually said. At the same time, what Jesus did preach, teach, and perform, if his claims were not justifed, would constitute a serious lie. The claims, if not accepted, would provoke his own rejection.

In thinking about Jesus' Christology, it is important to distinguish between functional and ontological categories. Did the original Christology think of Jesus as God in action, or as God in flesh? Some pluralists hope that an action Christology will free them of the burden of an objectionably high Christology. But does it? I think not, for even if what Jesus claimed was only in the category of a functional rather than an ontological Christology, the claim would still be too high for theological pluralism to absorb. If Jesus were only a Spirit-anointed functionary of the kingdom of God, for example, it would still be the case that this function as emissary of the kingdom issued in a movement of world evangelization, something which pluralists wish to avoid. For, if Jesus pointed the way to the coming messianic banquet and saw himself as strategic for getting a seat at the table (and who can deny this?), then we would still have a divisive truth claim to deal with which is universally applicable. The function or action in question would be so decisive that the issue of an ontological bond between Jesus and God would still eventually and inevitably surface.

I am arguing here in a minimalist way, not saying all that I believe about Jesus' claim myself. But it seems true that if Jesus' claims were to be taken in a functionalist sense, as distinct from a metaphysical sense (something I myself do not do), they would still be too high to permit removing normativity from Jesus' Christology. Getting rid of the Incarnation category, while shocking to church tradition, would not solve the problem that the uniqueness of Jesus poses to interreligious harmony as the pluralists see it. For Jesus cannot play the pivotal role, which even the pluralists grant he probably played, without running into the problem of normativeness and universal relevance all over again.

Jesus played a prophetic role for his followers, and the legitimacy of that role became a central issue in his career. Was he sent by God or not? By the end of his public ministry, Jesus had generated the conviction in his disciples that he occupied an honored place in the plan of God, as God's agent in the end times. Whether this was true or not was the question which followed him into his death and beyond.

My argument permits a possible application that is worth commenting on. What if a person today were to confess Christ on the basis of a functional understanding of Jesus that was derived from the synoptic Gospels and did not move further ahead to confess him in the full incarnational sense? That is to say, what if they accepted Jesus more in the sense of Luke than of John? How would we regard such a Christian? This is not just an idle question, since it would be easier for Jews and Muslims to accept Jesus in those terms rather than under the incarnational category. Their difficulties with Christianity in fact lie not with biblical language so much as with the technical creedal formulations of later church tradition.[21] Though this would be an abnormal case, I suppose that the person who held to the Christology of Luke but not of John would relate to Jesus in a saving way, just as people in Luke's narrative do, even though they would probably not be regarded as fully orthodox Christians in terms of church tradition. It would not be a question of their denying the doctrine of Incarnation in the metaphysical sense, but of preferring the dynamic biblical language as more understandable than later formulations.[22]

There may be debate then around the messianic self-consciousness of Jesus. Discussion swirls around the question of which sayings actually come from his lips, and what sort of finality he laid claim to. But there is less room for debate when it comes to the post-Easter doctrine of the Christ. No one can deny that after the Resurrection the person and work of Christ is described strongly in terms of uniqueness and finality. If Jesus was raised up by God and the bonds of death were broken, then the pre-Easter claims are validated and worship is the natural response. Jesus has been exalted to the divine glory. He has become God's agent of eschatological salvation. Resurrection begets worship, and worship spells divine status for the risen Lord. As Stephen was dying, he had a vision of the glory of God and of Jesus standing at his right hand, and prayed: "Lord Jesus, receive my spirit" (Ac 7:59).

Antony Flew, an atheist, stated this in the course of a debate on the resurrection: "We are agreed that the question whether, in that literal understanding, Jesus did rise from the dead is of supreme theoretical and practical importance. For the knowable fact that he did, if indeed it is a knowable fact, is the best, if not the only, reason for accepting that Jesus is the God of Abraham, Isaac, and Israel."[23] Church Christology develops out of Jesus' claims, as confirmed by the Resurrection, and could scarcely have failed to develop in the direction of uniqueness and finality.[24] The Nicene Creed in 325 AD did little more than to declare in a formal manner what was involved already on Easter day.

What then happened in the apostolic writings was that the person and work of Christ was described in all sorts of ways to bring out its decisive importance for all humanity. These ways are obvious to any reader of the New Testament and need not be labored. Jesus gave up his life on the cross on behalf of sinners (1 Co 15:3). He rose on the third day to become the firstfruits of the dead who slept (1 Co 15:22). He ascended on high where he now reigns at God's right hand far above all principalities and powers (Eph 1:20–21). Jesus is our living, reigning, and coming Lord. Jesus, the Jew from Nazareth, crucified and risen, is an exalted being, the agent of God, supreme over all other claimants. All nations must therefore be summoned to worship at his feet (Mt 28:19). Jesus is Lord—this is the heart of the New Testament message.[25]

The Epistles do not provide promising material for a theology of religious pluralism. The early church went out into its world of religious diversity and called upon people to decide about Jesus Christ. If we had asked them why they were disturbing the status quo, they would probably have asked us in return what is so great about the status quo? People are changing their religious affiliations all the time—why shouldn't Jesus Christ be part of their decision-making process? It is no different today.

Far from seeing the lordship of Christ as a barrier to the unity of humankind, or a further cause of division, the early Christians saw it as the basis of racial unity not otherwise achievable. The irony of pluralist theology is that, while removing this possible basis of racial unity in the name of racial unity, it does not explain the alternate means. According to the New Testament, Jesus Christ broke down the walls, made us all one, and created a new humanity (Eph 2:13-15). This unity is not something which we have to achieve by devices of our own, even if we could do so. It is a reality—Christ "created" one new man—which is realizable through preaching and embodying the kingdom of God. The gospel presents a possibility for racial reunification that should not be dispensed with prematurely, not until we know what is to replace it. A generic deity is not going to be able to do the job. The pluralists are right, that humanity does need to be reunited in itself and reconciled with God. But one must ask, how is this likely to happen? The gospel gives us an answer: Jesus has broken down the walls that divide. Is it wise to let this possibility go until there is something better in the wings?

What about the category of Incarnation itself? Following the fourth Gospel, Christians have confessed Jesus Christ as the Incarnation of God and the Word of God, in the sense of metaphysical fact. We have said that Jesus is unlike any other human being in this respect. He alone is the God-man, the *deus homo*. But was this development in Christology necessary, and do we need to perpetuate it? Theological pluralists feel strongly that in the interests of interreligious peace and harmony we should not do so.

I agree that, whatever the other New Testament witnesses say about Jesus, however exalted the claims they make, however close they come to saying precisely this, it is only John who names the coming of Jesus "incarnation." It is he who who identifies Jesus as Word of God incarnate, the preexistent Son of God, come from eternity into history. By doing so, John provided a framework for much subsequent discussion around the mystery of the person of Jesus Christ. His is unquestionably a powerful and influential truth claim which goes beyond what Jesus said about himself and even beyond what other New Testament witnesses say.[26]

Incarnation, then, is not the normative category for Christology in the New Testament. But there are other ways of dealing with the significance of Jesus alongside it. There might even be dangers for the church, were it to make the Incarnation its only operative Christology, ignoring the other possibilities. The biblical witness is richer in its Christological reflection than one line of interpretation, and this richness should not be lost or become inoperative.

On the other side, the category of Incarnation is an important way in which a New Testament witness characterizes the meaning of Jesus, which is at the same time a most influential one historically. As long as it stands in the canon of scripture, it will prevent efforts to drop finality claims for Jesus Christ. It will block efforts to argue exegetically that Christians need not interpret Jesus as someone of final importance for the whole race. Incarnation language stands alongside the other modes of interpretation testifying to Jesus as the Savior of the world. It coheres with them and does not contradict them.

In summary, Jesus was first experienced as God's agent bringing near the kingdom of God. The claim was tested by his death and vindicated by the Resurrection. At that point it was clear that Jesus shared the divine glory and was a proper object of the church's worship. All of this happened in the Jewish monotheistic context and requires nothing from the hellenistic world to explain it. The gospel story leads to the conclusion that Jesus has been exalted to divine glory, and legitimated by God himself as the object of Christian devotion. The New Testament witness to Jesus Christ, taken as a whole and not just the Incarnation category by itself, makes truth claims concerning the uniqueness and finality of Jesus Christ as agent of the kingdom of God, living Lord, coming King, and Word made flesh. This witness calls for commitment to a Christ who is normative for the whole world and not just for his followers. The proposition "Jesus Christ is Lord," is metaphysically and not just existentially true. It is a claim about reality, and Jesus' position within that reality. It says that Jesus stands with God at his right hand in his dealings with the human race. When we say "Jesus is Lord," we mean not only that the stories of Jesus communicate the power of new being, though they do so. We mean that it is propositionally the case that Jesus is definitively and unsurpassably the Lord of the universe.[27]

Theological pluralists, if they are Christians, do not have an easy row to hoe. It is difficult for them to revise church Christology downwards because the apostles make such a comprehensive claim for the finality of Jesus Christ. Jesus for them is a person like no other. Not only do the texts say this, but it is true even from the standpoint of other religions. Jesus is incomparable to every religious leader. Second, Jesus did a work in his life, death, and resurrection like none other. This is what the texts say, and it is true also from the standpoint of other religions. Jesus is the incarnate one who died for the sins of the world and rose again unto endless life. One can question this or that text and ask whether Jesus said every logion attributed to him, but the overall picture is nearly undeniable. How each detail in the picture is taken may be debatable, but the picture itself of a universal Savior figure is undebatable.

But would the uniqueness of Jesus have to mean exclusivity? Not necessarily. Was not the Buddha a unique religious figure in his own way? There is room in the world for many unique people, even many religious leaders. Buddha points to truths and values that we would do well to weigh, just as Jesus does. Could not the claims of Jesus and the Buddha, though different, be complementary rather than contradictory? Yes they could be, and in some ways they are. But it would be a mistake to deny a level of incompatibility and competitiveness too. Jesus proclaimed a loving, personal deity, while Buddha considered such talk futile metaphysical speculation. Jesus also placed himself in a pivotal role vis-à-vis the coming of God's kingdom, which has no parallel in the Buddha's thinking. This makes a choice between Jesus and Buddha difficult to avoid, however complementary they are in other ways. The New Testament says that Jesus is decisive in the redemption of the world and unique in ways that cause him to stand out. He gave himself a strategic place in regard to anyone's position in God's kingdom, and the apostles bolstered that claim. His uniqueness is not just a uniqueness others can share with him. It involves a distinctive role in the coming of God to rule, and in the redemption of the world. As Paul would put it, "For he [Christ] must reign until he [God] has put all his enemies under his feet" (1 Co 15:25).

REINTERPRETING NEW TESTAMENT CHRISTOLOGY

Theological pluralists have a problem with Christology. Were Jesus to be decisive for all nations, that would be unconducive to dialogue and cooperation among the religions. Therefore, ways must be found to reinterpret historical data so as to eliminate finality claims from Christology. They must be diminished so they do not constitute a barrier to interreligious peace. Pluralists hope there is a way to read the New Testament without coming up with a Christ who has to be normative for everybody in the world. They need a way for Jesus to be unique for his followers, but not necessarily for others. If his uniqueness could be relational, for example, this would create fewer problems. Pluralists think that belief in the finality of Jesus Christ stands in the way of our appreciating other religions and getting along smoothly with them. They intend to correct the problem.

Different solutions have been proposed. The least radical involves shifting the emphasis away from metaphysics in the direction of action/functional categories. The problem could be eased, in the minds of theological pluralists, if we would just learn to view Jesus as God's love in action and present him as one who assists people to find access to the grace of God. Why not put the emphasis on Christ's prophetic office, then stress the way he reveals the Father's character and will for humans in his own life and teachings? This would shift the emphasis away from Jesus as a metaphysical oddity and toward the impact he had on people, the way he shaped people's understanding of what God is like. Instead of repeating the idea that God entered history in Jesus from the outside in a miraculous way, we could explain how Jesus functions as a window into God's very nature. As Jesus himself said, "Anyone who has seen me has seen the Father" (Jn 14:9). In this way, one can speak about the importance of Jesus without having to talk about his preexistence, or about the Trinity, or about Incarnation in a metaphysical sense.[28]

The late J. A. T. Robinson took this tack. He claimed that it was God's love that was incarnate in Jesus of Nazareth, not the divine substance. Jesus was special because God was acting in and through him. He became the image for us of who God is. Incarnation imagery supplies an effective mythic expression of the way we relate to God through him. Jesus is the clue to the nature of God as personal love, not the absolutely unique embodiment of God's being. He is unique in degree but not in kind.[29]

The idea of Jesus embodying God's love for us is true as far as it goes. But not going farther creates severe difficulties. First, unwanted claims of finality tend to attach themselves to action Christology, even though the claims are functional. Even when the Christ-event is taken only as disclosure, it is still viewed as decisive disclosure. But if decisive for us, why not for others? If it is decisive for us in our cultural setting, why not also in other people's settings? Second, functional Christology has a way of not remaining functional. Edward Schillebeeckx also places emphasis on Jesus' role in communicating God's love, but then he goes on to posit an ontological bond between Jesus and God his Father also. Substance and action categories are brought together in his final assessment. For, he reasons, if Jesus presents us with God most human, are we not also in the presence of unfathomable mystery?[30] Third, there are texts that present ontological teaching about the person of Jesus elsewhere in the New Testament, so that moving to action Christology does not really get one off the hook. It cannot account for the entire biblical witness, even though it can account for some of it.

A second possible way to correct the "problem" of high Christology in the New Testament allows one to accept the higher-than-functional claims that are made for Jesus and still dispense with universal normativeness. With reference to the "once and for all" language of the New Testament for the decisive work of Jesus, Paul Knitter comments that, "To close one's eyes to such proclamation is either psychologically to repress or dishonestly to deny what one does not wish to face." We cannot prevent the biblical witnesses from saying what they meant to say.[31]

Nevertheless, Knitter does try to evade the proclamation in another way. First, he explains the expressions in terms of the culture of the early Christians, saying it was natural for them to speak of their religious experiences in the ways that they did. Being a culturally conditioned way of speaking, their words tell us more about their social setting than about the actual person of Jesus. Second, their high praise of Jesus is more an expression of love and devotion to him than truth claims as such. It is rather like our saying, "My wife (or my husband) is the kindest and most loving person in the world." This is not a scientific statement based on research but rather love language. By looking at these claims in this way, Jesus can be relationally unique (like a spouse is relationally unique), unique in the way Christians experience God—but not unique in a universal sense, in the sense of being normative for other people who may experience God in different religious contexts. The confession, "Jesus is Lord," would express what Jesus means to us without carrying any implication that everybody in the world must worship him or come to God by way of him. This confession is our way to honor God, but need not be taken as a judgment on other confessions made by other people.

This approach allows one to admit that the New Testament witnesses make extraordinarily high claims for Jesus. Yet, one does not have to deny or excise them. The key is to reinterpret their significance in the experiential and confessional terms of love. Because they are culturally conditioned and psychologically rendered, the claims for Jesus turn out not to be truth claims in the ordinary sense, in which the church has understood them historically. The problem of high Christology vanishes.[32]

The approach is ingenious and possible, if not entirely plausible. But there are problems in the following areas. First, the New Testament writers appear to be stating, as far as one can tell, what they consider to be facts and truths. They are not only sharing religious feelings, but conveying what they took to be information as well. In a famous text, for example, Paul tells his readers about Christ's identification with their humanity and God's raising him up from the dead (1 Co 15:1–11). How fair is it to forbid Paul to make these claims by categorizing them as only what he could not but have said, given his culture and personal life-history? Surely we ought to take him more seriously than that. We need to listen to what he wants to say, and consider whether or not what he claims is true. Reducing the Resurrection to an event of experience only, when Paul obviously thought it was more than that, is unfair.[33] Just because it is easier for us to think of the Resurrection as the ongoing presence of Jesus rather than the transformation of a dead man, we are not entitled to impute this view to the early Christians. If they wanted to say more than that, we should let them. Such a hermeneutic is being driven by a modern agenda imposed on the text.[34]

Second, there is also something of a justice issue involved here. What right does a modern interpreter have to alter what the biblical witnesses intend, so as to make it mean something else? What right has he or she to change and reduce the meaning in this way? To transmute claims about Jesus, as Savior of the world and risen from the dead, into a description of what was going on in their culturally conditioned psyches is illegitimate. Suppose one turned this same argument on pluralists and reduced their claims in this same way? Are their claims for God similarly derivative from the psyche? Is it their love for God that makes them think there actually is a God? To argue in this way constitutes an unacceptable put-down. People have the right to make claims others do not like or accept without having others change and distort their meaning to suit themselves. New Testament claims for Jesus ought to be taken seriously, the same way Knitter's claim about God ought to be. It is inconsistent to apply a noncognitivist bias to claims for Jesus and not to claims for God.

Third, the suggestion is very dubious that Christians might

confess a nonnormative Jesus without losing anything important in their faith. Knitter posits our living, and even dying, for Christ with the knowledge that the truth of the gospel is our truth, but not necessarily the truth for the world. It is as though we could confess that Jesus is Lord while harboring the reservation that maybe he is, and maybe he isn't. How can Christ's resurrection be true for us and not for the world? The faith of Christians would be fatally damaged if it came to be accepted that the risen Lord were our myth of meaning and not more than that.[35]

A more radical approach to the problem of high Christology in the New Testament is adopted by John Hick.[36] First, he outright denies any uniqueness claims on the part of Jesus. He realizes that hesitating on this point would leave a thread of continuity between Jesus and the later developments, giving it a toehold of plausibility. This is certainly a wise move methodologically, if a risky one exegetically. Second, like Knitter he transposes all the uniqueness claims made on behalf of Jesus by the New Testament witnesses onto the level of noncognitive love language. Third, he attempts to locate the Christology of the Incarnation in a hypothetical context of the development of traditions. Using Buddhism as an example, he points to the process by which religious leaders are deified over time out of respect. Fourth, he adds that there are various insuperable logical problems with belief in Incarnation. This supplies a philosophical backup objection should all else fail.

Unfortunately, none of his points sticks firmly. First, one cannot deny Jesus' claims to uniqueness on the basis of critical exegesis. While granting his point about Jesus not making explicit claims to Incarnation, the implicit claims Jesus does make solidly ground the more-developed views of his person after the Resurrection. Not easily sidestepped, they entail the high view of Jesus which issued in the faith of the church. Second, transposing claims for Jesus' uniqueness made by the biblical witnesses onto the level of noncognitive love language is an unacceptable put-down of their sincerely held beliefs. It is rooted in hostile presuppositions against the truth of what they are declaring. Neither just nor fair, it refuses to take them seriously. Third, there is Christological development in early doctrine, and the Incarnation is noticeable in that development. But the Christology being developed there is already very high, with the event of Jesus' Resurrection, and constitutes an unpacking of what is implicit from the beginning.[37] The centuries of development envisaged by the Buddhist analogy do not exist in this case. Fourth, as to whether belief in the Incarnation is rational or not, two things can be said. First, the problem of finality is much larger than belief in the Incarnation. In many other ways the biblical witnesses lift up Jesus as Lord of the universe. Second, not everyone is as impressed as Hick by the logical problems of believing in the Incarnation. A large number of thoughtful Christians find the belief coherent, even true and magnificent.[38]

The New Testament quite effectively resists attempts of this type to rid it of the unwanted belief in the finality of Jesus Christ. Efforts to revise Christology downward are difficult to accept because they go against the evidence, and they appear to be based on special pleading and hostile presuppositions. It is impossible to bring it off in an exegetically convincing way. One cannot make the New Testament teach a non-normative Christology. There may be nothing wrong with trying—one learns a lot from conducting exegetical experiments. But in terms of results, the effort to rid the New Testament of the doctrine of the finality of Christ must be pronounced a failure.

TAKING OFF THE GLOVES

Why do people go to such lengths to establish a non-normative Christology against all odds? What fuels this passion? What dynamics drive the discussion? On one level, there is a healthy dynamic, stemming from the desire not to limit salvation to a minority of the race. I agree with this, though that does not in my opinion require one to deny the Incarnation. There must be another dynamic at work. I see it as the ideology of pluralism.

According to this ideology everybody knows that religions are relative to the cultures of which they are a part. No one should say that one religion is better than another. This does not involve truth and knowledge, for these are not involved at all except in the sense of existential truth, which would be relative to each individual. This is a dogma of modernity. To reject it is to invite being considered narrow-minded and bigoted. Everybody knows that Christianity is the religion proper to Canada, just as Hinduism is the religion proper to India. It is unacceptable for religions to make claims of universal validity. It goes against the grain of popular consciousness. Christianity cannot be regarded as superior in truth, and it cannot be considered the point of convergence for other religions. At most, it can only be relatively the best religion for a certain population at a given time. It would be unfair for truth not to be equally and simultaneously present to everyone. It cannot be accepted that it would arise in a particular historical situation. We have to assume that ultimate reality is known vaguely by everyone, even if not clearly by anyone. The assumptions of modernity require us to say that God is unknowable by mortals, and all claims to know the Real are humanly generated myths. Only in this way do we all stand on level ground, something that modernity requires.

This is the deeper reason why pluralists object to a high Christology. Though they may try to make their point exegetically, what drives them has little to do with the Bible. Exegesis is more of a strategy for bringing on board more conservative Christians, who respect the Bible and tradition. Pluralists know that they are a minority in the churches. Therefore, in order to win a hearing for theological revision they will have to make out a biblical case for it. In actual fact, however, the reason for rejecting the finality of Christ is not exegetical but rather that Christ's finality does not fit into the modern mindset.

A major problem with imposing religious relativism on religions in general, and on Christianity in particular, is its unfairness. It rules out people's most precious beliefs in things normative. It asks Muslims, in effect, to deny that the Koran is central to God's purpose. It asks Jews to deny that God spoke definitively through Moses. It asks Christians to deny that Jesus is the Incarnation of God in history. Is that a reasonable or even a practical thing to ask people to do? Obviously it is not.

Enlightenment dogma may ask this of people, but we cannot. All religions make truth claims which are salty and distinctive, just as all philosophies and biologies do. Religions do not simply say the same things as one another about God, humanity, salvation, and hope. To say that they do is intellectual dishonesty. There are intractable differences of doctrine, and therefore choices to be made. To wave a wand over religions and declare that they are saying the same thing is nonsense. This is sloppy pluralism, false tolerance, and indifference to truth.[39]

There must be a greater concern for truth. Muslims, for example, cannot be asked to drop their convictions about the Koran out of politeness and civility. Even to make such a request is a refusal to take their beliefs seriously. Only a person for whom the doctrines mean very little would think up an idea like this. Liberals in the religions treat religions as putty to be shaped however one wishes, and adapted to a desired cultural shape.

Truth claims in religion must be taken more seriously than that. They must be viewed like claims in science or philosophy or medicine. In those areas, there is no leveling down, no denial of real differences, no overlooking of bad mistakes. Instead, there is a concern for truth and a willingness to search it out in the midst of disagreements. The suggestion that Christians or Buddhists should give up their most precious beliefs for the sake of politeness is a form of intolerance on the part of the people who claim to be so tolerant. No one is in the position to refuse religious communities the right to hold distinctive convictions.[40] As Rabbi David Novak has commented: "The moral impotence of religious relativism comes out when one faces what for both Judaism and Christianity is the greatest of all God's demands: martyrdom. For if one is to die as a martyr rather than abandon one's own faith for anyone else's, how can one justify this ultimate sacrifice if the other faith is as true as one's own?"[41]

The only feasible way to promote interreligious dialogue is to invite people to approach the dialogue from the perspective of their own covenant relationship with God. We can only approach universality from the point of our own particularity. This does not mean these commitments can never be discussed. On the contrary, they must be. But it does mean that relativism cannot be the basis of dialogue.[42] The first Christians lived in a religiously plural world and when they made claims like "Jesus Christ is Lord," they did so in the awareness of the differences. They made the claim anyway because they believed it to be true, not because they did not know what they were doing.

What we are up against is Enlightenment dogmatism masquerading as toleration. The commitment to relativism and the commitment to Jesus Christ are both faith positions that need to be tested. The one cannot set the rules for the other to bow to. Neither is right a priori. Christians believe that in Jesus we find a particular healing for the whole world. One can deny it and try to refute it, but one cannot rule it out of court from the beginning.

Besides being unfair, religious relativism is also incoherent. If all beliefs are historically conditioned, what about belief in relativity, which is so obviously a product of late modernity? Belief in relativism did not come out of nowhere. It does not have the status of revelation. How is it that one can be relativistic about everything and not about relativism itself? How logical is it for a person claiming to be free of dogma to harbor a dogma against dogmas? It is self-refuting for a skeptic to say that skepticism is certain, or for an agnostic to say with certainty that God does not exist. A relativist cannot make any absolute claims at all and be consistent, and that includes the claim that "all claims are relative, there are no absolutes in history." It is the very people who hold vociferously to relativism who are such dogmatists. But how do they know God did not call Abraham to be the source of blessing for the nations? How do they know Muhammad is not seal of the prophets? How do they know Buddha did not have the answer? On the basis of relativism they cannot know this, yet they pretend to know. They know what they know on the basis of relativism accepted by faith.

In theological pluralism we are up against a metareligious conviction, an attitude which is not at all open-minded or tolerant to non-relativist ways of thinking. Though presented as the way of tolerance, pluralism as an ideology is not tolerant when it meets with those who believe that there is truth and that it is possible to attain it. True pluralists respect other people's convictions and do not demand they discard them. They recognize and respect the real differences in religions and do not pretend these differences do not exist, or do not matter, or have no merit. True pluralists do not even despair of finding truth through religion, and wish to pursue truth in genuine dialogue.

Theological pluralism is not what it appears. As with Hindu tolerance, it can be a covert form of monism. When John Hick declares, "All religions are varied responses to ineffable divine reality,"[43] how does he know that? It is a very Eastern way of thinking. It is not something just obviously true. If in fact the divine is so ineffable and unknowable, how does one know any path is valid? If the Real is unknowable, how can one say that all religions are valid paths to salvation? If God is unknowable, then one cannot say *anything* informative about *any* religious path. Hick's pluralism is really an apologetic for the monistic path which is agnostic about the Real. This is not open or tolerant to other faiths. It would be better if we assumed that the religions embody various truth claims not to be swept aside but to be probed and weighed.

This debate is not between those who do and those who do not want to promote racial unity, peace among nations, and harmonious relationships among the religions. This debate is over the basis for such unity and peace. To ask about the oneness of humanity is itself a religious question. Christians believe that this oneness is based on God's creation of humanity and redemption in Jesus Christ. The Good News is that Jesus has made us one, so of course we want to tell the whole world about that (Eph 2:15). The unity of the race, therefore, does not have to be invented but appropriated. The Gospel offers a basis for the salvation and unification of humankind. It may even offer the best hope there is for it. Though a contested claim, it would be folly to discard this possibility, especially in the absence of an obviously better basis on which to achieve it. If there is a better basis somewhere else, then let us hear about it in the context of truth-seeking dialogue. One thing is sure, relativism does not provide a better foundation for it. Relativism puts us back to square one, back to the unknown God and to tribes in conflict. Before we agree to drop our Christology, we should be sure there is something to replace it with that has some teeth in it.

In the Revelation we read of a scroll which contains the divine purposes for history. No one can open it except Jesus. Without him we would not know what was written on it. Only the lion of the tribe of Judah is worthy to open the scroll and its seals (Rev 5:5). The purposes of history are bound up with him. I realize that it may be embarrassing to pluralism to say that the unity of humankind and its salvation are tied up with a single figure, Jesus Christ. But the possibility that the world's destiny may be tied up with Jesus cannot be ruled out. This is not a claim for the superiority of Christianity as a historical movement over the other religions. I am only contending that the uniqueness of Jesus is central to the Christian message, and interreligious dialogue will not be served by trying to deny that.[44]

DOES A HIGH CHRISTOLOGY ENTAIL NARROWNESS?

What disturbs people most is not high Christology itself but the thought that such a belief entails a narrowness in divine salvation and what this belief may say about our attitude to other people. It is this that causes pluralists to take extreme measures such as revising Christology downwards. Although most church members would not think this a right or practical thing to do, and are not attracted to any kind of relativism or syncretism, nevertheless they feel the same pressure pluralists feel and they want better answers from traditionalists than they have been getting. Church members understand what motivates the pluralists, even if they are uncomfortable with their proposed solutions.

What has to be said forthrightly is that a biblically based Christology does not entail a narrowness of outlook toward other people. The church's confesssion about Jesus is compatible with an open spirit, with an optimism of salvation, and with a wider hope. Sensitivity to religious pluralism does not require radical revision of our doctrine of Christ. God's decision to deal with humanity through the agency of Jesus does not mean or imply that his plan is lacking in universal implications. According to the New Testament, the work of redemption, which spans all ages and continents and comes to fullest expression at a particular point in history, also issues out again into universality. The pattern is certainly unusual and distinctive. If, as C. S. Lewis said, the Christian message were something we were making up, then we could have made it less surprising. Nevertheless, the salvation of the world through Jesus Christ is not an incoherent idea but something true, beautiful, and satisfying. It stands almost alone in offering hope to a broken world.

The spirit and wisdom of the Second Vatican Council is worthy of commendation in these matters. The Council made clear that God's grace is global, and that the belief in the Incarnation complements and does not cancel that fact. Faith in the triune God gave the bishops the wide scope of their sympathies. If God be the Father, maker of heaven and earth, who identifies himself with humanity in the person of his son Jesus Christ who entered history for our sake and subsequently poured his Spirit out upon all flesh, then we are not dealing with a small operation in his plan of redemption. As stated in the preface to the Council's *Decree on Missionary Activity*, "The present historical situation is leading humanity into a new stage. As salt of the earth and light of the world, the church is summoned with special urgency to save and renew every creature. In this way all things can be restored in Christ and in him humankind can compose one family and one people."

The achievement of Vatican II was in showing Christians that it is possible to hold to the finality of Jesus Christ and at the same time give qualified recognition to the positive religious worth of other faiths. The bishops prove that it is not necessary, in order to recognize God's work among nations, to deny central elements of the Christian faith—such as a high Christology or world missions.[45] Instead, one can say that a high Christology "mandates both an openness to other religious traditions and a responsible ministry of evangelism on a worldwide scale."[46]

The Vatican Council knows no other salvation than what God has given through Jesus Christ and no other hope than the hope of the Gospel, imperfectly embodied as it is in the church's life and message. It knows no other basis of hope for humanity than the hope founded in the work of Jesus Christ for sinners. But at the same time, the Council views the whole world as lying within the circle of God's grace and the object of his loving care. One may be "outside" the church, but one can never be "outside" God's love. The Council knows how to distinguish the ontological necessity of Christ's work of redemption from the epistemological situation of sinners. There is no salvation except through Christ but it is not necessary for everybody to possess a conscious knowledge of Christ in order to benefit from redemption through him. The patriarch Job, for example, was saved by Christ (ontologically) without actually knowing the name of Jesus (epistemologically).

The Council seeks to foster bonds of unity between the church and other religions in the interests of God's saving plan for all nations, recognizing that God is at at work among them causing much that is true and noble in them. At the same time, "she proclaims and must ever proclaim Christ, the way, the truth, and the life, in whom men find the fullness of religious life and in whom God has reconciled all things to himself" (*Declaration on the Relationship of the Church to Non-Christian Religions*, par. 2).

Some Catholics, thirty years after the Council, are moving in directions which seem mistaken and dangerous. For example, the papal encyclical *Redemptor Hominis* (1979) declared: "The human person—every human person without exception—has been redeemed by Christ." In such a statement, the distinction is not preserved between redemption objectively provided and redemption subjectively appropriated. It is made to sound as if the benefits of the gospel are automatically applied, apart from faith. If so, the need of conversion seems to have been undercut.[47] Similarly, it is common now for Catholics to speak of other religions as vehicles of salvation.[48] Such views further erode the need of conversion to Christ and have led to a diminished urgency for evangelism in the church. Let the reader note that The Second Vatican Council does not say such things. It maintains a wiser caution. Catholics and evangelicals alike should heed its more conservative judgments.[49]

The basis of an open attitude to all peoples theologically is the doctrine of the triune God and of his prevenient grace.[50] Let us review the matter briefly. First, we confess the lordship of God: "We believe in God the Father almighty, Maker of heaven and earth." God, the Creator of the world and Lord of all history, is the mystery of our being and present everywhere. "For in him we live and move and have our being" (Ac 17:28). God is within and God is beyond all human structures and institutions. God is the unity in the midst of all the diversity. He is the gracious God, the God who loves the world so much that he sent his Son to be redeemer of the world. There are not two gods, an angry Father and a gracious Son, but one God, the Father of our Lord Jesus Christ. God the Father is present everywhere in his graciousness, not only where Jesus of Nazareth is named. God is present and at work in every sphere of human life, secular as well as sacred. He is free to act outside as well as inside ecclesiastical structures. We live in one world, which is the creation of the one God. There is no other source from which anyone draws life, and the mystery which surrounds us is the God who loves us in Jesus Christ. God has the whole world in his hands. He sees the sparrow fall. He sustains our life in the world. God is love.

The church also confesses: "We believe in Jesus Christ his only Son our Lord." The life of Jesus is the point in history where God's secret plan for the creation is disclosed, where what he has been doing hiddenly on a grand scale becomes visible and explicit. In Christ, the mystery hidden for ages is revealed and we are made aware of the gracious God who makes all things new. The Incarnation does not weaken but seals and strengthens our confidence in the universal salvific will of God. From the Old Testament Scriptures we learn about God's global reach of grace, and through the Son we receive definitive confirmation of that grace. The Incarnation underlines and highlights the universal salvific will of God. Through our living Lord, now exalted in the heavens, and through the outpoured Spirit, God is working to make all things new. Although God is present everywhere in his graciousness, his purpose and will are not everywhere clearly perceived. The coming of Jesus, far from shutting the door to universality as some suppose, opens it widely and decisively. Now one can connect the light that has enlightened everyone coming into the world with a stronger light that has come with Jesus, the embodiment of the logos which is at work in the whole world.

It is important to remember that the Logos, which was made flesh in Jesus of Nazareth, is present in the entire world and in the whole of human history.[51] Though Jesus Christ is Lord, we confess at the same time that the Logos is not confined to one segment of human history or one piece of world geography. The second Person of the Trinity was incarnate in Jesus, but is not totally limited to Palestine. In a real sense, when the missionaries take testimony about Jesus to the world, they take the gospel to places where the Logos has already been active. They will discover noble insights and actions which are the result of God working among the peoples.[52]

Evangelicals tend to be unitarians of the second person and often not fully trinitarian. We need to realize that our insisting that God is embodied and defined by Christ does not mean that God is exhausted by Christ or totally confined to Christ. God the Logos has more going on by way of redemption than what happened in first-century Palestine, decisive though that was for the salvation of the world. Recognizing the cosmic Christ is a way to balance the exclusive and the inclusive biblical texts and can be the key to broadening our

Christian attitudes. Acknowledging the Logos at work in the wider world is the way to confess the Incarnation without it being a hindrance to openness.

We also confess: "We believe in the Holy Spirit, the Lord, the giver of life . . . who has spoken through the Prophets." The Spirit is the mysterious presence, the breath and vitality of God in the world. It is important for us to consider siding with the Eastern churches in an ancient dispute about the Spirit over the question of whether the Spirit proceeded from the Father and the Son (filioque), or from the Father only. Most people today may consider this a futile and useless question, but it is not when considered in this context. What makes it important in the context of religious pluralism is that, according to the Eastern view, the Spirit is not tied to the Christ-event exclusively but rather can operate in the whole world, which is the Father's domain. This provides another way of thinking about God being active in the world at large. God is active by his Spirit in the structures of creation, in the whole of history, even in the sphere of the religions.[53] The breath of God is free to blow wherever it wills (Jn 3:8). The economy of the Spirit is not under our control, and certainly it is not limited to the church.[54]

The triune God is a missionary God. The Father sends the Son and the Spirit into the world (Gal 4:4–6). His heart reaches out to embrace it. He gives himself up in becoming human and thus moves history toward redemption. Here is the basis of the unity of humankind and the salvation of the world. There is no hint of the grace of God being limited to a single thread of human history.[55]

CONCLUSION

The appeal of theological pluralism and the drive to revise church Christology downward derives from outrage at restrictivist thinking. Pluralists think it spells relief, but in actual fact it spells disaster and is quite unnecessary. A trinitarian theology supplies the broad and adequate basis we need for openness and hope. Those texts used to support pessimism and exclusivism are being read out of context. Of course there is no other name given to us by which to be saved (Ac 4:12), but Peter is referring to messianic salvation including physical healing through Jesus' name. He is not denying premessianic occurrences of God's grace. Certainly Jesus is the way, the truth, and the life, and no one comes to the Father but by him (Jn 14:6). No one else can show us the way to find God understood as Abba, Father. But in saying this, Jesus is not denying the truth about the Logos enlightening everyone coming into the world (Jn 1:9). He is not denying God at work in the wider world beyond Palestine and before his own time.

Why was Karl Barth, a great trinitarian theologian, not more open to general revelation, to prevenient grace, and to other religions? Why did he not recognize the meaning of the trinity for the wider work of God? It was due to what is called his Christomonism. A strong defender of the filioque, Barth could only see God reaching out to people in and through Jesus. To maintain this position, of course, he had to ignore a good deal of scriptural material. Barth is proof that a high Christology can be used to entail narrowness and justify pluralist fears in that regard. But it seems to me that a trinitarian theology does not point in the direction of narrowness.

These two axioms do not enable or require specific deductions with regard to the view we should take concerning other religions. For example, it does not require Karl Rahner's deduction. Although he is correct in saying that we may expect God to be seeking lost sinners, he may be mistaken to dogmatize about the role the world's religions play in this. We cannot know by way of deduction that religions will necessarily be the main sphere of life in which God deals with people. On the other hand, it does not require Karl Barth's deduction either. Although he is correct in insisting that God's grace comes to humankind in Jesus Christ (Rahner would agree with him), he may be wrong to state so dogmatically that religions as such are always negative. Why would God, who is present everywhere, absent himself so totally from the sphere of religion, the very realm in which people search for ultimate answers? These are sheer speculations, isolated from the scriptural data.

The triune God is free to work out the application of his love and salvation for humankind in the ways he chooses. We have proved in these two foundational chapters on a theology of religions that God is seeking all sinners, and he has provided for them all in Jesus Christ. We have not found anything specific about religions themselves. In order to arrive at more specific results, it will be necessary to consider other relevant data, especially scriptural and phenomenal data. As in most matters, it is safer to rely on empirical investigation than on grand theory. What we have concluded from chapter one is that God loves the human race; and from chapter two, that God was in Christ reconciling the world to himself. We have not yet learned what role (if any) the other religions play in the outworking of the drama of redemption.

Three

Religions Now

P eople everywhere both inside and outside the church are asking similar questions: why are there so many religions? Why have these continued to flourish, even after the coming of Jesus Christ? What are we to make of them? Will Christianity displace or absorb them? Should we ignore or cooperate with them? May we think of God working in and through them? Questions like these have taken on central importance for people in our generation.

It has been difficult to answer such questions satisfactorily in the past because the Christian traditions until recently have tended to view other religions as spiritual and theological zones of darkness. Church leaders have not been willing to recognize divine light shining in them. The comment that Luther made on this is typical: "All worship and religions outside Christ are the worship of idols."[1] Perhaps this is the sort of religion Luther and others chiefly experienced, religions manifesting corrupt aspects and not inviting favorable judgments. But the attitude of unrelieved negativism no longer seems fair or right. With the publication of the sacred books of the East a century ago, with increased travel and electronic communications, with an increase of direct knowledge into the human religious situation, the issue of religions outside Christ has to be reopened and reexamined.

Therefore, in this chapter we will be turning to the Bible to search out information possibly relevant to settling some of these issues. I have found (somewhat to my surprise) that the Bible offers a more balanced view of religious life than my tradition had allowed for. In particular, I was struck by the discovery of a much-neglected biblical theme, the holy pagan tradition. Because it is important to our subject, we should retrieve it.[2]

In the past, it has been possible for Christians mostly to ignore other religions, just as other religions ignored Christianity. This was due chiefly to the fact that Christian communities in the West were isolated from firsthand contact with religious communities elsewhere in the world. However, with the world becoming smaller, it has become impossible to ignore the religious values of hundreds of millions of people who have faith outside the Gospel. We cannot live any more in splendid isolation, cut off from these people. We meet them on a day-to-day basis. Christian love itself dictates that we show a more serious interest in all aspects of their lives, including their religious experiences and beliefs. Not only are they loved by God just as we are, there are also elements of truth and nobility in what they believe and what they do that cannot be denied. In the past, we have accepted that there was much to learn from a pagan philosopher like Plato or Aristotle. It should not prove too difficult, then, for us to open up a dialogue with believers and thinkers of other faiths. In principle, it should not be impossible to open up some positive relations with them.

In the first two chapters, we considered the basic Christian truth claim in its dialectical two-sidedness: salvation for the whole world *through* Jesus Christ. This gave us two parameters within which to think about the other religions. As we begin now to do that, let us take up a new set of questions: How does God relate to religious people of other faiths? How should we think of religion as it exists in the world around us? What does Scripture say about our approach to people of other faiths? Underlying all this will be our concern about the universality of God's saving plan, and how the multitudes who seem to be left out of it actually have access to it.

The next three chapters take up the specifics of our theology of religions. This chapter considers the status of religious experience as it presently exists in history. The next reflects on the possible futures of religions in relation to Christ's victory over the powers. Chapter five ponders the question of the eschatological destiny of the unevangelized, insofar as it can be known this side of eternity.

There is a range of possible attitudes to other religions that is worth reviewing as we get started. First, there are secularists who consider all the religions deceptive and untrue. These are people in the tradition of Nietzsche, Feuerbach, Marx, and Freud, who maintain that religions represent the curious human practice of self-delusion and self-deception. This is a totally negative view of religion, the view of only a minority of people historically but a view growing in popularity in the Western societies. It is an odd position to hold, considering how pervasive religion is in all cultures across time and space. It leads one to ask why, if materialism is true, people deceive themselves so consistently.[3]

At the other end of the spectrum are pluralists and inclusivists who hold that religions are all more or less true and valid, despite their great differences. They take them as true either in the sense of their saying basically the same things deep down, or in the sense of their being appropriate for the people who invented them within their own cultures. The idea is that each religion can and should be appreciated as the expression of a valid response to God. Practically no religion should be judged hopelessly false or harmful. This position too is odd, though in a different way from the secularist, in that it requires denying a great deal of wickedness and error which crops up fairly regularly in the sphere of religion. Since philosophies are not equal in validity or practicality, why should religions be?

Between the two extremes are some middle positions which claim greater support. Closer to the skeptical view is the traditional position which judges religions false with one exception: one's own religion. Like Karl Barth, conservatives usually judge Christianity true and other religions false. Though reflecting a commendably high estimate of the finality of Jesus Christ, this is an odd position in that it is so positive about the religiosity of Christians, while so negative about the religiosity of everybody else. One would suppose that people who are themselves religious would be more open and sympathetic toward other people of faiths, especially when considering the threat of secularism against any and all religions. Conservatives have not yet seen the need for cobelligerency on this matter.

The position I prefer is a middle one which couples the church's confession of Jesus Christ with genuine openness to the truth and the goodness found in other religions. It is the official position of the Catholic church since the Second Vatican Council, and one which seems to be growing in popularity among both mainline and evangelical Protestants. This view combines belief in the gospel as God's saving truth for all nations with a recognition of premessianic

truth and goodness in other religions. It holds that belief in the
finality of Jesus Christ does not entail narrowness or exclusiveness on
our part toward other faiths. Our Christian faith does not rule out
listening to other people in the hope of learning from them and
recognizing God's hand upon them. At the same time, it does not
trivialize the truth question, pretending there is agreement where
there is not, nor does it overlook error and darkness where that
exists.[4]

What I and other evangelical theologians confront is a restrictivist
control belief so common in our communities that effectively denies
the universal salvific will of God. It seeks to suppress biblical
evidence that God has such a will, along with any evidence that he is
working broadly in history. This opposition comes at every stage.
There is objection to appealing to a Logos Christology; to appreciation of the positive value of general revelation; to the concept of the
Spirit at work in the wider world; and to a view of the significance of
individuals like Melchizedek and Cornelius. The reader will have to
decide who is right, and who is listening to the Bible most carefully.
Let us heed Paul's advice in 1 Thessalonians 5:21-22: "Test everything. Hold on to the good. Avoid every kind of evil."

WHAT IS RELIGION?

Religion is not an easy word to define. Augustine ran into a
similar problem when asked to define the word "time"; he thought he
knew what time meant until someone asked him to explain it. It is
similar with the word "religion." You think you know what it means
until asked to define it. In defining religion, I make a distinction
between subjective and objective religion. Subjective religion refers
to existential faith, piety, or the fear of God. Objective religion refers
to cumulative traditions such as Christianity and Buddhism, insofar as
they are institutions and cultural movements. The Bible does not use
the word religion very often, either of personal religion (Jas 1:26–
27) or objective religion (Gal 1:13–14). To speak as we do of, for
examples, Sikhism and Jainism, is modern coinage and quite an
abstraction. In this chapter I will emphasize religion in the subjective
sense. In the next chapter we will explore religion as objective.

Subjective religion refers to the heart response to God, to that sphere of human consciousness in which ultimate commitments are decided. As subjective, religion is a universal dimension of human life where questions of truth, meaning, and value are asked. It is the sphere of ultimate concern, where people contemplate the highest good and worship God as they understand him. Tillich's definition of subjective religion suits me. He said that "Religion is the state of being grasped by an ultimate concern, a concern which qualifies all other concerns as preliminary and which itself contains the answer to the question of the meaning of our life. Therefore, this concern is unconditionally serious and shows a willingness to sacrifice any finite concern which is in conflict with it."[5]

Religion in the subjective sense is the Bible's main concern. Jesus, for example, does not relate to religions as abstractions. He relates to persons in their uniqueness at the level of their heart needs. One does not find him stereotyping the woman at the well as a member of the Samaritan sect, and then raising religious differences between it and his own type of Judaism. Rather, Jesus treated her as a real person, offering her living water to satisfy her inner longing. Thinking about religions as objective risks losing sight of the uniqueness of persons and of judging their interior life as a fixed quantity known by an external label and not as something dynamic and capable of change. According to Hebrews, it is faith or subjective religion which God is most concerned about: "And without faith it is impossible to please God, because anyone who comes to him must believe that he exists and that he rewards those who earnestly seek him" (Heb 11:6).

THE BIBLE'S VIEW OF OTHER RELIGIONS

Evangelicals have read the Bible on the topic of other religions using the control belief that says there is little truth or goodness in them. Influenced by it myself, I was surprised by what I found when I surveyed the text afresh on this question. I found a valuational spectrum running all the way from the sort of religious experience that is false and vile, to the sort of religious experience that is noble and uplifting. Religion according to the Bible is deeply ambiguous, a fact that resonates with my own experience. Religion sometimes appears in the form of naked self-justification, and at other times functions positively, both vertically in relation to God and horizontally in fostering community. Scripture and experience agree about this; religion can be life-sustaining and spiritually enriching, or it can be delusory and destructive—and everything in between. The extremes can even occur alongside each other in the same religious traditions. In a congregation of any faith, one will find saints and hypocrites kneeling together, some responding to God out of a pure heart, others using religion to mask their rebellion and wickedness. In every religion, some respond to the truth set before them while others hold it down in unrighteousness. Religion can facilitate one person's approach to God, and at the same time be a means of escaping God for another. Let us delve into this phenomenon.[6]

A. False Religion

I have decided to examine false and vile religion first, because of the danger of being simplistic and naïve about religion. A biblically informed Christian cannot be a fan of religion in general because darkness can masquerade as light. Paul wrote that "Satan himself masquerades as an angel of light. It is not surprising, then, if his servants masquerade as servants of righteousness" (2 Co 11:14–15). Religion is not necessarily positive. There is much in it that can enslave and blind people. Placing faith in false gods is denounced in Scripture because it has dire consequences. For example, fanaticism and bigotry commonly are products of religion. A threat to world peace arises from Catholic against Protestant in Northern Ireland, Hindu against Muslim throughout India, Sikh against Hindu in the Punjab, Hindu against Buddhist in Sri Lanka, and Muslim against Jew in the Middle East.

John writes that "The light shines in the darkness, but the darkness has not understood it" (Jn 1:5). According to this text, there is light and there is darkness, and one must do justice to both sides. On the one hand, we should celebrate and honor whatever goodness and truth there is anywhere, even in the context of other faiths. On the other hand, we must not blind ourselves to the ways in which religions enslave and darken the minds of men and women, distort their perceptions, corrupt their wills, and harden their hearts.

It is not my intention, in starting with the dark end of the spectrum, to cancel the positive signals that the recent Vatican Council sent out to the world community of religions.[7] Rather my intention is to correct a certain naïveté, the love affair that some people today have with religion in general. I contend that it is wrong and unsafe to view religion through rose-tinted glasses as something wholly positive. Let us keep our eyes open; religion can be cruel, destructive, and an abomination to the Lord (Am 5:21).

There is also a strategic reason for my starting at the dark or negative end of the spectrum. It arises out of the fact that one reason for writing this book is the desire to persuade evangelicals to embrace a position of greater openness and generosity toward other faiths. Since evangelicals understand already the dark side of religion, they will want to know whether I see this aspect too. It would not work for me to begin with a defense of religion as possibly something noble and uplifting. My argument would not get off the ground.

In showing the dark side of religion, I will take some examples from Old and New Testaments, and then refer to some religious phenomenology that confirms them.

1. Canaanite religion is certainly presented in the Old Testament as a false and destructive faith, so bad indeed that it deserved to be wiped out, according to the biblical historians. At any rate, here was a religious path that did not lead to God and one that the world would have been better off without. I realize that some wince at the harshness of this judgment and denounce the Old Testament for making it. But I also wonder whether this is not due to the fact that Western peoples seldom encounter truly nauseating religious cults close up. (This is now changing as society degenerates into neo-paganism.) We would not be so shocked by these judgments if we experienced the sort of thing the Old Testament is referring to: the world of idolatry, child sacrifice, fertility cults, sacred prostitution, blood-soaked rhetoric, snake worship, demons, necromancy, gods without moral character, magic, divination and the like. God told the Israelites not to have any relations with those religions. It would only corrupt their relationship with him. We have no reason to doubt the truth of this.[8]

The reader can confirm Scripture's judgment by becoming acquainted with Canaanite, Ugaritic, Moabite, Hittite, Philistine, and Phoenician religions—or by reflecting on the biographies of such popular deities as Baal, Anat, Moloch, Dagan, Chemosh, and Astarte. A closer look at these gods and their practices would remove some of the regret one might feel initially at the perishing of these religious cults. The regret might even turn to anxiety that they have not completely perished but might reappear to blight the world again. The gods of violence, debauchery, cruelty, power, and materialism do not die off so easily. They seem to go into remission only to rise again at the opportune time.[9]

Goddess worship has actually come back into vogue in modern culture, taking delight in its Canaanite roots. In cases like this it would be wise to consider why the Old Testament preferred male imagery over female imagery for God, and why it warned against worship of the goddess instead of just ritualistically denouncing it. The "queen of heaven" (Jer 44:17) is likely to turn out to be a blood-thirsty monster, unfit for any kind of worship, feminist or otherwise. More likely, the goddess may prove to be the impersonal matrix from which the world has emanated. The point is that switching from male to female imagery for God will improve nothing. Susanne Heine warns that the turn to goddess spirituality is a mistake that promises to nullify the gains women have made in church and society in recent years.[10]

2. A second example of bad religion is Israelite religion itself. This was far from flawless, as presented in the Old and New Testaments. Israelitism is as mixed a blessing as heathenism; the prophets speak out strongly and repeatedly against Israel's infidelity and religious practices. Jesus viewed his own rejection against this very background and found it no surprise. He knew a crisis awaited him from the beginning. Startling though it may seem, even a religion founded on the basis of a divine covenant and election can become corrupted and actually keep people away from God rather than facilitating their coming to him. The Old Testament nowhere suggests that being an Israelite by birth in any way validates one's response to the word of God. Even a religion with large doses of revealed truth, like Israel's, failed dismally again and again, according to the Hebrew Scriptures.[11]

Is it possible that, due to such a failure, Yahweh is portrayed on occasion as cruel and peevish? What else can be the meaning of the side of God seen in certain texts of the Old Testament (like Ex 4:24)?

Does this stem from the human side of Scripture? Two factors make that seem possible. First, no Christian would picture God in a way that suggests a course correction. Second, the reason they would not picture God as cruel and peevish is because of Jesus Christ. When James and John asked, "Lord, do you want us to call fire down from heaven to destroy them?" Jesus turned and rebuked them, saying (according to some manuscripts), "You do not know what kind of spirit you are of, for the Son of Man did not come to destroy men's lives, but to save them" (Lk 9:54–55). It appears that the Old Testament did not always capture the divine nature with full accuracy. Does this not also illustrate the failure of religion in Israel's case?

3. Religion is also viewed negatively in the New Testament. Jesus never spoke more harshly than when he condemned Israel's religious leaders (Mt 23:1–37). He lamented an almost total lack of understanding of God's nature and purposes on the part of Israel's leaders, whom he called "blind leaders of the blind" (Lk 11:37–52). He was disturbed by their love of ritual, of status, of honorific titles and robes, of externals, of legal niceties. Such religion was human unbelief and rebellion. Alongside the finest of impulses lay dark hypocrisy and wickedness. People most knowledgeable of the things of God turned out to be farthest from the kingdom of God, while penitent publicans and sinners outside strict observance of the law were closer to the kingdom. As if to seal this point, it would be the most religious people who asked for Jesus to be crucified—the guardians of revelation, not the atheists.[12]

4. Paul criticizes religion in numerous places, too. There is in religion a misguided religious passion, an unenlightened zeal for God (Ro 10:2). When the Thessalonians were converted, Paul likened it to a turning from idols to serve the true and living God (1 Th 1:9). To Colossian believers, he said that becoming a Christian is like being delivered from the dominion of darkness, transferred into the kingdom of God's beloved Son (Col 1:13). In a speech recorded in Acts, Paul declared that Gentiles need to have their eyes opened and to turn from darkness to light, from the power of Satan to God (Ac 26:18). Paul knows full well that religion can be the path of deception, and he expresses the fear lest Christians be deceived and believe a false gospel foisted on them (2 Co 11:3–4). He speaks of false apostles, deceitful workmen, who disguise themselves as

apostles of Christ, adding, "And no wonder, for Satan himself masquerades as an angel of light" (2 Co 11:14). Even the Christian religion can be nothing but empty form, lacking in power and reality (2 Ti 3:5). Paul personally encountered religious functionaries on his travels who were possessed by demons (Ac 13:6–12). When Paul surveyed the religious pluralism in the city of Athens, his first reaction was one of disgust ("His spirit was provoked within him" Ac 17:16). Far from delighting in what he saw, he was greatly troubled. Of the Gentiles, he said in one place that they were "without hope and without God in the world" (Eph 2:12). One cannot accuse either Paul or Jesus of viewing religion uncritically through rose-colored spectacles. They saw the dark side very clearly.

The church has to take this critique of religion seriously. No one is immune from being religious in unacceptable ways. Anyone can fall into error and corruption under the guise of religion. Not even receiving messianic light guarantees avoiding religious disaster. Darkness and iniquity can hide as comfortably under a Christian banner as any other. One can go to hell as easily from church as from temple or mosque. Peter says that judgment begins at the house of God (1 Pe 4:17). It is a sobering thought that among the seven churches of Asia in the book of Revelation, only one (Philadelphia) escapes condemnation from the risen Lord (Rev 2–3).

The conclusion to be drawn is that religion may be dark, deceptive, and cruel. It harbors ugliness, pride, error, hypocrisy, darkness, cruelty, demons, hardheartedness, blindness, fanaticism, and deception. The idea that world religions ordinarily function as paths to salvation is dangerous nonsense and wishful thinking.

This is not difficult to accept, for this line of biblical teaching on religion is unfortunately regularly confirmed in ordinary experience. It is perhaps noteworthy that, though the Greek Fathers were prepared to accept the idea that God was at work in the lives of pagan people, they had little good to say about the religions of antiquity. Justin Martyr, for example, praised Socrates for listening to the voice of the Logos, but he opposed the religions of his day just as Socrates had opposed them in his time. Justin regarded religions as inspired by Satan. He said their gods were "wicked and unholy demons whose actions are inferior to those of mere men who set their hearts on virtue" (*Apology*, I, 5). I do not think his harsh judgments were due to prejudice but to bitter experience. What he encountered in the religious realm of his day had little noble aspiration or moral goodness in it.[13]

Anyone can provide a formidable list of religious expressions that are evil, whether from the history of religions or from personal experience. There are so many candidates to choose from, like the religions of the world that offer social stability but no hope of redemptive transformation, or religions that instill fear of death and malevolent spirits, the observance of taboos and placation of the gods. Generally favorable toward religion, John Hick describes this preaxial religious outlook (which concerns itself more with the preservation of cosmic and social order than with salvation) which still persists and does not die out.[14] Was the blood of countless human sacrifices in Aztec religion much worse than the practice of voodoo among the population of Haiti, a religion of sorcery and magic, of charms and spells?[15] How different are the all-too-human gods of the Ugarit or Greek pantheons from the millions of deities of popular Hinduism, including such as Kali, Krishna and Shiva? There is so much that is evil in religion. The caste system continues in India to this day, sanctioning a pious neglect of the poor. Islam continues its intolerance toward the non-Muslim world, and its violence against Muslims who wish to forsake Islam. How can one forget the picture of the Muslim plunging the knife in the Israeli woman, crying, "Allah akbar!"

There are so many evil sides to religion that a fulfillment paradigm (the idea that religions point people to Christ) is out of the question. Religions are not ordinarily stepping stones to Christ. More often, they are paths to hell. Rahner's theory of lawful religion, the idea that people approach God normally through the religions available in their social context, is naïve speculation. It is a nice idea in principle, but oblivious to the realities staring us in the face. Part of a responsible theology of religions must be an unambiguous judgment against idols of our creation and deceptions of the Evil One. Approval of religion can never be more than qualified because the temptation to domesticate God and use him to justify all kinds of evil purposes is overwhelmingly documented. As in Jesus' day, it is often the noblest representatives of religion who reject God's action emphatically, while ordinary people welcome it.[16]

A tragic failure of theological pluralism is the way it impedes making necessary judgments about truth and error, goodness and corruption in the religions. If God is unknown and all paths equally valid, a person is not in a position to evaluate whether a belief or behavior is true or false, healing or destructive. As a result, error and vileness tend to go uncontested, and there remains no way for differentiating wholesome from poisonous spiritual food.

Theology knows why false religion exists. It is created by the unholy trinity: the world, the flesh and the devil. It arises from the human capacity to ruin what is noble, and to refuse light when it is offered.[17] This means that human alienation also appears in the sphere of religion. Underneath the misuse of freedom lies a mystery of iniquity, a dark alienation of humanity from its source, an alliance with invisible powers at war with God. Satan is the deceiver of the whole world. His conspiracy exploits sin's potential in the sphere of religion (Rev 20:3).[18] All who achieve holiness, whether in the church or outside it, achieve it not as a result of their own efforts but by the grace of God, which they received by faith.

This has been the easy part. It is easy to accept the reality of false religion. It is much harder to accept the possibility of noble religion existing outside of Christ. To this we turn.

B. True Religion

According to the Bible, there also exists among the nations religious faith which lies at the other end of the spectrum. It recognizes faith, neither Jewish nor Christian, which is nonetheless noble, uplifting, and sound. We came across this faith earlier in the category of pagan saints, believers like Abel, Enoch, Noah, Job, Daniel, Melchizedek, Lot, Abimelech, Jethro, Rahab, Ruth, Naaman, the Queen of Sheba, the Roman soldier, Cornelius, and others. These were believing men and women who enjoyed a right relationship with God and lived saintly lives, under the terms of the wider covenant God made with Noah.

How should we understand a term like pagan saint? The Latin word from which our term *pagan* comes meant a country dweller or a rustic, much the way *heathen* in early English meant a person who lived out on the heath, or wasteland. Pagans or heathens were persons who lived in the country outside the city and mainstream of society. From these beginnings, these words picked up some very pejorative meanings: irreligious, nasty, brutish, amoral. A "pagan" soon became despised, unclean, a Gentile, an outsider. In the evolution of the term, we glimpse something of a cultural chauvinism or superiority being birthed. In choosing to use the terminology of pagan saint, I am registering a protest against viewing people outside the church as normally or necessarily unbelieving or unclean. I take the term the way Gregory the Great used it, when he called Job "a just pagan" and in the sense of Jean Danielou's title, *Holy Pagans* (1957).[19]

Expanding on what was said before, I want to point to biblical support for the idea of pagan saints outside the church. One reason this is important is strategic. Pluralists like John Hick notice the reluctance of orthodox Christians to admit the idea of pagan saints, and they use this as a basis for abolishing the classical consensus itself. Hick actually states that a major reason for his own "Copernican revolution" was precisely his encounter in Birmingham with saintly people of other faiths.[20] Evangelicals ought to reply with a question: How does this in any way threaten classical theology? Both Scripture and experience tell us there are pagan saints outside the church due to the work of the triune God in the world. God's being revealed definitively in Jesus Christ does not imply that he is not working in the wider world. His working in the wider world is rooted in a covenant with the race through Noah. All nations are blessed with revelation. God's grace is given in every context. But does the worldwide working of God enter the religious life of the nations, or is it always outside of religion?

For Protestants, in contrast to Catholics, the possibility that God might be working in the other religions is seldom countenanced. After all, if saintliness is possible apart from any religious cult, then God's grace might well occur outside rather than inside the religious sphere when operating in the wider world. There is no need to posit God's working in the other religions. The question arises, Is there evidence in the Bible for seeing *any* positive features in the religious aspects of cultures due to God working in this sphere?

One piece of evidence favoring this idea would be the fact that Israelite religion borrowed extensively from Mesopotamian, Egyptian, and Zoroastrian sources for its literature and laws—without being worried about being contaminated by it.[21] But there is more explicit proof than that. An example of it appears in the encounter of Abraham with Melchizedek (Ge 14:17–24). Melchizedek, named priest of God Most High (El Elyon was the name of his god), blessed the patriarch by his deity and received Abraham's tithe in return. Abram then uses the name of Yahweh for his deity, thus accepting the equivalence of Yahweh and El Elyon, and the validity of Melchizedek's worship. The meaning of this pericope is clear. Here we have Abraham accepting the blessing of a pagan priest, and giving tithes to him. It is as though the moment God called Abram to become the father of a chosen nation, he let him meet a king and priest from Salem in order to teach him the lesson that his election did not mean the exclusive possession of God. By introducing him to Melchizedek, God was giving Abraham a positive experience of the religious culture around him, to tell him not to be puffed up or feel superior. It reminds one of the lesson God taught Peter through Cornelius, and it is also reminiscent of the Lord's word through Amos: "'Are not you Israelites the same to me as the Cushites?' declares the Lord. 'Did I not bring Israel up from Egypt, the Philistines from Caphtor and the Arameans from Kir?'" (Am 9:7). This incident in Genesis 14 makes the point that religious experience may be valid outside Judaism and Christianity. There are also other examples that signal the same kind of openness and generosity of spirit.

Abraham soon had another encounter that confirmed this same lesson (Ge 20:1–18). Abimelech, king of Gerar, is presented by the Genesis narrator as a man of faith and integrity who acts more like a man of God than Abraham does. Anxious about what Abimelech (who was, after all, a pagan) might do to him, Abraham lies about Sarah being his wife, thinking that Abimelech would probably kill him and take her into his harem. The patriarch admits that he thought there was no "fear of God" in that house (Ge 20:11). He was completely wrong. Abimelech truly feared God, much like pagan Job had, according to other Scriptures, and proved to be a man of complete integrity. This encounter proves beyond any doubt that the fear of the Lord may occur in the hearts of people who live far beyond Israel's borders.

A series of incidents recorded in the Bible conveys the same lesson. Moses met a man named Jethro, priest of Midian, out in the wilderness (Ex 18:1–12). Already a believer in God, Jethro heard of the great things the Lord had done for Israel in bringing them out of bondage in Egypt. He concluded that Yahweh must be the greatest of the gods. To celebrate this, Jethro offered up a sacrifice on Israel's behalf in which all the leaders of Israel partook. This passage also tells us that God makes himself known outside the covenant community and has saints in the wider world. Balaam the soothsayer offers another glimpse into this principle (Nu 23–24). Whether personally a saint or not, Balaam was a pagan prophet who took the name of Yahweh on his lips and uttered true insights into God's will for Israel (Nu 23:8). It shows that God may reveal his purposes for Israel even to a non-Israelite prophet.

There are also passages that teach this lesson in the New Testament. The Magi who came from the east to worship the Christ child likely were pagan astrologers (Mt 2:1–12). Something in their religious culture must have pointed them to Palestine making them want to seek the coming one and open their treasures to him.[22] They had the kind of faith Jesus later would admire in the Roman centurion (Mt 8:10).

The most influential story of this sort in Scripture is about Peter's meeting with Cornelius and the lesson he learned from it (Ac 10). Cornelius was a pious, godly man, whom God used to convince the apostle that there is no partiality with God in his dealings with humanity. Peter needed to learn that God loves Gentiles as well as Jews, and that God has many ways of working in the world, not only one way. Before he heard the Gospel, Cornelius was a God-fearing believer. Luke describes him as "devout and God-fearing; he gave generously to those in need and prayed to God regularly'" (Ac 10:2). Like Job in the Old Testament, here was a Gentile in a good and acceptable relationship with God. Cornelius was one of those men of faith outside the covenant communities of Judaism and Christianity. God was present with him in the religious sphere of his pagan life.

This ought not surprise us, given other things that Luke says and records in Acts, like Paul's response to the Lystrians: "In the past, he let all nations go their own way. Yet he has not left himself without testimony: He has shown kindness by giving you rain from heaven and crops in their seasons; he provides you with plenty of food and fills your hearts with joy" (Ac 14:16–17). Elements of truth and goodness exist in pagan cultures like theirs because God has been with them and has not failed to reveal himself to them. Similarly, Paul told the Athenians: "From one man he made every nation of men, that they should inhabit the whole earth; and he determined the times set for them and the exact places where they should live. God did this so that men would seek him and perhaps reach out for him and find him, though he is not far from each one of us. 'For in him we live and move and have our being.' As some of your own poets have said, 'we are his offspring' " (Ac 17:26–28). Paul quotes favorably the word of a pagan philosopher, and it becomes part of our biblical text to celebrate the fact that such people as this have insight into the truth of God and his ways. The passage tells us that God providentially orders human history so that sinners might seek and find him.

The crown jewel in the Cornelius story is Peter's statement: "I now realize how true it is that God does not show favoritism but accepts men from every nation who fear him and do what is right" (Ac 10:34–35). Peter is saying that those like Cornelius who have faith in God, wherever they may live in the whole world, are accepted by God in the way Abraham was accepted, on the basis of faith.[23] In addition, by ennunciating the crucial principle of impartiality, the text has even more to offer, namely, that there are criteria for recognizing true religion among pagans. After all, a person might ask, how would I recognize godly religion among the heathen if I met it? How could Luke and Peter recognize a holy pagan like Cornelius? Peter gives us two briefly stated criteria, one cognitive ("one who fears God") and one ethical ("one who does what is right").

The first criterion tells us to ask, if we are trying to discern the spiritual condition of pagans, Does this person fear God? Obviously, Abraham came to the conclusion that Melchizedek and Abimelech feared God truly (though under another name), and Moses concluded the same thing about Jethro. We must be discerning in this matter— some outside the church do and some do not worship the true God in their religions. Some intend the same reality Christians intend when they believe in God (as personal, good, knowing, kind, strong, etc.). But others do not. When Jews and Muslims, for example, praise

God as the Creator of the world, it is obvious that they are referring to the same Being. There are not two almighty creators of heaven and earth, but only one. We may assume that they are intending to worship the one Creator God that we also serve. The same rule would apply to Africans who recognize a high God, a God who sees all, gives gifts to all, who is unchangeable and wise. If people in Ghana speak of the transcendent God as the shining one, as unchangeable as a rock, as all-wise and all-loving, how can anyone conclude otherwise than that they intend to acknowledge the true God as we do? On the other hand, clearly this would not be the case with a Zen master who intends to place the void over against a theistic belief. As Hendrik Vroom comments, "If a Zen master says that belief in God is only halfway to ultimate wisdom because the thought of a self-existing being, distinguished from the world in which we live, is naïve and betrays attachment to the self, then I do not see a philosophical ground to conclude that Zen and Christianity refer to the same divine or void transcendent."[24] The proof that people commonly intend the same deity as Christians worship is seen when the Bible is translated into the languages of the world. The word "God" normally can be rendered by a word already known to the people in their own languages as referring to the same Supreme Being. People fear God all over the world, and God accepts them, even where the gospel of Jesus Christ has not yet been proclaimed.

The second criterion tells us to ask, Do people pursue righteousness in their behavior? Peter knew what Jesus said about testing prophets: "By their fruit you will recognize them" (Mt 7:15–20). Spirituality is disclosed in morality. God is pleased when people's lives reflect his will for behavior. Verbal profession is not enough. "Not everyone who says to me, 'Lord, Lord,' will enter the kingdom of heaven, but only he who does the will of my Father who is in heaven" (Mt 7:21). Paul says the same thing. "To those who by persistence in doing good seek glory, honor and immortality, he will give eternal life" (Ro 2:6–8). One can make a faith response to God in the form of actions of love and justice. As Irenaeus states, "The Lord did not abrogate the natural precepts of the law by which man is justified, which those who were justified by faith and pleased God did observe previous to the giving of the law . . ." (Irenaeus, *Against Heresies*, bk. 4, chap. 13:1).

This is not easy for Protestants to accept, reluctant as they are to apply the ethical criterion for fear of seeming to support salvation by works. This is why they place most weight one-sidedly on the cognitive criterion, neglecting the ethical. We need to reconsider this bias and take more seriously the fact that profession by itself may mean nothing, or even less than nothing. As Paul said, "They claim to know God, but by their actions they deny him. They are detestable, disobedient, and unfit for doing anything good" (Tit 1:16). God takes the ethical criterion very seriously, and so should we.[25]

Peter places the two criteria together in association. What if only the ethical criterion is apparent in a person? What if the person seems genuine according to the ethical criterion, but not a believer according to the cognitive one? Would that be enough? Vatican Two went out on a limb stating that God will save even the atheist who, though rejecting God (as he understands God), responds positively to him implicitly by acts of love shown to the neighbor. The pertinent text reads: "Those also can attain everlasting salvation who through no fault of their own do not know the gospel of Christ or his church, yet sincerely seek God and, moved by grace, strive by their deeds to do his will as it is known to them through the dictates of conscience. Nor does divine Providence deny the help necessary for salvation to those who, without blame on their part, have not yet arrived at an explicit knowledge of God, but who strive to live a good life, thanks to his grace. Whatever truth or goodness is found among them is looked upon by the church as a preparation for the gospel. She regards such qualities as given by him who enlightens all men so that they may finally have life."[26] Evidently the bishops are of the opinion that a person's orientation to God may be revealed by moral actions alone, even if they are not accompanied by any profession. This goes beyond anything Peter says, but given the emphasis in the Old Testament prophets, they may be justified in their use of the nonpartiality principle. As Jeremiah says, "He defended the cause of the poor and needy, and so all went well. Is that not what it means to know me?" (Jer 22:16). A person may know God without it coming to verbal expression.[27]

Evangelicals have surely neglected the significance of the holy pagan tradition in the Bible which informs us about God being at work in the wider world. Evidently God has faithful people in the world and is educating the race in more ways than one. We have tended to ignore this line of teaching in Scripture because of a control belief which blocks it out. If we do see it, then we underinterpret it, taking Job or Jethro to be rare exceptions rather than a sign of hope in the larger context of a hermeneutic of hopefulness.

What the Bible tells us about other faiths being sometimes noble and truthful is confirmed in experience as well, just as John Hick said. One would have to be closed-minded not to recognize any spiritual or ethical fruit in the lives of men and women of other religions. In his book *Eternity in their Hearts*, Don Richardson documents many similarities of belief between Africans and ourselves, calling those beliefs redemptive analogies and bridges which make the gospel accessible to pagan peoples. (It is less clear to me that Richardson thinks people can have a right relationship with God on the basis of these analogies.) C. S. Lewis also detected and remarked on common elements in the religions which reveal the revelation of God in the wider world.[28] In *The Last Battle* of the Narnia series, Lewis records this encounter between a pagan named Emeth and Lord Aslan:

> Then I fell at his feet and thought, Surely this is the hour of death, for the Lion (who is worthy of all honour) will know that I have served Tash all my days and not him. Nevertheless, it is better to see the Lion and die than to be Tisroc of the world and live and not to have seen him. But the Glorious One bent down his golden head and touched my forehead with his tongue and said, Son, thou art welcome. But I said, Alas, Lord, I am no son of Thine but the servant of Tash. He answered, Child, all the service thou hast done to Tash, I account as service done to me. Then by reason of my great desire for wisdom and understanding, I overcame my fear and questioned the Glorious One and said, Lord, is it then true, as the Ape said, that thou and Tash are one? The Lion growled so that the earth shook (but his wrath was not against me) and said, It is false. Not because he and I are one, but because we are opposites, I take to me the services which thou hast done to him. For I and he are of such different kinds that no service which is vile can be done to me, and none which is not vile can be done to him. Therefore, if any man swear by Tash and keep his oath for oath's sake, it is by me that he has truly sworn, though he know it not, and it is I who reward him. And if any man do a cruelty in my name, then, though he says the name Aslan, it is Tash whom he serves and by Tash his deed is

accepted. Dost thou understand, Child? I said, Lord, thou knowest how much I understand. But I said also (for the truth constrained me), Yet I have been seeking Tash all my days. Beloved, said the Glorious One, unless thy desire had been for me thou wouldst not have sought so long and so truly. For all find what they truly seek.[29]

To mention examples of our own, how can one fail to appreciate the noble aspects of the Buddha, whose ethical direction, compassion, and concern for others is so moving that it appears God is at work in his life? Gautama resembles the sort of "righteous man" whom Jesus told his disciples to receive (Mt 10:41). He taught people that a man's proper relationship to the created world is not to give it ultimate value or devotion, because much human suffering derives from that. He also spoke of a power he called the *dharma*, which seems to be a gracious and good power and which promotes redemption and salvation. Granted, being anti-metaphysical in reaction to Hinduism, the Buddha did not teach personal theism with force or clarity. Nevertheless, though this was not his direction, there is something rather close to it in his teachings. There is in *nirvana* a quasi-personal aspect, a sense of possible friendship and intimacy with the good and the lovely, and there is the blessing of spiritual insight suggestive of revelation. In other words, I think we should not overemphasize the impersonal character of Buddha's faith. Of course, Buddhism is not Christianity and it does not try to be. But how does one come away after encountering Buddhism and deny that it is in touch with God in its way?[30]

The theistic Saiva Siddhanta literature of Hinduism, to take another example, celebrates a personal God of love. It expresses the belief that all God's actions in the world are intended to express love for his creatures and to lead them into loving union with himself. Or, what else can we make of the emphasis on grace and faith in the Japanese Shin-Shu Amida sect?[31] Who can deny the striking similarities between the prophet Muhammad and the Old Testament prophets? Would not admitting this have momentous consequences for our witness to Islam?[32] Obviously, these and all such parallels occur in diverse contexts which affect what is being affirmed. Nevertheless, it will not do just to dismiss it all a priori. Religions do not present only the way of human self-justification. At times they also announce the grace and love of God. When they do, this Christian, at least, rejoices.

Partly this is a question of the mercy of God toward sinners. Some question whether God would put up with a religion that was grossly deficient. Would God accept people whose beliefs fall far short of the complete truth? Yes, I think he would. For Scripture often hints at how merciful God is, even in the realm of religion. With liberality Yahweh permitted the nations to worship him in ways not proper for Israel to do (Dt 4:19). God allowed Naaman the Syrian leper, after his healing, to worship in Rimmon's temple because of the delicate circumstances he was in (2 Ki 5:18). Paul says that God permitted the nations to walk in their ways in past generations (Ac 14:16). He said that God overlooks the times of human ignorance (Ac 17:30) and passes over former sins (Ro 3:25). Is it possible that we have made God out to appear stingy? Should we not rather be thankful for the wideness of his mercy, for his not expecting the same thing from everyone, and for his accepting conceptual shortcomings in theology? Where would any of us be if God were not as merciful as that? This is the God who accepted Abram's faith in spite of its great shortcomings. Paul had learned through his own experience how merciful God is: "Even though I was once a blasphemer and a persecutor and a violent man, I was shown mercy because I acted in ignorance and unbelief" (1 Ti 1:13). If God did not accept people whose religious faith was deficient, who among us could stand before him?

Nothing that has been said here denies the uniqueness and finality of Jesus Christ. He said, "I am the way and the truth and the life" (Jn 14:6). Jesus *is* the only way to God the Father, to God who is boundless love. His is a unique disclosure without any rival at all. But this does not deny the reality of the knowledge of God that people possessed before Jesus came, or of that knowledge they possess today where he has not yet been named. When Peter says, ". . . there is no other name under heaven given to men by which we must be saved," he is not denying premessianic revelation and salvation, but rather he is saying that there is nothing comparable to the blessings of the messianic age which have been poured out on us in these last days (Ac 4:12). None of these texts should be taken to annul the grace of God that has penetrated human history along other channels and at lower levels from the beginning of time—before the messianic revelation was given. That would be a perverse use of the texts.

But how do we explain theologically the existence of truth and nobility that is sometimes found in other religions? One explanation is rooted in the fact that religions flow out of human aspiration, that is, from the center of our religious human nature. Here, atheists have a good point. If there were no God, there would still be religions. The need for God is so great within us that we would project gods even if none existed. God created humankind as naturally, inherently, and incurably religious. It is our nature, made in the image of God, to seek him. There is a universal urge to transcend—a basic capacity to experience the sacred. There is a drive to discover the basis of the meaning and worthwhileness of our lives, and to deal with our finitude and death. All persons know God precognitively, and most acknowledge him cognitively as well.[33]

Paul made this same point in his comment about the Athenians: "I see that in every way you are very religious" (Ac 17:22). This is true of humanity as a whole and not just Athenians, and Paul went on to explain why. God arranges things in life "so that men would seek him and perhaps reach out for him and find him" (Ac 17:27). Now that the Christ has come, the times of ignorance are over and people are expected to respond to God's love in Jesus (Ac 17:30). The Gospel comes as the fulfillment of the religious quest in all those who have sought God by faith. It may not fulfill the religions as such, but it does fulfill the longings of the soul.

If God created us to seek him and expects us to do so, what can Paul mean when he says that "there is no one . . . who seeks God" (Ro 3:11, citing Pss 14; 53)? That does not sound as though Paul believes humans are religious beings naturally seeking God. Is this a contradiction? I think not. First, Paul cannot be denying that millions of Jews and Christians (to mention no others) have sought and found God in the course of human history. The Old Testament gives many examples of them. Today there are hundreds of millions of believers who have sought God and found him. Paul must be saying something a little different. Second, Paul is surely not denying a large number of verses which invite us to seek God and promises to reward those who do. Isaiah says, "Seek the Lord while he may be found; call on him while he is near" (55:6). Jeremiah prophesies, "You will seek me and find me when you seek me with all your heart" (29:13). Hebrews states, "God . . . rewards those who earnestly seek him" (11:6). Again, Paul must be meaning something a little different. The solution is found when we recognize that Paul in Romans 3:11 is referring to the fool described in Psalms 14 and 53, the text he cites. Paul is saying that sinners left entirely on their own without the prevenient grace of God do not naturally seek God. When they act as sinners under the power of sin, apart from God's grace, they do not seek him. Those who seek God do so because of a divine work within them, not because they are free of the tendency of sinners to deny God. Apart from divine grace sinners do not have the inclination to seek God, but under the influence of prevenient grace they may choose to do so. Calvinists use the idea of common grace to account for goodness and justice in sinners, while Wesleyans prefer to speak of prevenient grace. Either way, it means that the grace of God mitigates the effects of sin in human life and preserves the creature from self-destruction.

A second reason why religions exist and sometimes may be positive and good is due to the prevenient grace of the triune God seeking sinners. Jesus tells us that God the Father is boundlessly generous and always seeking the lost (Lk 15). Although we cannot predict what God will do in his generosity, we can be sure that he seeks lost sheep because that is his nature. We know and confess that God loves the whole world, not just Western nations, and that he holds the whole world in his hands. God is everywhere active in pursuing the plan of redemption disclosed in the gospel. There is not one God who created the world and who is severe and uncaring, and another God who redeems humanity and who is kind and forgiving. A wedge cannot be driven between the God of providence and the God of the Gospel. God in his common grace supports the structures that keep life human: laws, morality, government, and culture. Even religions and their symbol systems are structures that give people dignity and hope. God is moving the world toward its fulfillment in Jesus Christ.[34]

Sent by God, the eternal Son and Logos upholds all things by his power and enlightens everyone coming into the world. The Logos is at work in the whole world like a schoolmaster bringing people to Christ. As Moses suffered for Christ without knowing him

(Heb 11:26), and as the Israelites drank from the rock in the wilderness which was Christ (1 Co 10:4), so the Logos is at work in the whole of reality. Those who respond belong to the larger people of God. The Logos connects Jesus of Nazareth to the whole world and guards the Incarnation from becoming a limiting principle.[35]

God the Spirit also proceeds from the Father and is present in the whole world. God's breath flows in the world at large, not just within the confines of Christian movements. The Spirit of Jesus is at the same time a cosmic force hovering over the waters and giving life to every creature (Ge 1:2; Ps 104:30). The Spirit is the overflow of God's love. We see his activity in human culture and even in the religions of the humanity.[36] The doctrine of the Trinity means that God, far from being difficult to locate in the world, can be encountered everywhere in it. One needs to take pains and be very adept at hiding *not* to encounter God.

World religions reflect to some degree general revelation and prevenient grace. Just as God himself is present in the world, so too is God's reality and revelation. Since God never leaves himself without witness (Ac 14:16–17), people always have divine light to respond to. Paul asks in Romans 10:18, "Did they not hear? Of course they did." Because of cosmic or general revelation, anyone can find God anywhere at anytime, because he has made himself and his revelation accessible to them. This is the reason we find a degree of truth and goodness in other religions. What an opportunity to engage this truth and to sort out the various claims in the knowledge that God is revealing himself to humankind. He wants people to know him.

Some object to this appeal to cosmic revelation on two grounds. First, that cosmic revelation has only a negative function, that is, that God gives it to ensure the damnation of sinners and not their salvation.[37] But this idea does not make a lot of sense. Why would God, the Father of our Lord Jesus Christ, do such a thing? Is there not one author of both general and special revelation? Is the God of creation not also the God of redemption? As Dale Moody comments, "What kind of a God is he who gives man enough knowledge to damn him but not enough to save him?"[38] The idea suggests confusion about God's intentions toward sinners.

The second objection is that general revelation offers no help because no one ever responds favorably to it anyway. Therefore, even if it were graciously intended, it would not have any positive results. Restrictivists contend that sinners do not respond to general revelation or prevenient grace. But this objection is not very convincing either. Job, Enoch, and Noah all seem to have responded to them. Peter states that a person can be acceptable to God on the basis of it (Ac 10:34–35). Paul speaks of the law of God written on the heart, and the possibility of being accused *or* excused on the day of judgment by responding to it. The objections cannot be sustained. Jesus Christ is now drawing all persons to himself just as God has always been actively doing from the creation of the world.

According to the Bible, persons can relate to God in three ways and covenants: through the cosmic covenant established with Noah, through the old covenant made with Abraham, and through the new covenant ratified by Jesus. One may even speak of salvation in the broad sense in all three circumstances. That is, insofar as salvation connotes a relationship with God, there is salvation for people in all three of the covenants. Of course, there is a more complete saving knowledge of God in the new covenant than in the old, and more in the old than in the cosmic covenant, but a relationship with God is possible in the context of all three covenants. In all three, God justifies Jews and Gentiles on the ground of faith, the condition for salvation in all dispensations (Ro 3:30).

It would be better not to speak of anonymous Christians, though. The believing Jew of the Old Testament was not a Christian, and the believing pagan was not a Jew. The language of anonymous Christianity tends to obscure the differences that Jesus makes when he is known through faith in the Gospel. The full-strength salvation he brings is neither found nor available anywhere else. Job and Enoch, even Abraham and Moses, belong to that great cloud of witnesses which spur us on. But that does not make them Christians, anonymous or otherwise (Heb 12:1). Responding positively to premessianic revelation can make them right with God, but it cannot make them messianic believers. They must still wait for Messiah to come.

Faith is what pleases God. The fact that different kinds of believers are accepted by God proves that the issue for God is not the content of theology but the reality of faith. As dispensational theologians have observed, theological content differs from age to age in the unfolding of redemption, but the faith principle remains in place. No one can say exactly how much knowledge one has to have in order to exercise faith. In Job's case, even in Abram's, the amount was rather little. Charles C. Ryrie states that "The basis of salvation in every age is the death of Christ; the requirement for salvation in every age is faith; the object of faith in every age is God; the content of faith changes in the various dispensations."[39]

No one knows how many holy pagans there may be. Some missionaries tell me they have encountered people like Cornelius, but not many. Others are more hopeful. But we are not in a position to know how many there are. Only God can know people's heart-responses to him. All we know for sure is that people are free to respond to God anywhere in the world, thanks to his grace. This encourages us to be open to the work of God in the wider world as we proclaim the gospel and encounter outsiders.

WHAT MAY WE SAFELY CONCLUDE?

One should not try to assess the status of other religions by way of deductive argument. Barth was as mistaken to say that other religions *must* be unbelief as Rahner was wrong to say that they *must* be valid. Rather, one must approach the issue inductively. Having done so, what can be concluded?

In the discussion as ordinarily carried on today, a strong polarization exists between Protestants like Barth and Catholics like Rahner.[40] On one side, Barth insists that all religions are unbelief and cases of sinful hubris. Rahner, on the other side, says religions are lawful and vehicles of salvation. These two theological giants are probably right and wrong at the same time. The fact is that religions can be both atrociously awful and remarkably noble, depending on the circumstances. This is clear both from Scripture and experience. The Bible presents a spectrum from good to bad, from true to false, and our experience agrees that religion is most ambiguous and calls for careful discernment.

Evangelicals need to become more positive in relation to other religions than historically we have been. There are positive features in other religions due to God's presence and revelation. Partly this is because we need to live in peace with other nations as a practical necessity, but mostly it is because Scripture allows a more generous attitude towards them. Both of these factors tell us to put away the hostile attitudes of the past and learn to live more in love with the peoples of the world, talking together so that more of God's truth can enrich us all. As Vatican II says, "In this age when the human race is daily becoming more closely united and ties between different people are becoming stronger, the church considers more closely her own relation to non-Christian religions. Since it is her task to foster unity and love among men, and indeed among nations, she first considers in this declaration what men have in common and what draws them into fellowship together" (*Declaration on the Relation of the Church to Non-Christian Religions*).

Being more positive does not require us to conclude that every religion is a vehicle of salvation or an ordinary way to salvation. Religions are part of fallen human culture. As systems of faith, they are often resistant to Jesus Christ and grossly deficient both cognitively and ethically. Vatican II was wise not to declare religions to be ways to salvation. They are a mixed bag and should not be evaluated a priori. Like psychology and anthropology, for examples, truth can be gleaned from them. (Is it not odd that some Christians make use of the latest trends in psychology and yet are not open to what religions discover?) Even faith-responses can be made in the context of other religions as in the case of Melchizedek and Jethro (both pagan priests). Their religions seem to have been vehicles of salvation for them. But it is not safe to overgeneralize from these cases. Religions may be under satanic influence rather than the divine Spirit. Religion may be human projection and not based in the revelation of God. There is no shortcut to the needed spiritual discernment.[41]

There is a middle way between the two prominent views in the present discussion. On the one extreme, we should reject the hyper-Protestant position on other religions that claims the divine action in Jesus Christ is the only divine action and the only revelation, and that religion is nothing but useless human activity. Religions are not all opposed to God to the same degree, and admitting that fact in no way betrays the unique role of Christ. The dark appraisal of other religions has cast over twentieth-century Protestant theology a long, deep shadow that needs to pass away. D. T. Niles, when he heard Karl Barth say that other religions were unbelief, asked him how many Hindus he knew personally. Barth replied that he knew not a single one. When Niles then asked him how he knew that religions were merely unbelief, Barth said he knew it as a presupposition. Believing that Christ is absolute, he deduced a position on the other faiths that they had to be a sinful grasping after idols.

But this deduction is false and unnacceptable. First, it labels religious people as rebellious unbelievers when, according to the Bible, some of them actually seek God and please him. Second, Barth is inconsistent in designating religion as such as unbelief because he himself grants the possibility of Christians being religious in ways involving grace and faith. Evidently then, religion is not always unbelief as Barth claims in rhetorical flourishes. Hendrik Kraemer sounds more open than Barth, but in the end he is really only less doctrinaire.[42]

Dialectical theology has a lot to answer for in this area. Though it performed a valuable function in proclaiming the transcendent majesty of God with fresh power, it marred this achievement by denying God's redemptive presence in the world beyond Palestine. Not that the religious sphere is necessarily the chief sphere in which God approaches human beings. It may be, as Jesus suggests, that one is more likely to encounter God in the course of ordinary human contacts than in religion per se. God often gets through to people in the course of secular life, in the home, at work, in the marketplace, in experiences of sickness, estrangement, disappointment, betrayal, and guilt. Jesus also implies that darkness and unbelief is often at its deepest in the realm of religion. But still this does not justify the conclusion that God absents himself completely from the religious sphere. Plainly he does not do so, even according to the Bible. Therefore, it is not necessary to approach the faith of other persons negatively.

At the other extreme, it is impossible also to accept certain contemporary Catholic views that other religions are inspired by God and therefore are ordinary ways of salvation. Vatican II did not declare this and surely it is not true.[43] To account for positive aspects, the Council relates the religions to the strivings of the human heart and to the divine presence. But the bishops did not declare religions to be the vehicles of salvation. They did not say that Buddhism, for example, has intrinsic value as a way to salvation, or that being a good Buddhist would make you an anonymous Christian. They did not say that Jesus is hidden in the religious history of humanity. These are the ideas of theologians like Rahner and others subsequent to the Council, and they represent large steps beyond it that we should not be taking.

Neither Scripture nor experience support such contemporary views. To do so would represent a move in a direction opposite to the Protestant tendency. It must not be forgotten that sin and Satan operate in the realm of religion too, that religions are adept at producing evil fruit both intellectually and morally, and that truth and error, good and bad, are both at work there. A mixture of positive and negative features is in them all, including Christianity as it has developed historically and become socially embodied. The Bible does not permit us to say that all religions are equal in saving power or are lawful cults until the Gospel arrives. Sometimes God is compelled to work in opposition to religion in order to reach people. Excesses in wanting to be positive to other faiths have brought Catholic theology close to heresy in recent years.[44]

But there is a middle way that allows us to be positive as well as discerning. In contrast to dialectic theology, which always refuses to be positive, and in contrast to recent Catholic theology, which is reluctant ever to name error for fear of jeopardizing the good feelings they want to encourage, the Bible permits us to be positive toward people of other faiths without being naïve about their beliefs and spiritual condition. On the one hand, it is possible to appreciate positive elements in other faiths, recognizing that God has been at work among them. On the other hand, it is not necessary to be blind to oppression and bondage in religion, Christ being our norm and criterion for measuring.

Spiritual discernment in the context of the believing community is what is critical in these areas. As John says, "Dear friends, do not believe every spirit, but test the spirits to see whether they are from God, because many false prophets have gone out into the world" (1 Jn 4:1). There must be a testing in the Spirit, a weighing of all utterances. The spiritually gifted need to judge whether a person is moving in the direction of faith or not. Is the will of the Lord being heard and done here? Is God at work here, or is this another spirit? Such questions cannot be answered on the basis of reason or exegesis alone. The community taught by God through the Spirit must exercise critical judgment in the realm of prophecy and all other such matters.[45]

The principle is that we ought not to judge people of other faiths harshly, refusing to see anything noble. Neither should we naïvely pronounce their religions vehicles of salvation. On the one hand, we should show respect for other faiths and enter into amicable dialogue with them. Having been negative long enough, it is time to be more appreciative. Religions play a positive role in human cultures and they deserve a sympathetic hearing. But, on the other hand, religions as institutions and symbol systems are not divinely inspired. They neither teach what Christianity teaches nor announce what the gospel proclaims. There are degrees of noble and ignoble elements in all the religions. The dharma of Buddhism may be an effective way of overcoming egoism and attaining inner peace and compassion, but it does not intend to lead people into a personal relationship with God. This is not its intention, even if we may hopefully detect something personal that is implicit in it. Salvation in this sense is something Jesus and not the Buddha opens up for humanity. Jesus is the way to the Father. This does not mean Buddhism has nothing to offer, or that Buddhists cannot move in Christ's direction from where they presently are. The same can be said of Islam. There is truth aplenty in it on which the sincere soul can feed. God can call people to himself from within Islam, but as a system it is not a reliable vehicle of salvation. On the contrary, it enslaves millions by its emphasis on works righteousness.

Given the state of the debate with its polarization between opposite assumptions (religions are good/religions are bad), a middle way is desirable. But such a debate is not very fruitful. There is another way to conduct it.

SUBJECTIVE RELIGION

The simple and necessary distinction that has to be made in order to make greater progress in this area is a distinction between religion as subjective and religion as objective. Wilfrid C. Smith in particular insisted on this sort of distinction.[46]He protested the way academics use the very term "religion" to refer to rival ideological systems, rather than to the human existential process of an individual's quest for meaning. He deplored the typically academic approach underlying this understanding of religion enabling the study of religious phenomena without becoming involved in them. Turning the tables, Smith does not want us to ask which religion a person belongs to, but what religion belongs to that person. This is the distinction between religion as a basic faith response of human beings and religion as a cumulative tradition of culture in which we live our lives.[47]

Using this distinction helps things fall together better than they do in the standard treatment. By subjective religion we refer to piety, faith, worship, and the fear of God, such as one sees in believers like Job, Abram, Enoch, and Noah. These were men who sought God and were rewarded for their faith (Heb 11:6). Though the content of their theology might have been pre-Christian and deficient from a later standpoint, they were moving in the direction toward God, no matter whether their religion helped or hindered their approach. By objective religion is meant religion as a cumulative, everchanging tradition, like Buddhism or Hinduism. The Bible does not often speak of religion in this way. The concept is something of a modern abstraction, though a useful one for limited purposes. Objective religion may or may not help foster faith in the existential sense. As with Christianity, one could be an adherent of the religion/church and not possess much personal faith.

Subjective religion or faith ought to be differentiated from objective religion, even though from within objective religion one might exercise faith in God. God calls on all persons to seek him, whether they seek him from within religion or outside it. There is enough truth in most religions for people to take hold of and put their trust in God's mercy. The religion may help or hinder—but ultimately it is what the person decides that counts.

Abraham's encounter with Abimelech can be considered in this light (Ge 20). The patriarch approached Abimelech on the basis of objective religion. He might have said to himself: "Since Abimelech is a Canaanite, I will assume (wrongly as it turned out) that there is no fear of God (subjective religion) in his house." The reader knows that Abraham was mistaken and that Abimelech happened to possess greater faith that day than Abraham himself possessed. Surely this is a lesson for us not to put people in institutional boxes but to relate to them as persons in terms of a heart response and faith direction. In another story, Jesus at the well does not judge the woman as a Samaritan member of a different religious sect but rather speaks to her need for living water at the level of heart religion. Arguing with Muslims about the relative merits of Christianity versus Islam as cumulative traditions is likely to get us nowhere. But speaking with Muslims about God, prayer, healing and the like may be a different story. In fact, on matters of personal religion Muslims are more ready to converse with us than our secular friends.

Buddhism as an objective world religion has a worldview and an approach to life which is not the same as the Christian approach. The Buddhist and Christian paths are different paths. But this does not tell us whether or not there is the fear of God in the context of Buddhism. We must not conclude, just because we know a person to be a Buddhist, that his or her heart is not seeking God. What God really cares about is faith and not theology, trust and not orthodoxy.

Of course, the distinction between the subjective and objective dimensions of religion should not be taken so far as to suggest that theology does not matter at all, as if one could ignore objective religion altogether and concentrate entirely on the subjective aspect. This would be ill-advised because religion as a framework and tradition influences religion as faith and trust. It would be wrong to drive a wedge between them. They cannot be kept entirely separate. Religious tradition will color and condition a person's outlook and as such it can help them. But it can also hinder. For example, the antimetaphysical tendency of Buddhist theology would not help a person trying to conceptualize God as loving and personal. The Muslim emphasis on works righteousness would not propel people to seek the mercy of God. The Hindu notion of illusion would not encourage people to take this life and its tasks seriously. Objective religion does matter, and it must be confronted on truth issues, even though subjective religion is more important to God. Nevertheless, it remains true that God's light shines everywhere in the darkness, and God's grace precedes all people everywhere. Objective religion, though it may hinder faith, cannot entirely prevent it. The light shines in the darkness and the darkness has not extinguished it

(Jn 1:5). People can respond to God on the basis of the light of revelation; therefore, we can approach every person with hope and Good News. Faith is always a possibility because of the prevenient grace of God, and the Good News itself is based on the decisive manifestation of God's love in Jesus Christ that fulfills and also corrects the other manifestations.[48]

It is not sufficient to consider religions as they presently exist in the world. This is because they are dynamic and cumulative traditions with great inner diversity. And it is also insufficient because, as with the whole creation, they are caught up in a sweep toward the kingdom of God along with all the powers of this age. We must go beyond what was said in this chapter. Of course, whatever truth and goodness is to be found in the religions now is evidence of God's work and not a denial of salvation through Jesus Christ. It is an anticipation of it. But we have to take account now of the fact that God is not finished with history yet, and therefore not finished with the religions. The historical situation is a dynamic and not a static one. Is it even possible that Christ wants to make the religions as objective, more pliable in God's hand, and more useful in mediating faith to people?

Four

Religions Tomorrow

In the last chapter emphasis was placed on religion as personal faith and on the propriety of approaching men and women as persons, not simply as representatives of the abstraction we today call religion. Nevertheless, religion has an objective side as well. Religions like Buddhism and Judaism are also cumulative traditions in the cultural history of humanity, and they have to be considered from that angle also. Let us then examine religion from the objective standpoint and retrieve another neglected biblical theme, that of the contest of the gods. We will draw from it practical consequences regarding engaging in truth-seeking dialogue.

As cumulative traditions, religions are not static entities frozen in their present condition. Hendrik Kraemer, in his view of the totalitarian nature of religions, was wrong to assume that they are. He overlooked their dynamic nature, and how they creatively interact with culture over time.[1] Christianity today, for example, is very different from what it was at the time of the Reformation. Its central confession may be the same, but many features have been added and there has been much more diversity over the intervening centuries. Whole new traditions have arisen, such as the Wesleyan and Pentecostal movements, which number today in the hundreds of millions of adherents. Everything in history is forever changing. We cannot assume that Islam, seemingly so monolithic, will always be what it is today. Not only so, but God himself is directing reality and ceaselessly shaping it toward the fulfillment of his purposes. We are obliged as Christians to regard religions as we ought to regard everything. They are in the context of the ongoing purposes of the Lord of history. This means change.[2]

Possibly the central theme of the Bible is the purpose of God to bring in the kingdom and realize sovereignty in the world. He has a plan for the fullness of time to unite all things in Christ, when history will witness the victory of God (Eph 1:10). It follows from this doctrine, since religions are part of historical and cultural reality, that God has designs on them—just as he has designs on everything else. It is safe to assume, even before reviewing the biblical evidence for it, that God will be working to bring those changing cultural entities we call religions into closer conformity with his purpose for the creation. God is not going to leave out anything as important as the religions from the work of transforming all things (Rev 21:5). Let us look at the religions now from the standpoint of God's will for history.[3]

Religious pluralism must be recognized as a fact of social reality. But this does not entail relativism. As in physics or biology, the existence of alternative truth claims does not mean there is no actual truth. It means that the truth has not yet been fully determined, and it points to the need for sorting out the various truth claims in an effort to discover what is really true.[4] People are searching for God, and they want to know the nature of transcendence. Although there is no present agreement about the answers (any more than there is in the sciences on numerous issues), people deserve to have their hypotheses about God taken seriously and not cavalierly dismissed. As Christians, we are convinced that God is revealing himself to humankind; therefore, we take claims at having attained insight into his revelation seriously, and we weigh them in relation to our own understanding. The fact that religions differ ought not to discourage us or cause us to give up on the search for truth. Let us explore other people's opinions about God with enthusiasm. Let us test their claims for any rational, moral, or religious power they may possess to make sense of things.[5]

PHILOSOPHY OF HISTORY

The setting for considering religions as dynamic, cumulative traditions is the biblical philosophy of history and hope. The Gospel instructs us to view historical movement in terms of a forward-looking process in which God is revealing his sovereignty over the world. As Pannenberg states, "In contradistinction to other peoples and their religions, Israel, in the light of its particular experience of

God, learned to understand the reality of human existence as a history moving toward a goal which had not yet appeared."[6] Their expectation was for a future redemptive action of God of which Isaiah spoke: "And the glory of the Lord will be revealed, and all mankind together will see it. For the mouth of the Lord has spoken" (Isa 40:5). It was the day the Lord enshrined in his prayer: "Your kingdom come, your will be done on earth as it is in heaven" (Mt 6:10). This the heart of the Good News. God's kingdom is coming, and preparations for it are now being made.

A forward look characterizes the church age, and central to it is the ingathering of the Gentiles. Christ calls the church to mission, to summon the nations into the kingdom in anticipation of the banquet feast to come (Mt 8:11). The kingdom of God, inaugurated in the ministry of Jesus, is now being extended throughout the world, principally through the mission of the church by which also history itself is being moved toward consummation. It is God's will that all the nations shall participate in the redemption and transformation of the world (Rev 7:9). Therefore, the central thrust of this present age is the ingathering of the Gentiles through the mission entrusted to us. The power of God that broke into history in God's agent Jesus is now continuing to impact the world through that mission and its realizing eschatology. Like the first Christians, we share the Good News of the coming kingdom and invite people to be caught up in its sweeping action. What God began to do in the event of Incarnation has to be fully accomplished at the end of history. "For he must reign until he has put all his enemies under his feet" (1 Co 15:25).[7]

Jesus said that "this gospel of the kingdom will be preached in the whole world as a testimony to all nations, and then the end will come" (Mt 24:14). Mission is an eschatological event. By means of it, invitations are being issued to the messianic banquet. God wants his house to be full (Lk 14:23). Therefore, all people everywhere are summoned to participate in the movement of the kingdom of God, and to become initiated into it. It is a day of Good News; we should not keep silent (cf 2 Ki 7:9).[8] A remedy has been found for the dread disease of sin that afflicts humanity. The coming of Jesus and his life, death, and resurrection has opened up a messianic history in which God is bringing everything under his rule and transforming the whole world. Oscar Cullmann says, "The missionary proclamation of the church, its preaching of the gospel, gives to the period between Christ's resurrection and parousia its meaning for redemptive history; and it has this meaning through its connection with Christ's present lordship."[9]

Religions as cumulative traditions have to be viewed in this context like everything else. The sweeping action of the kingdom of God, through the mission of the church, will inevitably overtake them. The Gospel cannot be preached to all nations without encountering the religions. Therefore, the church cannot escape a confrontation with the world religions—nor is it the will of God that we should escape it. There is no alternative to the encounter, unless we are not serious about reaching the nations. More than that, on account of its mission, Christianity has in fact become the catalyst for the rise of the increasingly common religious situation of humankind. Not only persons are changed through missions, but history itself is forever altered.

Earlier we saw reason for hope, and an optimism of salvation, about the ultimate future of God's universal salvific will and his work in the wider world. Now we add a reason for penultimate hope as well, in God's plans for the future of history and for religions as part of that history. God's plan aims not merely at rescuing a few souls from hell but rather at historical transformation whereby his sovereignty is reestablished in the universe. This means that any moment of the present is indecisive in itself, owing to the fact that God's plan for the whole of history has not been fully worked out. Any present moment lies somewhere in the middle stages of a divine project not yet fully in operation. Therefore, we act in faith toward the future even of the religions, and we are filled with hopeful expectation of what God may be planning to do.

The nations are in the valley of decision (Joel 3:11–15). They are caught up, whether they like it or not, whether they know it or not, in a plan of God for history that will sweep them before it. This does not leave any room on our part for despair or fatalism. It is simply an area of reality where God's will is not yet fully implemented, including the sphere of other religions. Christians are summoned to live in hope, and despite present circumstances, to expect to see God glorified, particularly in those areas where resistance to his will is strongest.

RELIGION AND THE POWERS

Bringing history to consummation in Jesus Christ is not easy because it is so strongly resisted. The Gospels make it plain that the kingdom encounters opposition and creates intense conflict. History itself is a battleground between divine and demonic powers. Jesus in his ministry (and still today) is challenging the other gods in the name of the higher sovereignty which the Father has given him (Mt 12:28; Lk 9:1).[10]

The religions are caught up and involved in this conflict as Christ challenges the gods to account, and as he challenges the powers of this age to repentance and submission.[11] God's plan to make all things new, to bring the powers of oppression under Christ, to transform history and culture, necessarily includes in its scope the religions. If Christ can transform culture, he can transform its religious dimension as well. Christians have been able to see God at work transforming cultures, as in the abolition of slavery, or the civil rights movement, but have tended not to be open to the possibility that God might be at work changing religions. This is inconsistent.[12]

To get at this let us review the Pauline doctrine of the powers and Christ's victory over them.[13] I think we may find that the category will prove fruitful when applied to the problem of objective religions.[14] St. Paul believed that behind what exists and all that happens on earth stand invisible and spiritual forces. He does not say much to indicate what he thinks about their exact metaphysical nature. For example, are they the angels of Daniel 10, which play a role in the life of nations? Paul is reticent to speak speculatively about this matter, unlike certain of the Jewish apocalyptic writers of his day. Nevertheless, despite the reticence, he makes three points about the invisible powers: God created these powers to structure life on earth; the powers fell into idolatry and they attempt to impede God's purposes; and Jesus (the strong man) triumphed over those powers through the Cross and Resurrection and he can consequently bind and impact them.[15] Let us take them up one at a time.

First, Paul says the powers were created by God and are therefore not evil in themselves (Col 1:16). The world is good. Apparently the powers were created for the purpose of performing positive, life-enhancing functions in the creation. As God's servants, they were intended to help implement the will of God for humanity in areas like law, language, morality, and ideology, for the purposes of sustaining and preserving human life.

Second, Paul says the powers have become sinful and destructive and are presently out of conformity with God's will (Eph 2:1–2; 6:12). Instead of promoting God's purposes for history, they form roadblocks to them. Instead of supporting humanization, they search out and destroy life. They wish to bring God's creation into ruin. One can perhaps see their rebellion manifested today in such aberrations of culture as Naziism, Marxism, racism, sexism, materialism, and secularism. The powers, created by God but fallen, need to be confronted, tamed, and reassigned to other duties. When people sin, they are yielding to the powers of evil. When we serve the Lord, we are caught up in spiritual warfare with our former masters.

Third, Paul also claims that Jesus Christ has won a victory over them in the Cross and Resurrection, and is now in a position to impact them as far as their functioning in history is concerned (1 Co 15:24–26; Eph 1:20–22; Col 2:15). I believe one can see that this victory was manifested, for example, in the fall of the Roman Empire, which crucified Jesus and cruelly persecuted the church in the early centuries, or in the fall of communism, which fiercely persecuted and oppressed the church in the twentieth century, or the humanizing features that belong to the Western democracies owing to a degree of Christianization.

In any case, we are in the midst of a cosmic struggle that affects not only individuals but social, political, and religious structures as well. Religions ought to be considered in this same context. They represent powers that Jesus Christ is challenging in the coming of the kingdom of God. If the gospel is true, if Jesus is Lord, the future of rebellious gods and powers is in doubt. He has been given a name higher than theirs. I am sure that the New Testament doctrine of the powers is not an esoteric concept to be demythologized, or just a doctrine of fallen angels which does not affect history. It is a way of speaking about the structures of the present age and the spiritual forces which shape our earthly life. We have become quite accustomed to thinking about Christ impacting social and political structures. Is it not time to begin thinking of him impacting the religions too?

Not only can religions be seen intelligibly in the context of Paul's doctrine of the powers, this is specifically suggested in the Scriptures. Observe how the Bible itself calls angels, powers, and principalities by the term "gods" or "mighty ones." Hear the exclamation of the psalmist: "Ascribe to the Lord, O mighty ones, ascribe to the Lord glory and strength" (Ps 29:1). These "gods" are not divine in the way Yahweh is God. They did not create the world but rather were themselves created by Yahweh. They represent fallen spiritual powers of the creation and need to be called to repentance. But they are not so insignificant that we can afford to pay no attention to them. Though we are not accustomed to thinking this way, the Bible does not deny the existence of other gods. It only questions their sovereignty, calling on them to worship the Lord. It is not that other gods do not exist, but that they are mortal beings, created by and subordinate to the Lord. And they are called upon to acknowledge that fact. "All . . . worship him, all you gods!" (Ps 97:7).

This fact encourages us to consider world religions in relation to the three points in the Pauline powers doctrine. Religions play a positive role in society, giving cohesion to life and sustaining civility and community among men and women. Religion is part of human culture, informing the beliefs and attitudes that help people cope with their environment. As such, they help to make human life more decent, and they may be seen as the gifts of God's common grace. Where would our society be if those of good will, whatever their faith, did not cooperate in backing decency and justice?

Religions unfortunately also enslave, deceive, and keep people from God, just as the powers do. Through their influence in culture, they can hurt and destroy life instead of enhancing it. In the last chapter we referred to many examples of this, such as child sacrifice, widow burning, voodoo, false otherworldliness, and fanaticism.

Jesus Christ is Lord over all powers, including other gods, being exalted high above every name. Therefore, he can challenge religions and can call them to account. He can address their rebelliousness and expose their darkness. As Christ confronts dark dimensions of culture and transforms them over time, so he can impact the religions whose destiny it is to be subordinate to God. The future of other "gods" is to do God's bidding. They must not be placed before God, or be worshiped as absolute. However, they have a valid role to play in the life of the nations and they are expected to perform it.

CONTEST OF THE GODS

This spiritual warfare can be considered under the aegis of a contest of the gods, a neglected biblical theme I want to retrieve. In the polytheism of the ancient Greeks, known to us through the epics of Homer, we receive a vivid picture of the struggle and competition among the gods of Olympus. Similarly, in Zoroastrian religion, one finds a basic dualism between two cosmic powers fighting with each other. In the case of Israel's religion, there is no other God for Yahweh to compete with, other than the fallen powers. Nevertheless, there is still competition. Joshua calls on the people to decide between Yahweh and the gods their father served beyond the river (Jos 24:14). Elijah challenged the people by asking, "How long will you waver between two opinions? If the Lord is God, follow him; but if Baal is God, follow him" (1 Ki 18:21). This gives us the clear picture, not of religions as equally valid paths to God, but as competitive truth claims. The various religions and their gods appear to be vying for people's allegiance. Competition in religion is not only biblical, it is empirically evident. Vital religions always compete with other's claims. If you can find a religion that is not competitive, you will have found a religion on its last legs. A dynamic religion always wants to tell its story, which adherents think is the best story ever told, and the one most worthy of commitment.

According to the Bible, history is the theater of a contest of the gods. Gods are in conflict with one another. There operates a kind of survival of the fittest among them. Some go down to defeat, while others move into ascendancy. This may be a novel way of thinking since most of us are hyper-monotheists—we have gotten rid of most of the beings in between God and ourselves. But in biblical thinking, not only are there beings intermediate between God and ourselves, these "gods" are mortal and do not live forever. They become extinct almost like animal species. History is a graveyard of the gods. The living God will outlive them all, proving himself to be the true God. Since this moment of revelation comes at the end of history, and will not be clear to everyone until then, our missionary task in the meantime is testing the proposition concerning God's identity and conducting the contest. We say: let the claims be made, let the information be shared, let the issues be weighed, and let dialogue take place. World missions promotes the contest of the gods and useful competition between the religions concerning the nature of reality.

There are reasons why Western intellectuals have difficulties taking these ideas seriously. One reason is the inability to impute reality to middle beings between God and ourselves.[16] Another is uncertainty about Christ's ability to change other religions. Partly this is due to the illusion that religions are unchangeable, bound entities. But a passing acquaintance with religion, including Christianity, tells us that religions are not static complexes but are continually changing and full of diversity. They are not separate circles of religious culture which always stay the same and have no overlap with the others.[17] Their changeability is what makes them vulnerable to being transformed by the living Christ. Religions as part of culture are dynamic traditions, continually interacting, absorbing, and changing.[18] Hinduism, for example, is really a collection of religions and is most remarkably variegated. It represents the religious conceptions of the Indo-Europeans, augmented by traditions of monistic thinking, and spiced with bhakti devotion among the common people.[19] Buddhism too has undergone enormous developments during its long history. Originally skeptical and metaphysically reserved, Buddhism later produced all of the lush abundance of a popular religious movement.[20] As for the Christian religion, it has thousands of denominations as well as numerous sects striving to be denominations in its penumbra. Given this openness to change, religions are vulnerable to being impacted by Jesus Christ, as the Spirit moves history towards consummation. Thomas Finger writes that "the major doctrines and practices of the non-Christian religions, systematically considered, are as incompatible with authentic Christianity as are the overall complexes of which they are parts. Eschatologically considered, however, as God calls people and as the kingdom impacts them, these doctrines and practices can be loosened, as it were, from their original complexes and be refashioned to express something different."[21]

Some oppose missions because they worry that if the gospel is taken to another culture it will spoil the stable socio-religious system in place there. This idea smacks of Western academia, wanting to keep exotic tribes unchanged for the sake of anthropological study. But it is a shallow idea, which ignores two factors. First, in a paternalistic way, it denies people the opportunity to decide about their own lives, assuming it would be a bother for people to be told about the grace of God and the possibility of a new beginning. Second, it ignores the fact that history is sweeping everything before it, that traditional cultures are not going to remain unchanged no matter what we do. Peoples are now in the process of tremendous change—the only question is, what will the change be? Multitudes, if they do not convert to Jesus Christ, will convert to something or somebody else, most likely to secular materialism. Individuals ought to have the opportunity to consider the Gospel when they are making up their minds.[22]

ILLUSTRATIONS OF CHANGE IN RELIGION

Let us consider some examples of changes in religion. The God of Israel, for example, triumphed decisively over the gods of the Ancient Near East. Baal, Astarte, Rimmon, Tiamat, Moloch, Melqart, and Chemosh, among others—they are all gone. But Yahweh lives in the devotion of hundreds of millions of Jews and Christians.[23] Belief in the Ugaritic, Egyptian, Assyrian, Greek, and Roman pantheons has pretty well disappeared. Those deities, notoriously promiscuous, fratricidal, and perverse, have passed away. Religious claims which were made on their behalf for centuries have been dealt with by history. They failed in the competition between the gods. Toynbee noted that cultures and religions rise and fall. Of course, one may still wonder whether they perish for good. Has Aphrodite really gone, or is she reigning in Hollywood in the sex industry? Has Mars, the god of war, really gone, or just changed his address? What these gods represented certainly still exists: violence, blood, power, mammon, and sex. Old gods have a way of coming back again, making any victories over them penultimate, never ultimate. Nevertheless, even small victories are better than nothing.

The God of the Gospel has been impacting religions for centuries. The Christian message with its unique emphases on the holiness and love of God, the value of the individual, and the importance of social justice, has already caused other religions to put aside numerous gross practices such as headhunting, cannibalism, infanticide, temple prostitution, polygamy, widow burning, caste, purdah, karma fatalism, and holy war. Gods like Krishna have had to clean up their act, and be rendered in more decent ways. Christianity has a long record of producing reform in other religions.[24] The role of world missions is not only to plant churches but also to stimulate this sort of reform and renewal in other religions.

Though Marxism is a quasi-religion, it is an encouraging paradigm of what can happen to real religions. Communism held half the world in its grip for seven decades before collapsing in 1989 as a failed cult. Here was a powerful claim to truth, a comprehensive belief system, one reputed to be the wave of the future. For decades it was highly competitive, militarily dangerous, and a cruel persecutor of the church. Was there ever so audacious a myth, with so little hold on empirical reality yet so tenacious at resisting refutation in the minds of its adherents?[25] Nevertheless, it exploded, its claims were discredited, and its prophets become a laughing stock. Marxism in the Soviet Union fell exhausted in a matter of months without a shot having to be fired owing to its own deep failures and the spiritual faithfulness of millions of people through seventy years of oppression. Marxism was sprung open and exploded and, without external force being applied, was unmasked and overturned. Why? Because it did not have the resources of truth or goodness to sustain itself. I cannot think of a better example of a truth claim being so decisively refuted and repudiated in the competition of history. What happened to a quasi-religious system can happen to a religious system. The idol that demanded worship proved to have feet of clay, and it fell. It entered into the contest of the gods and failed. Communism is a failed god.

Does this also happen to "real" religions? Just ask yourself, where are the gods of the Ugaritic, Egyptian, and Greek pantheons today? They are dead and buried. Then ask, where is Yahweh? He is worshiped by a third of the world's people. Now, in a way, the gods of the pantheons are not completely dead. First, because what was good about them has been taken over by way of syncretism into Christianity itself. Second, because what was evil about them lives on under other names. But the main point is still valid: religions are not immortal or static, invincible or monolithic. They are immensely diverse internally, constantly changing, and vulnerable to being transformed by Jesus Christ, something that happens through world missions.

What can we expect to happen in history in this regard? Not having a crystal ball, we can be guardedly optimistic. The pessimistic view of history, which was based on the early return of Christ and held that Christ could not win substantial victories in history until the parousia has been refuted by events, if not by exegesis. The Lord did not return quickly, and the Gospel has spread to the four corners of the world changing the course of history. Thus being pessimistic makes no sense. On the other hand, an unqualifiedly optimistic view of history has not been materialized either, one that expects steady advancement of the kingdom in history until all Christ's enemies submit to him before the parousia. We have seen victories but also defeats; advances but also setbacks. The mystery of iniquity is such that once a victory is won, an ironical setback is also experienced. This suggests that a position somewhere between pessimism and optimism is the wisest view to take, and that what we should be on the lookout for is measured success. The continued power of sin means that there are always limits to our progress. We must struggle for our success. There will always be a certain deadlock until the great leap forward through the intervention of God.[26]

We can illustrate this outlook with reference to Islam, a religion which is certainly not disappearing. God is not finished with Islam yet. Her continuing vigor shows us that the contest of the gods is not finished but is going on full tilt. Christianity and Islam are two of the major combatants today, now that Marxism has conceded defeat. But Islam is still not stronger than Jesus Christ. Just because it has replaced communism as the most powerful competition and the fiercest persecutor of the church does not give it a higher name or greater power than Jesus Christ. Our prayer is that Christ will soon confront Islam and that she will open up to the Gospel for the sake of her peoples.

No one knows exactly what God will do. Contrary to our wishes, he may decide to let Islam alone, allowing it to harden its attitudes still more. Islam might become more hostile in the future or become more open to the Gospel, as has happened already with Islam in Indonesia. No one can comprehend God's ways in providence. Victory over Islam in our time is not assured. We simply do not know what God will do in the short term. All we know is that victories are possible and we can pray and work for them. What we know is that in the long term, if Jesus is Lord, he and not Muhammad will be vindicated. With John the Baptist, the prophet of the Arabs will have to say: "He must become greater; I must become less" (Jn 3:30).

Ultimately, we wait for the kingdom of God, the new humanity in a new creation. Penultimately, there will be ups and downs, progress and regress, success and failure, advances and setbacks, ironies and surprises, the cross and the resurrection. We are not privy to God's strategies prior to the end; we only know that at the end there will be a revelation of his sovereignty. This is all we need to sustain us. Secular newsmakers know nothing of the contest of the gods, though it is the number-one story of the age and the deepest stuff of all history.[27]

COMPETITION IN RELIGION

If one reason for dismissing the idea of the contest of the gods is the fact that many do not take the idea of the demonic seriously, another reason is that the notion of competition in religion is unappealing. A contest of the gods implies that competition is central to religion. Remembering wars of religion, people prefer to play down the category of competition rather than lift it up as important. Like it or not however, competition is in fact prominent in religion, and it is easy to see why.[28] Given a plurality of conflicting religious claims, competition and even conflict among them cannot be erased. Any serious claim to truth, whether in religion or in science, will try to convince others of its validity, to convince others to decide in its favor and not against it. Only a moribund religion or a lackadaisical science cares nothing about competition. Vital religions compete. Jay Newman comments:

> As a religious activity, religious competition is just one of many such activities, along with such things as worship, theological reflection, and philanthropy. The sacred works of the world's living religions do not teach people to be competitive in the way that they

teach people to love the Divine and love their fellow human beings. However, in urging people to lead a certain kind of life, and to work to make their fellow human beings lead that kind of life, these sacred works (and the clerics and laymen who disseminate and interpret the teachings of these works) force those who would be faithful to compete religiously. Religious competition is not a minor concomitant of the religious life. It is central to religious life, this relentless struggle against heathens, pagans, infidels, materialists, cynics, perfidious corruptors of the faith, weak and incompetent defenders of the faith, and those who would allow the faithful to be assimilated into an unbelieving world. The only people who will not witness for their faith are those who have none, and to witness is to compete in the purest and clearest sense of the word.[29]

Competition between religions and denominations is distasteful because it can become cutthroat competition leading to bitterness and hatred. Competition sounds like a destructive trait for a noble enterprise like religion to have. However, competition does not have to be nasty or brutish, and the danger of it becoming so cannot change the fact that competition in religion is inescapable. No good would be accomplished by wringing our hands or trying to eliminate it altogether. Religions vie with each other for commitment and resources. A religious monopoly would be no answer, even if it were possible. Hispanic Catholicism in sixteenth-century Europe was no improvement on competition. The real challenge is to try and regulate religious competition so that it produces good results, to foster healthy competition which furthers the search for truth in which all religions are engaged. Since competition cannot be eliminated from religion, we need to channel it in directions which will promote good and not evil.[30]

The notions of spiritual warfare and religious competition need to be brought together in our minds. The New Testament alerts us to spiritual warfare as characteristic of this present age, and our experience confirms that competition is central to the way serious religions relate to one another. In associating these two ideas, we may be on the track of a better way to reconceptualize the relationship between Christianity and the other religions, and to reconceive our strategy for conducting those relations.

What then does spiritual conflict mean in actual practice?

Sometimes it involves sharp confrontation, as when there is a power encounter between God and the forces of Satan. An example of this is described when Saul, fresh into his first missionary journey, encountered at Salamis a magician named Bar-Jesus, or Elymas, who sought to prevent the proconsul Sergius Paulus from the faith (Ac 13:4–12). Discerning his spiritual condition, Saul said to him outright: "You are a child of the devil and an enemy of everything that is right! You are full of all kinds of deceit and trickery. Will you never stop perverting the right ways of the Lord?" Whereupon the man was struck blind for a time and the proconsul came to faith when he saw the power of the Lord at work.[31] This is often the form that spiritual warfare takes when people need deliverance from satanic oppression or, when they need a demonstration of God's power to be convinced of the truth of the Gospel, as is often the case in folk Islam today.[32]

But it would be a mistake to think that spiritual warfare occurs only in that highly charged mode, when it occurs in calmer ways as well. In other situations during his missionary work, Paul entered into religious competition by way of dialogue, through the exchanging of ideas, and through respectful sharing (Ac 17:16–31; 19:8–10). Spiritual warfare on this level is more familiar to us. Intellectual life, for example, is competitive. Books are written to put other scholars straight. Book reviews are written to settle some score, or point out some neglected truth. Publishing is highly competitive but publishers usually do not come to blows. This competition of ideas is a very good thing because it facilitates greater apprehension of the truth. To try to deny competition in religion would be futile anyway. Rather we should endeavor to make competition work in fairer and healthier ways.[33]

TRUTH-SEEKING ENCOUNTERS

The way to foster healthy forms of religious competition is to include truth-seeking encounters within our understanding of mission and its activities. Various kinds of actions are appropriate in mission, including proclamation, church planting, healing, exorcism, nurture, and works of love. Truth-seeking dialogue should also be one of them. Such dialogue is neglected but is important to Christ's impacting other religions.[34] In dialogue, the contest of the gods becomes incarnate in flesh and blood, and truth claims meet in real people.

The biblical basis for truth-seeking encounters as a proper action for Christian missions is seen in the ministries of both Jesus and Paul. Jesus at the age of twelve, for example, is found sitting among leaders in the temple, listening, asking questions, and showing understanding (Lk 2:41–52). In later encounters with people, Jesus continued to use dialogue in his approach. One does not find him practicing formula evangelism, or taking a canned approach. His remarks to people were always directed to real situations, and he spoke to real needs. Jesus does not hurl Bible verses at people but rather listens carefully to them, addressing their concerns. Jesus related the Gospel to issues that were important in actual life. He looked beyond the externals to the heart of a matter. He did not allow a person's association with another religion to prevent him from seeking heart faith in them. When he told his disciples, "As the Father has sent me, I am sending you" (Jn 20:21), he was telling them to go and identify with people, showing them God's love.[35]

Paul's practice of engaging in dialogue as an integral part of his missionary strategy is especially instructive. Week by week he engaged the Jews in discussion in the synagogues, seeking to persuade them to consider the claims of Jesus as the Christ (Ac 9:29; 17:2–4). He also presented the faith at the Areopagus, the intellectual marketplace of Athens, making several converts, including Dionysius and Damaris (Ac 17:34). But most impressive of all, Paul spent two whole years in daily interaction with people in a rented facility in Ephesus (Ac 19:9–10). Luke describes Paul teaching, arguing, pleading, and holding discussions for five hours a day (according to the Western text). If someone had asked him why he was not out on the street winning souls instead of spending all this time doing theology and apologetics, Paul might have answered that what he was doing was more important in the long run. Wrestling with the Greek thinking, learning how to tell the Christian story in Asia Minor so that people would understand it, and outthinking the pagan philosophers—this was very important work in the mission. Paul must have thought that Asia Minor would be better reached by means of a process of in-depth dialogue and the laying of intellectually solid foundations.

The results of this strategy of dialogue are reflected in the Colossian letter, where one finds pagan phrases employed in Christian ways. As an apologist to the Greeks, Paul met his opponents on their own ground, using their terms in his own theology, in order to show that the truth they were seeking lay in Jesus Christ. As F. F. Bruce comments, "This employment of the technical terms of erroneous teaching in what has been called a 'disinfected' sense helps to explain the difference in vocabulary which many have felt between this epistle (and Ephesians) on the one hand and the Galatian, Corinthian and Roman epistles on the other."[36] Evidently Paul built upon the truth people already possessed and discussed new issues in relation to that truth. Paul had, in addition to a practical bent for strategy, an eye for the impact of the gospel on world history and culture, and not just for how many churches he planted or how many souls were saved.

If we hold the Apostle in high esteem, we must take seriously interreligious dialogue as part of the strategy of missions. Paul was prepared to begin the conversation with people to see where it would lead. In dialogue, he was ready to move to their territory, to their comfort zones, to preach Christ to them. It was part of his stated desire to be all things to all men (1 Co 9:22).[37] Religious pluralism did not bother Paul at all. The fact that people believed different things in no way deterred him from picking up on the conversation wherever possible. True to his own particularity, Paul was also open to the other person, and he was prepared to work from agreements and learn from disagreements.[38]

Paul's willingness to go the second mile in mission is instructive for us. If we are not prepared to identify fully with the concerns of Muslims (for example), we are not likely to see a breakthrough in the mission to Islam. God cannot impact an unreached culture if his people are not willing to be involved at costly levels. Paul was a missionary prepared to enter into serious dialogue with people. We should not be surprised that all the residents of Asia heard the word of the Lord, both Jews and Greeks.

One reason why the Spirit can use truth-seeking dialogue in mission is because it is an excellent way to get at issues in the presence of disagreement. On a level playing field, issues can be compared and evaluated in the presence of those who differ, without anger and without anyone losing face. Interreligious dialogue is similar to what happens in physics, biology, philosophy, or anthropology. Competitive claims to truth are weighed in each other's presence for their possible contribution to knowledge. Worldviews such as theism, polytheism, atheism, deism, or panentheism cannot all be true at the same time, but they are serious claims to truth which deserve to be weighed and debated. Assuming that no one wants to be committed to illusion rather than truth, dialogue is the best way to negotiate the important disagreements. It does not need to be disagreeable itself.[39]

There are several reasons why dialogue in religion can be amicable and not hostile. One stems from the love commandment. If we love people, we will want to understand them sympathetically. Love does not say that because people are "outside" the truth that they are unclean and beyond talking to. If we care about people and truth, we will want to explore other people's convictions, weigh their claims, and judge their intentions fairly. A second reason is more practical. Amicable dialogue is simply the best way to pursue disagreements. It offers us some hope. A third reason derives from the fact of general revelation, which says there is God-given truth in the world to be found and built upon. Because of this general, divine revelation, all sorts of positive connections and bridges can be constructed.

We need to transcend our fear of dialogue and the polarization surrounding it. On the one hand, there are traditionalists like Martyn Lloyd-Jones and Karl Barth who refuse to dialogue at all. After all, they say, belief cannot argue with unbelief, it can only preach to it.[40] This is certainly not Paul's view, and it is most insensitive to those with doubts, questions, and alternative convictions. On the other hand, there are religious liberals who love to dialogue so much that they never seem to get around to arguing issues of central truth, such as the claims concerning the person and work of Jesus Christ that eventually must be answered. Perhaps for this reason evangelicals have shied away from interreligious dialogue. Perhaps they disapprove of the direction dialogues often take in ecumenical circles. What good are dialogues (they wonder) that prevent crucial issues from being discussed, or that give the impression of relativism?[41] But dialogue does not need to be like that. Bad dialogue should not drive out good dialogue. Rather than a moratorium on dialogue itself, we need to stage dialogues of the proper kind. We could do that with a good conscience. Theologians in the past did not hesitate to engage Plato and Aristotle in their work. All that is needed is for us to enlarge the circle of conversation partners and include leaders like Buddha and Muhammad in the circle. When we do so, we are likely to find that these new conversation partners stand closer to us not only in the topics they want to discuss but also in religious temperament than the secularists we have been taking so seriously for so long. Since we found it possible to converse with atheists in the past when pursuing our theology, it should not be overly traumatic to begin talking to people of other faiths.[42]

NOT A RELATIVIST

Before launching into an examination of the nature of truth-seeking encounters, we should pause to notice two features of Paul's approach to dialogue. In modern parlance, we could say that he was neither a relativist nor a fideist. Let us examine this because it is also important for us to reject both relativism and fideism if we hope to get anywhere in dialogue.

First of all, Paul was a cognitivist and not a relativist when it came to handling differing religious truth claims. This is clear from observing his practice of arguing and persuading in evangelism, and from reading his letters where he expounds and defends the truth. Paul, when he proclaimed the Gospel, was a cognitivist. That is, he shared with people what he took to be knowledge of reality. What he proclaimed, Paul thought to be true. These were not just his private convictions, or beliefs that meant a lot to him existentially. He took truth more seriously than that. Truth was something that was true for everyone. Paul intended to make truth claims, and he respected other people's intention to do the same thing. Since he respected truth and since he knew there were rival claims, Paul was committed to a process of sorting out the positions in dialogue.

Had Paul been a relativist, the truth claims being put on the table would have been thought of as only superficially distinct from each other. The various beliefs would been regarded as culturally conditioned, as functions of the birthplaces of their advocates. Beliefs that reflect culture do not need to be taken seriously as truth claims. One assumes that people cannot help believing what they believe since beliefs are culturally conditioned. Therefore, they should not be weighed as if they were convictions that might just be true to reality. They can best be interpreted as existentially moving symbols. Thus, any dialogue conducted on a relativist basis would not be a truth-seeking encounter but a sharing of the subjective events of the heart. There would be no place for argument or persuasion in it, and no real dialogue would take place. It is important to see that relativism threatens and does not enhance dialogue. In effect, relativism equates all beliefs, values, and standards as culturally conditioned. It is indifferent to real differences between convictions. It leads to cheap tolerance which trivializes and prevents truth seeking.[43]

Because there is no truth to pursue, relativism literally kills the possibility of dialogue and dooms useful discussion. What is there to talk about, if we have already agreed to judge truth claims as culturally conditioned beliefs? Relativism also prevents one from confronting evil and falsehood in religion. And, because contradictory things can both be true simultaneously, it leads to absurdities like God's being both personal and impersonal, good and evil at the same time. The Christian pluralists cannot have it both ways. If the God of love is the basis of their pluralism, then God must in reality be personal and not impersonal. A choice has to be made; a truth question is involved. Either there is a God or there is not. Either God is personal or he is not. Either God is loving or he is not. Either the Koran is the Word of God or it is not. There is no way to get around the truth of such propositions, that is, if religion is more than a subjective attitude.[44]

In his early work, John Hick stoutly defended an understanding of religious claims in cognitive ways. He held that religious experience, in particular, points to God and gives us some real knowledge of God.[45] He held out the possibility of something he called eschatological verification, according to which we will all know the truth at least at the end of history. He was still sure that the personal and loving God of the Christian faith would be revealed as the true God in the end.[46] Nowadays Hick sounds less sure. He seems to be retreating from the cognitivity of religions claims, perhaps because he wants to include everybody and leave nobody out. But for nobody to be left out means viewing different claims as non-fact-asserting. This is because, if metaphysical or historical truth were involved, everyone can not be right. For some such reason as this, in the latter stages of his work, Hick has become a full-fledged Kantian. He now holds that God cannot be known, and that the various religions ought to be respected as valid attempts to name God, there being no way to test the validity of the varying claims. Thus Hick's characterization of the object of faith has become more and more vague as he has sought to accommodate the diverse claims of the world religions into a single framework. The erstwhile defender of cognitivism in religion has shifted towards a position difficult to distinguish from relativism.[47]

Ironically, allowing the God-concept to become vague undercuts the primary reason Hick has given for being a religious pluralist in the first place, namely, the universal salvific will of God. But how does John Hick know God has such a will? Does a loving and personal God even exist? My theory is that Hick personally does still believe that the Christian God will in the end turn out to be the true God. But he cannot say much about this in certain circles for fear of arousing opposition from pluralists like Joseph Campbell, who differ with him on this very point.[48]

It is important not to be relativistic because the sine qua non of good dialogue is that we respect other people's convictions as serious truth claims. If we do that, dialogue can be a way to make progress toward the truth. The various claims about God, self, and salvation are seriously intended by the religions, and they are not identical with each other. Therefore, there has to be an intellectual, experiential, and moral contest among the religions as we all struggle to reach truth in these matters. Elijah was right to demand that the people decide whether Yahweh or Baal is God. Both cannot be, for they cannot both mediate salvation. We cannot place alchemy, witchcraft, and child sacrifice on the same level as belief in God the Creator. We dare not say "anything goes" in theology or elsewhere. There must be a discerning of spirits.[49]

Love, not relativism, is the reliable foundation for dialogue—

love coupled with respect for the possible truth of what the others believe in. Dialogue works when participants care for truth while respecting one another. Tolerance does not require relativism.[50] Relativism actually threatens tolerance by assuming a dogmatic stance that frowns upon all nonrelativist positions. It reeks of Enlightenment ethnocentrism. It is a meta-theology of not-knowing, which then dictates to others what they may claim and what the terms shall be of any dialogue. Relativism does not lead to genuine conversation, but to a new type of intolerance toward all those who take truth seriously. It is secularism in disguise, and it must not be permitted to take over the study of religion. Paul sets a better example by holding that truth really matters, that one choice is not as good as another, that differences need to be sorted out. He was in fact a real pluralist (not a covert relativist under the guise of pluralism) who recognized real differences and thought they were worth talking about.

NOT A FIDEIST

By fideism is meant the position that beliefs are held without having any reasonable basis for holding them, apart from the decision of faith itself. Fideism holds that faith stands independently of reason. Faith's epistemic rights are such that it does not need to have reasons or arguments in its defense. One can believe in God, for example, without having any publicly affirmable reasons for doing so. Fideism reminds one of agnosticism because both accept the notion that there is no rational way to know whether religious claims are true or false. The difference is that, unlike the agnostic, the fideist makes a leap of faith by an act of sheer volition.[51] Paul was not a fideist in matters of religion. This is plain from his efforts to persuade people to accept the Gospel, and also from his willingness to give evidence for his beliefs—such as the belief in the resurrection of Jesus.

Fideism threatens truth-seeking dialogue much the same way that relativism does. Though fideism does not deny that religious truth claims differ, or that they are ultimately either true or false, it does deny that there is any way to sort them out or to validate or falsify those claims. Under fidiesm, one is free to believe this proposition or that proposition, but one is not able to say which one is right. A dialogue among fideists would result in stalemate because there is no way to arrive at any truth. There is no way to resolve anything. There is an absence of data.

One would expect fideists to be modest in their claims, given their lack of supporting argument. Ironically this is not always so, because having no arguments does not make the claims less ultimate or less important. Fideism means that, since you cannot convince anyone by reason, you have to resort to something else; and this is usually straight dogmaticism. For example, it is both annoying and at the same time perfectly understandable that a person like Barth, who makes the strongest claims to being right in modern theology, happens to be the one who refuses to offer anything rational to back up his claims or submit them to any kind of public testing. The popular parallel to this would be the television preacher who renders his convictions in a very loud voice, hoping the viewing audience will not notice the total lack of any solid basis for those convictions.

Paul is not a fideist in religion. He is ready to give a reason for the hope that is in him (1 Pe 3:15). He thinks faith has content and is verifiable in principle. There are reasons for belief in the Resurrection, for example. One reason is Christ's appearing to five hundred brethren at once (1 Co 15:6). Paul maintained that the Resurrection was evidence for the truth of God (Ac 17:31).[52] For Paul, faith was not a blind act of the will without any grounding in reality. Because he had confidence in the truth of the Gospel, Paul was able to expose himself to truth-seeking encounters without being intimidated and without being anxious about the outcome. He did not have to retreat intellectually. He was prepared to test for truth. Truth that is trivialized or sacrificed on the altar of religious unity is not in anyone's best interests.

How could Paul have engaged in open dialogue? How could the Apostle, having placed his hope in Jesus, have entertained other truth claims as seriously as dialogue requires? It sounds as though he would have had to pretend to be neutral, or to bracket his convictions during such exchanges. Would Paul have done that? Can we imagine Paul to have been open to conversion to another religion, or open to being convinced that another path was superior to the way of Jesus? Surely he would have had to be open to this if he expected others to be willing to reconsider their own faith commitments. How did Paul bring this off?

The answer may lie in the analogy of a scientist who is committed not only to the truth but to a particular scientific paradigm. He knows where he stands but is prepared to enter into contest with rival claims. Truth is worth the risk, vulnerability, and intellectual adventure of not knowing where the conversation may lead. Taking risks is how we grow and learn things in life. How exhilarating to read a powerful book opposing what one already believes. Iron sharpens iron. Religious faith is not identical to scientific faith and its claims are less easy to test. Nevertheless, it does have a cognitive side that invites investigation. As for the possibility of being converted, people do not go into dialogue expecting to surrender one faith and accept another. Rather, they are more likely to become stronger in their own faith as a result of dialogue. But the risk of openness is present in honest dialogue, and we should not be afraid of it. If Islam is not true, the Muslim should want to know it. If Christianity is not true, the Christian should want to know it.[53]

A STRATEGY FOR TRUTH-SEEKING ENCOUNTERS

Evangelicals are leery of dialogue because they think it means overlooking differences, searching for shallow consensus, avoiding tough issues, and refusing to ask hard questions. Above all, they think fretfully that dialogue is a substitute for evangelism, and that means not proclaiming Christ as Savior of the world. But dialogue does not have to mean any of these things. There is not one normative type of dialogue, for dialogues come in different varieties. One kind likes to share common religious experiences, another to discuss truth claims, another may focus on the practical concerns of living together in the same world. One can have the kind of dialogue one wants. Evangelical dialogue would be the kind that arises from caring about other people, the willingness to listen respectfully, a preparedness to step into their shoes and try to understand. It would mean clarifying differences where they exist, engaging in serious conversation, and seeking genuine communication. Proper dialogue means going beyond relativism and fideism to talk about the Gospel and the alternative truth claims together.[54]

Evangelicals are real pluralists who recognize the integrity of every religion and do not assume that they are all saying the same things when they are not. They are not unwilling to grant that some of the things others are saying also ring true for Christians. They recognize that a discussion of differences can be fruitful when it forces us into fresh thinking. Evangelicals know how people can serve one another in dialogue and yet not fall into syncretistic patterns. There are three elements that constitute good dialogue.[55]

The first element in good dialogue is the willingness to appreciate other religions, to honor their truth and to learn from them. There is nothing to prevent us from doing this. God has not left any nation without witness (Ac 14:16–17). Some of their own poets say true and valid things, according to Paul (Ac 17:28). Therefore, in the spirit of Vatican II, evangelicals should admit that other religions have positive contributions to make and a wealth to share. (The wealth their kings bring into the New Jerusalem, according to Rev 21:24, 26).[56] Other religions have resources for speaking truth and referring to realities that Christians need to learn about. As George Lindbeck says, "Whatever the faults of Hellenization, it must be seen as a process in which Christians learned much of inestimable value from ancient paganisms and from the cultures and philosophies that were their offspring."[57] Evangelicals cannot forsake the finality of Christ, but they can try harder to do justice to non-Christian truths and values. There is no reason why we have taken such a negative stance toward truth in other faiths, as if they had been given no valid insights. To say that religions are mere fabrications is to deny general revelation and God's prevenient grace. Recognizing truth in other religions does not take any glory away from Jesus Christ. For if all treasures of wisdom and knowledge are hid in him, the truth anyone possesses is a facet of the truth in Jesus, and the result of God's revelation to them.

Loving communication celebrates and does not deny areas of agreement where these exist. While insisting that religions are not saying the same, but significantly different things, we do not need to fall into the opposite error of supposing that religions are totally dissimilar, that they share nothing at all in common and have no overlap. It is equally wrong to absolutize differences and similarities. Though Christianity and Islam, for instance, are vastly different, they are not without important similarities. Christians and Muslims, together with large numbers of people from other traditions of the world, believe there is one God who created the universe and they admire the work of his hands. Christians do not have a monopoly on belief in one God. Even oriental religious systems with an absence of clear belief in a personal God do not lack for abiding insights into religious and philosophical truth. Even there the light shines and points to a greater light.[58]

Besides, because of the great variety within the world religions, we may find more agreeable features, and therefore more to build on, in one denomination or school of Buddhism or Islam than we do in another. In any event, it is normally possible to find some common ground when we engage in dialogue, to discover things to talk about and things to share. In an age of rising secularism, religious people need to stand together against the forces opposed to all religion.[59] North American society needs a broad religious vision that transcends differences in order to maintain the moral and physical ecology of the world we all inhabit.[60]

Sometimes to make dialogue work we have to admit problems in the way our own religion has been presented or perceived. Muslims and Jews, for example, insist that we be clearer about what we mean by the Incarnation and the Trinity. Rather than taking offense, we should try to clear up the difficulties if we can. Who would claim that in the history of doctrine we have never made mistakes? Dialogue is not monologue—teaching without listening, or giving without receiving. Dialogue is not an unpleasant duty. It has the real potential of renewing and enriching us.[61]

One reason Protestants in particular have been afraid of dialogue is that they have been terrified of syncretism. This fear may have been overworked. Religions influence and affect one another, and that is not always such a bad thing. There can be good syncretism. At this moment, Christians are influencing world religions through world mission. It is forcing Buddhism, for example, to take this world more seriously. On the other hand, Christians in the West need to become less materialistic and more spiritually Buddha-like. The interaction between Christianity and Buddhism has the potential of being mutually beneficial. Contacts can help us both. Christianity can be enriched through dialogue; it need not be corrupted by it. Far more than Buddhism, secularism poses a threat to Christianity by way of cultural influence. Against secularism, Buddhism is our ally. So there is good and bad syncretism, critical and uncritical, just as there is good and bad dialogue and good and bad contextualization (the respectable evangelical word for syncretism). Christians need dialogue as a challenge to catholicize our traditions by embracing and transforming through Christ all that is true, good, and lovely in other religions. If Aquinas can use Aristotle, why can we not use Shankara?[62]

There is no reason why not. In our approach to other religions, we ought to begin with appreciation not with criticism. Only our traditions prevent it—not our theology. Let us heed Max Warren: "We remember that God has not left himself without witness in any nation at any time. When we approach the man of a faith other than our own, it will be in a spirit of expectancy to find how God has been speaking to him and what new understandings of the grace and love of God we may ourselves discover in this encounter. Our first task in approaching another people, another culture, another religion, is to take off our shoes, for the place we are approaching is holy. Else we find ourselves treading on men's dreams. More seriously still, we may forget that God was here before our arrival."[63]

The second requirement of good dialogue is taking globalization seriously. No longer can we afford to do our theology and our apologetics in the isolation of Western ghettos outside of the global context. Just as it is unacceptable to do ninety-five percent of our outreach in Western countries, it is unacceptable to do ninety-five percent of our theological and apologetic work in dialogue only with Western intellectual currents. Why is Plato worth talking to and not Lao-Tzu? What makes atheism a challenge worth discussing and not monism? We can no longer afford to think parochially. We must begin to think and live globally, which means working dialogically and not monologically.

Systematic theology has to be done globally, in such a way that doctrines are considered within the context of the world religions. We must ask how other people regard their scriptures, how they cope with transcendence and immanence, how they view the human condition and salvation, who they think will save us, and what they hope for in the end. In the past, we have related our ideas to what Plato, Kant, Freud, and Whitehead may have said. It is time for us to relate our work to the deepest concerns of the nations that we want to reach with the Gospel. We will find that these people care more about what we are saying than Kant or Freud ever did.[64]

Apologetics has to be done globally also. We must explain why we believe in a personal God, why we confess the Incarnation, how salvation comes through the death and resurrection of Jesus, and what resurrection means in contexts where claims to the miraculous are common. In dialogue we must be prepared to explain what we believe and why. We have to stop taking refuge in the fortress of fideism and be concerned, not with whether this faith is true for me alone, but whether it is true to reality and for everyone.

Paul took several years to figure out how to reach Asia with the message (Ac 19:9–10). It may also take us years to become sensitive to how the Spirit flows in these other contexts, as God draws nations to himself. But it is incumbent on us to figure this out, if our theology is mission oriented as opposed to being merely a maintenance of traditions. Missionary theology is willing to make the effort and take the risks.

There is a third element in good dialogue which some would like to avoid because it is so delicate. It is the stage of dialogue in which critical questions are exchanged among the religions. If Christians are going to be self-critical about their claims, we have a right to ask others to be self-critical about theirs. The truth that the other person brings, and not just our own truth, has to be weighed. This stage cannot be avoided. People who dialogue are often too polite to press the issues of truth that need to be addressed. If a friend were killing herself by smoking or drinking, we would surely warn her. Love has the courage to confront. It is not love that fails to warn people of physical, intellectual, or moral danger. Truth matters. Ideas have consequences.

This approach would not be a completely new idea or experience. We are used to talking to atheists about God, trying to show them that the hypothesis "God exists" accords better with reality than the one that says "God does not exist." We are used to conversing with Mormons also, probing their claims for the Book of Mormon, or inspecting aspects of their remarkable (poly)theism as to its adequacy as a religious framework. And properly so, for it is inevitable, if we are serious about truth in religion, to engage such issues even at the risk of stepping on sensitive toes or causing misunderstanding. It is not easy to raise sensitive questions without appearing to be disrespectful. But it must be done.

David Novak, an Orthodox Jewish scholar, warns us away from dialogue on this level. He prefers to emphasize the practical concerns of living together peacefully in society. For him, questions like singular revelation through Moses, or the lordship of Jesus, are interior convictions of communities that cannot be discussed usefully with outsiders.[65] Novak is right that it is not easy to discuss such questions. This is why relativism and fideism are so appealing, because they leave aside such questions of ultimate truth. But we cannot accept this restriction on dialogue. None of us with the courage of our convictions should be unwilling to put everything on the table. To refuse to do so means that dialogue may degenerate into the relativism that critics of dialogue warn about. We can and we must talk about ultimate commitments in a spirit of love, openness, gentleness, and respect.

CRITICAL QUESTIONS

There are some critical questions to be discussed with Jews,[66] who must be challenged to respond to the fact that a billion and a half people in the world today believe in the God of Israel because of Jesus of Nazareth. God called Israel to be a light to the Gentiles, and this has happened in a surprising way (Isa 49:6). The light was not taken to the Gentiles by Judaism chiefly, but rather by the rejected One. It would seem as if Jews ought to face the possibility that the God of Israel sent Jesus to bring salvation to the world.

Furthermore, Jews should be challenged to reconsider the claims of Jesus and to explain their reluctance to take them more seriously.[67] What was it about Jesus that made it possible for God to use him to bring Israel's truth to the Gentiles? What is the meaning of his self-identification with the coming Son of Man (Da 7:13–14)? What is the meaning of the resurrection of Jesus, without which this worldwide penetration would not have occurred?[68] Jews love to venerate great rabbis, poring over the details of their lives, yet no rabbi has had the influence of Jesus of Nazareth on the world. Why is the signficance of Jesus ignored? And what of the sacrificial system of Torah in relation to the death of Jesus on Passover?

Christians are obliged to present Jesus to Jews as the unsurpass-
able Messiah, and we cannot retreat from this obligation. From our
standpoint, all people ought to reconsider Jesus' claims now, because
they will have to face him at the parousia.[69]

There are critical questions to raise with Muslims.[70] Although we
both worship the Creator of the world, we have to explore the
generosity of God; whether, in addition to issuing commandments,
he also reaches out in mercy to sinners and suffers in his love for
them. The God of Islam is a distant monarch who makes demands,
but does little of any cost to himself to save us from our failures.
Allah is said to be merciful, but how does this show? Why do
Muslims persist in dishonoring God by refusing his generosity to
them?[71]

Underlying this is Islam's optimistic view of human nature that
allows them to preach salvation on the basis of human works. The
problem goes beyond an irrational denial of the Cross as an actual
event to an outright denial of divine redemptive suffering. With Islam
we agree about the excellency of prophecy. But a prophet will not
suffice to save sinners.[72] There are questions, too, about historical
origins. Muslims think of the Koran as dictated to Muhammad by an
angel from a book kept in heaven, a book inspired down to every
syllable and inerrant in every line—a book so holy that one must
wash his hands before reading it. The naïveté that allows Muslims to
think in this unhistorical and noncritical way has to be confronted.
They have to face the fact that the Koran contains later material and
has a human history. The Koran's laws are those one might expect to
have been formulated in a given time and place. The laws are hard to
transfer to life today, and the rigidity of the system prevents it from
being flexible to changing times.

In addition, there are numerous ethical failures to address in this
religion of law. There is the continuing scandal of religious intolerance, the institution of holy war, the shariah code imposed on the
unwilling in Sudan, and the ideal of revenge and retaliation. What can
be said about Islam's social and political failures? Why is there no real
democracy among Arabs, or even one well-functioning modern
economy, despite all the oil money? Where is the doctrine that
celebrates the unique value of the individual and the equality of
gender? Why are women systematically suppressed?[73]

There are critical questions for Hindus too.[74] We must confront the circular character of Eastern thinking and the meaninglessness of the world that arises from it. The world is unreal, according to monistic ways of thinking, and this is a serious obstacle to the social betterment of the Indian masses. It is also a barrier to taking the individual seriously. Are individuals really merged into the one? Is evil really part of ultimate reality? Does Hinduism have resources within it to enable social transformation? Does it not need a higher view of man rooted in divine personality?

Ethically too, the meaning of karma as it applies to the poor and needy is a disturbing way of rationalizing power. It is a doctrine designed to persuade poor people to accept their place in the world without complaining. Then there is the caste system sanctioned by a religion that controls every aspect of life. Does it not destroy the basis for believing in the equality of people? And what of the economically and socially devastating cow worship?

There are also critical questions for Buddhists.[75] How was it that a religion that was originally anti-metaphysical was unable to keep god-beliefs away? Is it not because the religious instincts of people will not be suppressed? Is there not in Buddhist teaching about nirvana an inarticulate sense of transcendence suggesting the need of something more? Can Buddhists face the fact that the joy and worthwhileness of life cannot be dismissed as insubstantial appearance? How can Buddhists justify their indifference to the social needs of mankind? Is withdrawal from the world a legitimate response in the face of grinding poverty?[76]

Posing these questions does not mean that Christianity has no deficiencies. All religions are open to criticism. We have nothing to fear from mutual critical questioning. Although in this era of multiculturalism one is not supposed to ask critical questions about other people's beliefs, but rather honor every decision and allow each person to drink from his own well, we do not agree. No one who cares about truth can agree to suppressing questions that must be posed. These are not hostile questions, and there is just too much at stake not to raise them.

CLOSING REMARKS

How can we avoid triumphalism in this phase of dialogue? There are a couple of possibilities. One is to avoid being a hard rationalist in pursuing truth. Although we trust in Jesus Christ unreservedly, we admit that we only know in part, in finite, fragile ways. Unlike God's understanding, human understanding is partial and provisional. The full truth of anything will not be fully divulged until the end of time, when God reveals his glory. John Hick was right to speak of eschatological verification. At any present moment, we all experience doubt and uncertainty in some areas. We experience unresolved conflicts and contradictions that we hope will be resolved in the future. This does not entail relativism, but it does require epistemological modesty, a modesty which facilitates peaceable dialogue. It provides us a middle position between relativism and dogmatism. Truth will be resolved eschatologically. This means we will never fully resolve the conversation but patiently await the arrival of full knowledge from God.

An eschatological resolution of religious pluralism is a better and more scriptural resolution than a pluralistic reduction that leaves everybody completely uncertain about what is true. That leaves one with the depressing possibility that religions are only human constructions with nothing to offer by way of answers for the most important questions men and women have ever raised. Christians claim that God, the ever-debatable divine reality, has appeared in a definitive way in Jesus Christ. This is a possibility which cannot be ruled out a priori. It is the essential subject matter of our proclamation, and a topic for dialogue.

The other way to avoid triumphalism, and prevent unpleasant competition in dialogue, is to be modest ecclesiastically as well. Christians are waiting for the kingdom of God, not the hegemony of institutional Christianity over other religious institutions. It is the victory of Christ that we hope for, not the victory of the churches. We hold out to the nations the coming feast of God, not the requirement of church membership. The church is witness and servant of the kingdom, and subservient to it. We have been called to serve the world, not to seek our own glory.[77] Our primary desire ought to be to see people become followers of Jesus, whether or not they become baptized members of our churches. For in the kingdom of God there will be no Islam or Buddhism or Christianity, but only the triune God and the redeemed community. What God wants to do with the religions in history is his business. History is open-ended as far as these institutions are concerned. Nobody knows what Buddhism or Islam will be in the year 2100 A.D. No one has a map of the world's religions for that date and beyond. We should not pretend to know more than we do.

Let us remember that God is interested in more than just the salvation of individuals, and the planting of countless churches. God is renewing all things, including cultures and history itself. It is not for the purposes of short-term evangelism alone that we should engage in truth-seeking dialogue, because dialogue serves the mission of God in the sphere of historical transformation as well, and the effects of obedience may be larger than anything we intended for them.

This chapter tries to find a way between dogmatism and relativism. Holding to the finality of Jesus, it also allows some of what pluralists like Troeltsch argued for; it allows that the religions, including Christianity, are in a historical process. We recognize that revelation has entered into human history and is not unaffected by that history. Revelation sees movement toward the future and recognizes that before the end of time we will not be able to see everything clearly. Jesus is the prolepsis of the end of history, but until then we will not know what all that means.

Five

Hope for the Unevangelized

The question that Christians worry about and non-Christians ask about as much as any other is this: Is there hope for the unevangelized, or (as it used to be phrased) what is the fate of the heathen?[1] What about the eternal destiny of the millions who have never heard of Jesus? Will God extend an opportunity for salvation to them? Is it necessary for non-Christians to call explictly upon the name of Jesus in order to benefit from his work on their behalf? This is a real problem for those who believe that God is just and that he loves the whole world.[2] If God has grace for all, how do people benefit from grace if they have not been told about it? It is a question of coherence in theology. Is the universal salvific will of God frustrated by accidents of birth?[3] The subject we turn to now is eschatology. If the goal of history is for humanity to share in redeemed existence beyond the grave in fellowship with the triune God, is there any way that the unevangelized can share in it?

AN OLD AND PRESSING PROBLEM

Porphyry, an early critic of Christianity, identified the problem centuries ago: "If Christ declares himself to be the way of salvation, the grace and truth, and affirms that in him alone, and only to souls believing in him, is the way of return to God, what has become of the men who lived in the many centuries before Christ came?"[4] This is a painful question well stated. What about the millions who died before the Good News of the kingdom reached them? Is it fair to exclude them without them having a chance to be saved? How can heaven be a delight for anyone who knows that there are large numbers of people suffering in a hell that they had no possibility of avoiding? Why should they suffer for a failure to hear the gospel that was due not to their sins but to the sins of others? God wants his house to be filled (Lk 14:23); how can it be filled without them?

Elton Trueblood puts the same question to orthodoxy: "Such a scheme is neat and simple, but it is morally shocking and consequently not a live option of belief for truly thoughtful or sensitive persons of any faith. What kind of God is it who consigns men and women and children to eternal torment, in spite of the fact that they have not had even a remote chance of knowing the saving truth? What sort of God would create men and women in love, only to irrationally punish the vast majority of them? A God who would thus play favorites with his children, condemning some to eternal separation from himself while admitting others, and distinguishing between them wholly or chiefly on the basis of the accidents of history or geography, over which they had no control, would be more devil than God. In any case he would not even resemble Jesus Christ, and thus there is a contradiction at the heart of the system. The effort to glorify Christ as the only true revelation of God presents a conception of the divine that is incompatible with the picture which Christ himself gives."[5]

The eternal destiny of a very large number of people throughout history who have not had access to the Gospel, and who enter eternity not knowing Jesus Christ, is a pressing problem for theology. It pits access against urgency. If we say there is equal access to salvation for all, including the unevangelized, we will be charged with eliminating the urgency of mission. But if we preserve the urgency, people will protest that this means millions will go to hell without any chance to avoid it. No decision is free from serious objection. Supporting access, stalwarts will claim that the motivation for missions has been undermined and will oppose thinking in this direction. Supporting urgency, sensitive souls will worry about the fairness issue.

Therefore, some will play it safe and say nothing. They will opt for reverent agnosticism on the subject. Having stated his belief that the majority of the human race will be saved, John Stott then adds: "I remain agnostic about how God will bring it to pass."[6] Many try to duck the issue in this manner. But this sudden attack of modesty does not seem quite right. Isn't theology supposed to face tough questions as well as the easy ones? After all, it is not as if the Bible offers nothing to reflect upon.

THE BIBLE AND WESTERN INDIVIDUALISM

It is true that the Bible does not address this issue as often or as specifically as we would wish. This is because the Scriptures are more familiar with corporate thinking in regard to judgment than we are in Western culture. We think more in terms of the individual. It is instinctive for us to think immediately of the eternal destiny of individual persons, while the Bible prefers to address larger issues of justice and restitution, focusing much less on the judgment of solitary individuals.

This is quite clear in the biblical prophets who express hope for the salvation or judgment of whole groups of people at a time. This can be seen in the word of Isaiah: "On this mountain he will destroy the shroud that enfolds all peoples, the sheet that covers all nations" (Isa 25:7). Corporateness is visible when Jesus describes all nations (not individuals, one by one) gathering for judgment (Mt 25:31–46). God is going to put things right in history. He will cast the mighty from their thrones and raise up those of low degree (Lk 1:51–53). Liberation theology, for all its errors, has rightly called attention to divine judgment as the righting of historical wrongs. The millions who have been trampled down and victimized throughout their earthly lives, not because of their sins but by the sins of others, will be recompensed and vindicated on that day. Victims will be delivered and judgment will be visited on oppressors. Dives, who disregarded the poor man at his gate, will be in torment, while beggar Lazarus will go to Abraham's bosom (Lk 16:19–31). God's judgment means that wrongs will be put right, and justice will be done when God comes to judge the earth.[7]

This corporate emphasis contrasts rather sharply with the popular evangelical view of judgment which focuses on the much narrower issue of verbal assent to the gospel—or the decision for Christ. In particular, it contradicts an implication of the thinking that the unevangelized, most of whom have endured oppresssion and misery in this earthly life, will go on suffering in hell forever because they did not believe in Jesus, even though this is something they could not have done. The implication of popular eschatology is that the downtrodden of this world, unable to call upon Jesus through no fault of their own, are to be rejected for eternity, giving the final victory to the tyrants who trampled them down. Knowing little but suffering in this life, the unevangelized poor will know nothing but more and worse suffering in the next. Popular eschatology simply does not add up. What judgment in the Bible means, in part, is that wrongs are going to be set right and suffering will give way to fullness of life.[8]

The same corporate rather than individualist concern for judgment is apparent when Jesus instructs his disciples to pray for the coming of God's kingdom (Mt 6:10). This is a much broader hope for the future than just the destiny of individual souls. It is also visible in Paul when he anticipates Christ's victory at the parousia over the powers which afflict society and oppress sinners (1 Co 15:20–28). It appears again in Paul when he expresses concern about the fate of the whole race, Jews and Gentiles, not just the destiny of individuals (Ro 9–11). Similarly John in the Apocalypse expresses longing for the healing of the nations (Rev 21:24). These examples and others show that the Bible is more concerned about structural redemption than the fate of individuals in contrast to ourselves.[9]

But it would be stretching the corporate emphasis too far to say that the Bible has no interest at all in this issue of individual salvation. Lesslie Newbigin, for example, likes to emphasize that God will do what is right in judgment, and we do not need to worry ourselves about it. He points to texts like Luke 13:30 which say that judgment is going to catch us by surprise and contradict all normal expectations.[10] There is truth in what he says. But such an attitude can also be a cop-out to avoid answering a fair and urgent question in a responsible way. What kind of theologian refuses to speak about the possibility of salvation of the majority of the human race? Is such a person reticent on other controversial matters? Maybe he or she should find easier work. The Bible speaks to the issue of the destiny of individuals. It offers believers hope and the assurance of being with Christ after death. And there are also warnings of judgment to come upon individuals who neglect God's great salvation. Scripture speaks to issues of life after death, and our participation or nonparticipation in endtime salvation. God cares about those who have lived and died before the Gospel of Jesus Christ reached them. What are God's plans for these people?

GOD'S BOUNDLESS GENEROSITY

The context for discussing this question must be God's boundless generosity. In the first chapter, I argued against the fewness doctrine and in favor of a large outcome of salvation. We saw reason to think that a tremendously large number of people are going to be saved— the structural redemption of the human race in fact. John anticipates this large result: "After this I looked and there before me was a great multitude that no one could count, from every nation, tribe, people and language, standing before the throne and in front of the Lamb" (Rev 7:9). This must include a substantial number of the unevangelized.

The optimism of salvation is rooted in a word of Jesus that echoes an Old Testament background: "People will come from east and west and from north and south, and will take their places at the feast in the kingdom of God" (Lk 13:29). This reference is to the prophetic theme of the eschatological pilgrimage of the Gentiles to God's mountain, where they share in the messianic banquet and the life of the world to come.[11] This same image underlies the idea that the men of Nineveh will be part of the resurrection, and that the queen of Sheba will be there along with the blessed (Mt 12:41–42). The Gentile nations that responded to the poor will also inherit everlasting life (Mt 25:31–46). God's concern for the nations will issue in a large redemption.[12]

The same truth is likely present in other texts too, as when John says that the people who put Jesus to death will weep on account of him at his coming (Rev 1:7). Some interpreters assume this means they will weep in shock and dismay at their fate. But it could just as well mean that they will weep, not selfishly for themselves, but for what they did to Jesus by nailing him to the cross. Could John be saying that at least some of the people presently so hostile to the Gospel will come to the realization that Jesus is in truth the Messiah of Israel? This seems to be implied in other texts. "I will make those who are of the synagogue of Satan, who claim to be Jews though they are not, but are liars—I will make them come and fall down at your feet and acknowledge that I have loved you" (Rev 3:9). In yet another place John says that the people were so terrified by God's judgments that they "gave glory to the God of heaven" (Rev 11:13). Further, he anticipates the nations that Satan had deceived coming into the new Jerusalem with the glory and honor of their cultures (Rev 21:26). I do not agree that the book of the Revelation is a pessimistic book. God is bringing many to glory, not a solitary few (Heb 2:10).

But one might ask what Jesus could have meant when he said that "small is the gate and narrow the road that leads to life, and only a few find it" (Mt 7:14)? Are they few or are they many? To make sense of this text in the presence of the others, we can say that Jesus is warning the disciples away from speculation and urging them to choose the hard and unpopular path. At the time when he spoke this warning, the number of disciples was few and the conditions were arduous. However, in other contexts he encourages the disciples in the direction of the large hope, perhaps in order to encourage them. I do not think that this text about fewness can be used to cancel out the optimism of salvation that so many other verses articulate.

God allows us a generous hope, however we explain it, however the mechanics work. God boosts our morale by sharing with us the information that salvation will be large and generous in the end. This hope coheres well with the picture of God's love for the whole world and the universal covenant he made with all flesh.

We have to confront the niggardly traditions of certain varieties of conservative theology that present God as miserly, and that exclude large numbers of people without a second thought. This dark pessimism is contrary to Scripture and right reason. Not only does it contradict the prophetic hope of a large salvation, it is a cruel and offensive doctrine. What kind of God would send large numbers of men, women, and children to hell without the remotest chance of responding to his truth? This does not sound like the God whom Jesus called Father. When Indian evangelist Sundar Singh was told by someone that his mother, a saintly Sikh woman, would be in hell because she was not a Christian, his eyes flashed with indignation and he said, "Then I will ask God to send me down to hell so that I may be with her there." R.V.G. Tasker's reading of Matthew 5:22 leads him to conclude that Jesus is saying that "The man who tells his brother that he is doomed to hell is in danger of hell himself."[13]

If there is going to be a numerically large salvation, how will such an outcome eventuate? If Christ is the sole mediator between God and humanity, how can a large number be saved since only a small number in many periods of history, including our own, have heard of Jesus or been given an adequate presentation of his message? The only way this could happen would be if a substantial number of the unevangelized are saved in the end. But how can this be?

UNIVERSAL SALVATION?

Some posit universal divine reconciliation as the answer. If God would decide to save everyone, whether they heard and responded to his Word or not, then there would be no problem. The outcome would be both large and certain. Origen came up with this possibility in his work against Celsus. All will be saved in the end, said Origen, and the purpose of hell is purification (*Against Celsus*, IV, 13; VI, 25). Quite a number of modern theologians agree with him. John A.T. Robinson, for example, defends universalism as the only way to uphold the love of God. God will not give up on lost sinners. Christ will continue to suffer until the whole world is reconciled.[14]

Universalism is appealing, especially if the alternative is the fewness doctrine with hell defined as everlasting conscious punishment. One can feel driven to universalism under such circumstances. Appealing either to divine sovereignty or to never-failing divine persistence, the way of universalism can account for a large salvation outcome, while at the same time taking care of the problem of the unevangelized.

There are two well-trodden theological routes to universalism. Sovereign love is preferred by Augustinians, accustomed as they are to a God who saves people irresistibly. What Augustinians have to do to reach universalism is enlarge the scope of election to include the whole race, and then theologize in their usual way. God merely decides to elect all (and he could easily do it in his sovereignty), after which he proceeds to save them in the normal coercive manner. With the same argument that says no one can answer against God, all objections against universalism can be put aside. The preferred route to universalism for non-Augustinians is to appeal to infinite divine patience. God will keep on making his appeal to sinners even after death, until they finally yield to his grace. This approach results in universal salvation without destroying human freedom. God tires sinners out and wears them down with his mercy until they give in. After a thousand invitations the hardest sinner supposedly becomes tired of saying no. Jacques Ellul ordinarily accepts human freedom except in one instance—the freedom to be damned. That freedom God does not permit.[15]

But universal salvation for all its appeal has two serious problems. First, there are too many warnings about divine judgment falling on people to be ignored, warnings that suggest that rejection is possible. These warnings do not sound like idle threats, but like real danger to be avoided. When Jesus speaks of an unforgivable sin (whatever it is), he must be indicating that a person can place himself outside God's kingdom (Mk 3:28–30). What else can the following warning mean? "But unless you repent, you too will all perish" (Lk 13:5). The so-called universalist texts may not speak of a universalist outcome at all but rather of a universal opportunity to be saved.[16] In the light of all the warnings, this would seem likely.

Second, the theory does not allow for humans in their freedom to say no to God. If not, what is the meaning of any yes? How can the personal address of love, even God's love, be irresistible? How can a person be compelled to accept a gift from God or from anyone else? It is the nature of these relationships that they are freely accepted or else refused. Our relation with God, as well as our final destiny, are chosen by ourselves and not thrust upon us. God does not purpose to condemn anyone, but anyone can choose rejection.[17]

RELATED CONSIDERATIONS

Universalism feeds on the mistakes of orthodoxy. If traditional Christians hold to the fewness doctrine and deny universal access to salvation, then universalism will seem to many like a doctrinal improvement. Another error which promotes universalism is the traditional understanding of the nature (not the fact) of hell. The idea that hell means everlasting conscious punishment contributes much to belief in universal salvation. If the choice is between hell as everlasting torture and universal salvation, who could resist the latter? Sensitive persons would be practically forced to accept it, since they cannot accept that God would subject anyone, even most corrupt sinners, to unending torture in both body and soul as Augustine and Jonathan Edwards taught. If that is what hell means, many will conclude that there should not be a doctrine of hell in Christian theology.

There is a middle way, however. It is very probable that the biblical doctrine of hell does not entail everlasting conscious punishment. If so, the problem does not arise. John Stott, Michael Green, Philip Hughes, John Wenham, and Stephen Travis, among other evangelicals, have concluded that the evidence points to an understanding of the nature of hell as annihilation.[18] As E. G. Selwyn says, "There is little indeed in the New Testament to suggest a state of everlasting punishment, but much to indicate an ultimate destruction or dissolution of those who cannot enter into life: conditional immortality seems to be the doctrine most consonant with the teaching of Scripture."[19]

HOW CAN THE UNEVANGELIZED BE SAVED?

If God really loves the whole world and desires everyone to be saved, it follows logically that everyone must have access to salvation. There would have to be an opportunity for all people to participate in the salvation of God. If Christ died for all, while yet sinners, the opportunity must be given for all to register a decision about what was done for them (Ro 5:8). They cannot lack the opportunity merely because someone failed to bring the Gospel of Christ to them. God's universal salvific will implies the equally universal accessibility of salvation for all people.

But this raises a difficult question. How is salvation within the reach of the unevangelized? How can anyone be saved without knowing Christ? The idea of universal accessibility, though not a novel theory, needs to be proven. It is far from self-evident, at least biblically speaking. How can it best be defended?

In my judgment, the faith principle is the basis of universal accessibility. According to the Bible, people are saved by faith, not by the content of their theology. Since God has not left anyone without

witness, people are judged on the basis of the light they have
received and how they have responded to that light. Faith in God is
what saves, not possessing certain minimum information. Hebrews is
clear: "And without faith it is impossible to please God, because
anyone who comes to him must believe that he exists and that he
rewards those who earnestly seek him" (Heb 11:6).

People cannot respond to light that did not reach them. They can
only respond to revelation that did. Scripture and reason both imply
that no one can be held responsible for truth of which they were
inculpably ignorant; they are judged on the basis of the truth they
know. A person is saved by faith, even if the content of belief is
deficient (and whose is not?). The Bible does not teach that one must
confess the name of Jesus to be saved. Job did not know it. David did
not know it. Babies dying in infancy do not know it. It is not so much
a question whether the unevangelized know Jesus as whether Jesus
knows them (Mt 7:23). One does not have to be conscious of the
work of Christ done on one's behalf in order to benefit from that
work. The issue God cares about is the direction of the heart, not the
content of theology. Paul says that faith makes the difference. God is
the "Savior of all men [potentially], and especially of those who
believe [actually]" (1 Ti 4:10). This is the path I will take to explain
how the unevangelized gain access to God and are finally saved.

Many other theologians have held and defended the faith
principle. As we saw, Greek fathers like Justin and Clement held it.
Ulrich Zwingli held it.[20] John Wesley said that no one had the right to
sentence the heathen and Muhammadan world to damnation, and he
held that the unevangelized cannot be blamed for failing to accept
Christ if they have never heard of him. Some of them, he thought,
have been taught by God the essentials of true religion. Wesley did
not even rule out the salvation of modern-day Jews who have heard
the Gospel. Any such may be servants, though not yet sons of God,
and on them the wrath of God does not rest.[21]

A. H. Strong wrote:

The patriarchs, though they had no knowledge of a personal Christ,
were saved by believing in God so far as God had revealed himself
to them; and whoever among the heathen are saved, must in like
manner be saved by casting themselves as helpless sinners upon

God's plan of mercy, dimly shadowed forth in nature and providence. But such faith, even among the patriarchs and heathen, is
implicitly a faith in Christ, and would become explicit and conscious
trust and submission, whenever Christ were made known to them.[22]

Vatican II says the very same thing:

They also can attain to everlasting salvation who through no fault of
their own do not know the gospel of Christ or his church, yet
sincerely seek God, and moved by grace, strive by their deeds to do
his will as it is known to them through the dictates of conscience.
(*The Church*, chap. 16)

Evangelical apologist Stuart Hackett comments:

If every human being in all times and ages has been objectively
provided for through the unique redemption in Jesus, and if this
provision is in fact intended by God for every such human being,
then it must be possible for every human individual to become
personally eligible to receive that provision—regardless of his
historical, cultural, or personal circumstances and situation, and
quite apart from any particular historical information or even
historically formulated theological conceptualisation—since a universally intended redemptive provision is not genuinely universal
unless it is also and for that reason universally accessible.[23]

It would be unintelligible if it were not possible for all persons to
respond to the revelation given them, to renounce their sins and cast
themselves on the mercy of God. Abraham trusted in God every bit
as genuinely as we ourselves do, and he was saved in spite of severe
conceptual shortcomings. This is not to imply the unimportance of
making historical facts about Jesus known everywhere. It is essential
to make them known in order to clarify God's saving purposes for
humanity and to motivate individuals to make their commitment to
God in Christ. But we cannot reasonably suppose that a failure of
evangelization that affects many millions would leave them completely bereft of any access to God.[24]

Let me develop the scriptural basis for such a position. First,
there is the principle enshrined in Hebrews 11:6 that "without faith it
is impossible to please God, because anyone who comes to him must
believe that he exists and that he rewards those who earnestly seek
him." Referring as the author does to Abel, Enoch, and Noah,

Hebrews indicates that people are saved by faith, not primarily by knowledge. The Jews of Jesus' day knew more conceptually about God than their forefather Abraham, who knew relatively little. God accepted Abraham because he believed he would be given a son and heir. How little by way of knowledge God required of him! What God was looking for in Abram was faith, not a certain quotient of knowledge. God looks primarily for faith in persons. God is very generous in doing so, and keeps the window of accessibility to salvation wide open. The fact that the information possessed by the unevangelized is slight does not disqualify them from entering into a right relationship with God through faith.

By Christian standards, the knowledge Abraham possessed was certainly at a low level. But he gave as much of himself as he could to as much of God as he understood. How fortunate this is for all of us; for who has perfect knowledge? Whose knowledge of the things of God is not surrounded by oceans of ignorance? Though some have more to learn than others, the key factor is to be moving in the right direction in faith and to desire to know more of God's ways and to follow them.[25]

The same applies to a pagan believer like Job, who had a good will and put his trust in God even though inadequately informed doctrinally and morally. Job was a person who, provided with some valid information about what is good and true, assimilated it and acted upon it. Such people, having the desire for salvation, will surely receive it. This is not perhaps the view of the majority of Christians historically, but it is (I think) very nearly the consensus in the church today.[26]

Some offer a theory at this point about which I am not convinced, but I want to mention it because it may offer help with this problem. It is the notion of middle knowledge, a theory that postulates God's knowlege of things that did not happen but might have happened. For example, it is surmised that God would know what any person would have done under certain circumstances, even if the person never faced them. This would mean, in the case of the unevangelized, that God would know how anyone would respond to Jesus, even if they never actually heard of him. According to middle knowledge, God would know what persons would do even in hypothetical situations, and therefore what one would do if revelation reached them which did not in fact reach them. God would know whether a person would have accepted Jesus or rejected him by invoking middle knowlege.[27] The advantage of this theory is that divine judgment can be based on hypothetical states of affairs as well as real ones.

The idea is certainly intriguing—but there is also something wrong with it. First, is it the case that God has middle knowledge? He does not appear to have it in certain circumstances, as when he expresses consternation at Israel's responses and admits he does not know what she will do (Jer 3:7, 18:7–8). Second, does middle knowledge not mean determinism by implication, in that it posits free decisions being known solely on the basis of existing factors and not allowing for the possibility of agents doing genuinely new and unforeseen things? Third, middle knowledge applied to the question of the unevangelized has the interesting result of allowing certain persons salvation without exercising any faith at all, on the basis of God's estimate of what they would have done if they had had the opportunity. Thus, I myself hesitate to appeal to middle knowledge, but I mention it because it may possess an appeal for others.

While everyone will grant that it was possible to respond to God the way Job did in premessianic times, not everyone thinks that the possibility still exists. This latter hesitation needs to be confronted. Why would it make any difference if Job were born in A.D. 1900 in outer Mongolia? Why would God not deal with him the same way he dealt with him in the Old Testament? A person who is informationally premessianic, whether living in ancient or modern times, is in exactly the same spiritual situation. The same things apply to all such: "God will give to each person according to what he has done. To those who by persistence in doing good seek glory, honor and immortality, he will give eternal life." Paul adds the explanation too: "God does not show favoritism" (Ro 2:6–8; 11). Obviously the unevangelized can be saved by faith just like anyone else.

Second, the faith principle is also fleshed out in the holy pagans of the biblical story. These were people saved by faith without any knowledge of the revelation vouchsafed to Israel or the church. Though we do not know how many holy pagans there are in the world at any given time, we know they exist because of this scriptural testimony. Like Job and Abimelech, there are those who, due to an inner voice, come to a fork in the road and turn to God in faith. There is always a way, whatever the path, wherever that path leads, to come to God. It is always possible to move closer toward God than farther away. Those who desire God will be led by his Spirit to closer communion with him.

No one can deny the fact that the Bible presents these holy pagans as saved by faith, even though they knew neither Israelite nor Christian revelation. Abel, Noah, Enoch, Job, Jethro, the queen of Sheba, the centurion, Cornelius—all stand as positive proof that the grace of God touches people all over the world and that faith, without which it is impossible to please God, can and does occur outside as well as inside the formal covenant communities.

As Justin wrote, "We have been taught, are convinced and do believe, that God approves of only those who imitate his inherent virtues, namely, temperance, justice, love of humankind, and any other virtue proper to God who is called by no given name. If people by their actions prove themselves worthy of his plan, they shall be . . . found worthy to make their abode with him . . . We have been taught that Christ was the first begotten of God, and the Word of whom all mankind partakes. Those who lived by reason are Christians, even though they have been considered atheists: such as, among the Greeks, Socrates, Heraclitus and others like them." (*First Apology*, chap. 10, 14)

Dispensationalists have rightly opposed the notion that believers in other epochs needed to believe in the coming Savior in order to be saved. These people trusted in God, even though the content of their theology differed from our own. Charles Ryrie states it well when he says that "The basis of salvation in every age is the death of Christ; the requirement for salvation in every age is faith; the object of faith in every age is God; the content of faith changes in the varioius dispensations."[28]

Evangelicals often try to prevent this biblical truth from being taken seriously. Bruce Demarest sees the point but moves quickly to limit its relevance when he writes: "It would appear difficult to rule out the possibility that in exceptional circumstances God might choose to reveal himself in some extraordinary way independently of gospel proclamation."[29] Similarly, James Packer, after reviewing examples of God's generosity in this respect, adds this proviso: "We have no warrant from scripture to expect that God will act thus in any single case where the gospel is not yet known . . . living by the Bible means assuming that no one will be saved apart from faith in Christ and acting accordingly."[30] Millard Erickson has even less hope than these. He doubts if anyone has *ever* been saved by responding to general revelation, which was given only to make all people guilty.[31] What does "evangelical" mean when applied to those who seem to want to ensure that there is as little Good News as possible? The Bible offers them a strong basis for optimism, yet they decline.

Third, another class of people saved without professing Christ were the Jews who lived before Jesus was born. Forefather Abraham was saved by faith, as is clear in Genesis. "Abraham believed the Lord, and he credited it to him as righteousness" (Ge 15:6). All who have faith are sons of Abraham and are blessed with him (Gal 3:7). The Old Testament describes a large number of believing Israelites who trusted in God, though the Messiah had not yet come to them. Yet they exercised saving faith, as did Abraham, and experienced forgiveness, as did David. Their theological knowledge was deficient, measured by New Testament standards, and their understanding of God was limited because they had not encountered Jesus, in whom alone one sees the Father. Nonetheless, they knew God and belonged to the great cloud of witnesses who encourage us (Heb 12:1). Without actually confessing Jesus Christ, they were saved by his work of redemption.

J. N. D. Anderson comments on this: "It seems clear that believing Jews under the Old Testament dispensation enjoyed forgiveness and salvation through that saving work of God in Christ (dated, of course, according to the calendars of men, but timeless and eternal in its divine significance), by which alone a holy God can and does forgive the repentant sinner—little though can most of them have understood this."[32] What could be clearer proof of the faith principle that God saves people by faith on the basis of the light they have been given? Faith is our response to information about God in the direction of trusting and obeying him. Nobody can say how much or how little a person has to know in order to be saved.

Fourth, Jesus spoke about the salvation of the unevangelized in his parable of the last judgment when he says to those on his right hand, "I tell you the truth, whatever you did for one of the least of these brothers of mine, you did for me" (Mt 25:40). Who are the least of Jesus' brothers here? Some argue that they are the missionaries Jesus sent out into the world, the ones mentioned earlier (Mt 10:42).[33] That would mean that the fate of nations depends on the way they respond to Jesus' emissaries ("He who receives you receives me"—Mt 10:40). This would not speak to the issue of the unevangelized at all. This narrowing interpretation is possibly correct.[34]

But another interpretation is also possibly correct—the view that Jesus, speaking as a Jew with the Gentile world in mind, wishes to say (in the spirit of the Noahic covenant) that deeds of love done to needy people will be regarded at the last judgment as having been done to Christ, even though the Gentiles did not and could not have known it under the circumstances. This sense would call attention to who Jesus is in this portrait—the son of man standing in solidarity with the human race. And it would correspond well with Jewish thinking about the judgment. As the midrash on Psalm 118 says, "If he says, 'I have clothed the naked!' it will be said to him, 'This is the gate of the Lord—you who have clothed the naked, enter in the same.' "[35]

Joachim Jeremias agrees with this reading. He writes, "Jesus' audience must indeed have been surprised and amazed to hear such words. These words include not only those gentiles who received Jesus and believed on him, but also those who repented at the prophet's message, those who submitted themselves to the wisdom of God, and who showed kindness to the hidden and unrecognised messiah whom they encountered in the guise of the poor and suffering. Such would be numbered among the people of God at the last day, and would sit down with the patriarchs in the kingdom of God."[36]

To restrict the reference ("the least of these brothers of mine") to Christian missionaries seems unjustified and unlikely. Is Jesus not saying that one day all humanity will stand before him and that deeds of love shown to the poor will be accepted as if done to himself? Such a reading coheres well with the principle in his teaching that good works manifest one's basic attitude to God and that noncognitive responses to God count as much as cognitive responses do. Surely the text picks up on the beatitudes: "Blessed are you who are poor, for yours is the kingdom of God" (Lk 6:20). Serving the poor embodies what the love of God himself is, and it is accepted as the equivalent of faith.

The saying about the sheep and the goats refers then to humanity assembled in its entirety before Jesus in judgment. The Son of Man, because he is identified with humankind in every condition, receives the deeds done to the poor as deeds done for him, underlining his point about loving God through care for the neighbor. Those who confess Christ and those who do not are judged alike by the extent to which they walk in the way of the Son of Man.[37]

Fifth, the story of Cornelius in the book of Acts is also important evidence of the salvation of the unevangelized (Ac 10:1–48). Cornelius is the pagan saint par excellence of the New Testament, a believer in God before he became a Christian. He embodied in his very person the truth that Peter needed to learn: "God does not show favoritism but accepts men from every nation who fear him and do what is right" (Ac 10:34–35).

Peter was under the impression that God's plan was more or less restricted to Jews. He needed to learn otherwise. As Matthew Henry wrote on this text, "God never did, nor ever will, reject or refuse an honest gentile, who, though he has not the privileges or advantages that the Jews have, yet, like Cornelius, fears God, and worships him, and works righteousness; that is, is just and charitable towards all men, who lives up to the light he has, both in a sincere devotion and in regular conversation."[38]

Unfortunately, John Stott fails to see this meaning in the narrative. Limiting the scope of the text, he argues that the phrase "acceptable to God" does not mean accepted by God through faith but acceptable in a weaker sense. Stott thinks God found Cornelius only relatively better than other sinners, while still regarding him under condemnation. Citing Calvin, Stott states that the other sense would be a childish error.[39] Hardly so, since Luke is clear that Cornelius' prayers as a non-Christian ascended to God, and that God guided him in visions (Ac 10:1–3).

Another more plausible way to limit the text is the view that any soul like Cornelius who is genuinely seeking God will be evangelized through a special messenger before he dies. In other words, God will take steps to ensure that any person truly seeking him will hear the gospel before death and have an opportunity to be saved. This theory holds that persons who respond to the light they have will receive further light from God. There is something to be said for this theory. For one thing, the Cornelius account does illustrate that point. Cornelius was seeking God, and Peter was led to his side. Besides, things like this do happen in our own experience. Further, the theory can be commended for seeing the problem of accessibility and for answering it. It is a move in the right direction and (depending on the means used by God) it might even approach our own theory. If, for example, the divine messenger could be a vision or an inner voice, not necessarily a human messenger, then it could be part of my own theory.

But usually the theory calls for a human messenger, and that is the problem.[40] Regarding this version of it, there are factors that make us hesitate. First, it implies that Cornelius was not already in a right relationship with God before becoming a Christian. This means that Cornelius needed Peter in order to be saved from God's wrath. But this is not true. As Job in the Old Testament story, Cornelius did not need a special messenger to make him a believer. He was a believer already and not hellbound. True, he needed to become a Christian to receive messianic salvation, including assurance and the Holy Spirit, but not to be saved from hell. Second, the theory is not nearly adequate for the size of the problem. It might have been satisfactory for an Aquinas who, living in the Middle Ages, thought there were only a handful of unevangelized people in the whole world. But it is not satisfactory for us today because it cannot bear the full weight of the problem. How is a Christian messenger supposed to show up among the Mongols in the fifth Christian century? I have the distinct feeling that the special messenger theorists do not themselves believe that it often happens that the special messenger has to be sent, because it does not often happen that people call out to God for help. It would always be an exceptional divine action and not a normal one. Thus, it still leaves ninety percent of the race under wrath.

Sixth, another category of unevangelized are the babies (baptized or not) who die in infancy, or people who are mentally incompetent to respond to the gospel, even if they hear it. Since most Christians today grant that these people will be saved, they constitute a prime example of the unevangelized being saved apart from faith in Christ, apart even from faith in God in most cases. They are a practically uncontested example of unevangelized people being saved.

Historically, theology has taken a more pessimistic view than this. For example, Augustine taught that unbaptized babies who die are damned to hell, God holding them personally responsible for Adam's sin, though they had done nothing good or bad themselves. This kind of theology required a strong stomach, and before long efforts were made to soften this abysmal doctrine. Peter Abelard, for example, came up with the idea of "limbo" to ease the moral burden. Infants, he surmised, could not be either in heaven or in hell, but must be somewhere in between. Abelard is wrestling in effect with our problem of the fate of those who are in no position to respond to God through no fault of their own. Later on, the "baptism of desire" idea would serve the same function. Though the sacraments are the normal means of grace, the medieval theologians argued that it was really the disposition of faith to receive the sacraments that justified people. Therefore, there could be a desire for the sacrament even in the absence of it, a theory taught by the Council of Trent.[41]

Protestants also engage in the exercise of injecting mercy into theology. B. B. Warfield, following Zwingli, is typical of Protestants who feel pressure and seek relief from it. Logically, as a high Calvinist, Warfield should say there are elect and nonelect among even the babies who die, just as there are among the rest of the race. That would make sense in his system. Doesn't God derive glory from saving some and damning others? So why balk at babies? But Warfield does not say that. He is a universalist when it comes to babies.[42] Since he discovered no new biblical texts, I surmise that moral sensibility persuaded Warfield to revise the orthodox traditions. If only he had gone further and reconsidered his doctrine of the divine partiality in the salvation of adults! Why so great a compassion for infants who cannot believe, and so little for large numbers of others perishing without God lifting a finger to save them?

How is it that unevangelized infants are saved? First, they are saved because God reconciled the world to himself and this must include them (2 Co 5:19). Christ's transaction affects the whole race and alters its situation. Ordinarily this redemption would need to be ratified by persons in history. As Paul says, "Be reconciled to God" (2 Co 5:20). But if it cannot be ratified, one would expect this requirement to be waived or at least postponed. In the case of babies dying in infancy, the decision for God can come after death, since it could not have come before. This in turn may suggest that they are also given time to grow up and mature, so then a decision could be made. In this case, the salvation of all the unevangelized would not be certain. In Warfield's version there is no uncertainty because he has God declare all babies elect and therefore certain of salvation.

We have now refuted the restrictivist view that says that only those who actually confess Jesus in this life can be saved, be in a right relation with God, and be safe from eschatological wrath. On the contrary, the Bible teaches that many varieties of unevangelized persons will attain salvation. This will happen according to the faith principle. In the case of morally responsible persons confronted with the gospel of Christ in this life, they would surely turn to him in explicit faith. If they did not do so, it would prove that they had not been favorably disposed to God prior to that time, since Jesus is the culmination of divine revelation. Pre-Christian faith is valid up until that moment when Christ is preached, but not afterwards. When Christ is known, the obligation comes into force to believe on him. The unevangelized are expected to receive the Good News when it reaches them. God's offer becomes an objective obligation at that time, and refusal to accept that offer would be fatal. No hope can be offered to those declining God's offer to them in Christ.[43]

POSTMORTEM ENCOUNTER

Another way of conceiving universal access to salvation was entertained by some in the early church.[44] They proposed the idea that people would have an opportunity to respond to Christ after death, if they had not had the opportunity to respond before. Let us weigh this possibility alongside the faith principle and see if they can be combined.

The logic behind a postmortem encounter with Christ is simple enough. It rests on the insight that God, since he loves humanity, would not send anyone to hell without first ascertaining what their response would have been to his grace. Since everyone eventually dies and comes face to face with the risen Lord, that would seem to be the obvious time to discover their answer to God's call.

Logic aside, does the idea of a postmortem encounter have scriptural support? It seems to have some in Peter's word about the Gospel being preached to the dead, where the text sounds as if the dead are given an opportunity to respond to Christ (1 Pe 3:19–20; 4:6).[45] Pannenberg draws this meaning from the so-called "descent into hell" phrase of the Apostles Creed, which is based on these texts. He writes, "Salvation from future judgment is still made available to those who during their lifetime encountered neither Jesus nor the Christian message."[46] Undoubtedly there is something most pleasing about Jesus triumphing over Satan by taking away from him those he thought most surely his own and the saddest of all creatures. Could the meaning of the descent into hell be that the people who never encountered the Gospel in their lifetimes can choose to receive it in the postmortem situation? Such a possibility would make good the universality of grace and God's willingness that all should know it.[47] It would make clear that the most wicked of sinners are not beyond the scope of God's mercy, and that God is patient even with them. But it would not mean universal salvation, because the choice to be made is genuinely open.

C. E. B. Cranfield concludes that "It is a hint within the canon of scripture, puzzling indeed and obscure, yet at the same time reassuredly restrained, that the mysterious interval between Good Friday afternoon and Easter morning was not empty of significance, but that in it too Jesus Christ was active as the Savior of the world . . . it is a hint too that those who in subsequent ages have died without ever having had a real chance to believe in Christ are not outside the scope of his mercy and will not perish eternally without being given in some way that is beyond our knowledge an opportunity to hear the gospel and accept him as their Savior."[48]

Although the scriptural evidence for postmortem encounter is not abundant, its scantiness is relativized by the strength of the theological argument for it. A postmortem encounter with Jesus actually makes very good sense. Who can deny that all stand before God and give an account to him after death (Ro 14:7-12)? Will not all humanity experience such a postmortem encounter with the risen

Jesus who is Lord both of the dead and the living? Not only is a postmortem encounter possible, it would seem that it is inescapable.

But, one may object, it does not follow that this encounter will be a pleasant experience. Why should we think that there will be grace for the unevangelized? The reason to think so lies in the simple fact that God does not cease to be gracious to sinners just because they are no longer living. The God that sinners meet after death remains the same One who sent his Son to die for the sins of the world. Jesus, who was the friend of sinners, has not suddenly become their enemy after death. God has not abruptly ceased to desire the salvation of sinners, or that they come to a knowledge of the truth. Surely, the God who loves the world will always love it, even loving those who reject the gift of his love. If God is the gracious God of the Gospel, we know that wherever God is, there grace is. Therefore, when humanity stands before God, they stand before a God of mercy and love.

Now theology has strongly held that death is a cutoff point as far grace is concerned, based on the text of Hebrews 9:27: "Just as man is destined to die once, and after that to face judgment. . . ." It has been assumed that only decisions made in this earthly life count with God, not decisions made after death. If there were a postmortem encounter, it would render the decisions of this life of little or no effect. Perhaps it is time to reopen this issue and consider some fresh ideas.

Consider this. All humanity will stand before the only God there is, the God and Father of Our Lord Jesus Christ. That means that they stand in the presence of God's grace and can ask for God's mercy. The issue is not whether all will stand there (of course they will), or whether God is loving (of course he is), or whether they can ask for mercy (why not?). The question is whether sinners would respond to God on that occasion any differently than they have already responded in life on earth. There is no reason to think they would. Someone like Job, who loved God already in life on earth, would receive the Good News about Jesus gladly, because that is what he was longing for. Someone like Herod, on the other hand, who sought to kill the baby Jesus on earth, would only hate God all the more on the last day because he would see more grace in God to hate. The *opportunity* would be there for all to repent after death, but not necessarily the *desire*. At the judgment, believers from every age will love God more, while the wicked will love him less. The notion that there is a "danger" that the wicked will change their minds after death, receive Christ, and escape punishment for their earthly actions is a total misunderstanding.

To correct this misunderstanding, it is important to realize that heaven is not a bribe or extrinsic reward. It is not like receiving a million dollars for being good, or for returning the right answer to God's appeal. No, heaven is an intrinsic kind of reward—the way that marriage is the intrinsic reward of love and its very goal. It is not self-seeking to want to marry the one you love. Marriage would not even be desirable if one hated the other person. Such a union would be like hell. A prize is intrinsic when it offers consequences homogeneous with the actions being rewarded; it is extrinsic when it differs in kind from them. In essence, to desire heaven, which is life in the presence of absolute goodness, implies a love of goodness. Otherwise heaven would be hell.

Scripture does not require us to hold that the window of opportunity is slammed shut at death. The fate of some may be sealed at death; those, for example, who heard the gospel and declined the offer of salvation. But the fate of others is not sealed; babies, for example, who die in infancy. No one holds that death is the end of opportunity for them. The question is, would those who were capable of deciding for God in their lifetimes qualify for special treatment?

The issue in relation to postmortem encounter is not so much one of qualification as it is disposition. Humanity will appear in its entirety before God and God has not changed from love to hate. Anyone wanting to love God who has not loved him before is certainly welcome to do so. It has not suddenly become forbidden. No, the variable is the condition of the human souls appearing in God's presence.

One group that will have a grace-filled postmortem encounter with Christ consists of those who sought God during their earthly lives and loved him, though they had not heard of Jesus. Premessianic believers, accepted by God already on the basis of their response to the light they had received, will meet their Savior in fullness and clarity after death. Then they will be able at last to confess Jesus and put their trust in his righteousness. Job, for example, will meet Jesus after death and receive salvation from his outstretched hand. Before dying, Job had responded to God; therefore, after death Job will seal his faith by responding to Jesus. He will hear the word and believe on Jesus as Lord and Savior.

The same would be true of those Jewish souls who believed before Christ came. They trusted in God on earth and died before knowing about Jesus. Their response to God on the basis of premessianic revelation will be confirmed in the presence of Jesus after death. An informationally premessianic faith response made in this life will be improved and fulfilled when the person enters into the presence of the triune God. Even those who have known Jesus on this side of death will have their knowledge of God improved on the other side, since their knowledge too is partial.

The exegetical evidence may not be plentiful, but the theological argument is strong that those who have been seeking God in this life will have their knowledge of God updated when they enter into his presence. They want to know God better, and God wants to know them better. A postmortem encounter applied to this class of human souls means the completing of a faith decision already made on the basis of premessianic revelation and does not in any way diminish in importance the choices made in this life. It would in fact confirm those choices, since these are the ones who decided to move toward God in this life. Now they will meet the God they love in the fullness of his grace after death. For them a postmortem opportunity is firmly established.

Does this form of postmortem encounter diminish the urgency to take the Gospel to the world? Would someone like Job, who had already said Yes to God, not be best left unevangelized until the opportunity to receive Christ after death comes? Any evangelization they might receive on earth would certainly be less compelling than that! This question would have greater force if we knew who the premessianic believers were, whereas in actual fact they are mixed in with populations that need to hear the Gospel. Even if we did know their identity, we would be obliged to tell them of the greater light and salvation that they long for. I will raise the question of motivation for world missions at the close of this chapter.

A MORE LIBERAL APPLICATION?

What I have presented thus far is hard to deny. For some people the postmortem encounter with Jesus will be a blessed event. But is it possible that sinners who refused God in this world may have a second chance to believe in him? Can they change their minds after death and receive salvation? Is it possible that Hitler, a most wicked sinner, would be given the opportunity to receive Jesus Christ after death? Might it even be that Hitler could accept Christ and go to heaven, while some of his victims who do not respond to Christ perish? What an irony this would be, to have Hitler torture people in life and God condemn them forever! If those who reject God in this life and act wickedly receive an opportunity to respond to Christ after death, would it not be true that they are getting off very easily indeed? Would such a scenario not devalue all earthly decisions and render them meaningless?

But why would anyone assume for a moment that Hitler would accept Jesus the Jew after death? Is it not clear that his attitude toward Jews was definitively established on earth? How could one imagine that Hitler would change his mind, forsake evil, and love goodness in the afterlife? The answer can only be that people must be thinking of heaven and hell as extrinsic rewards. But heaven is not an extrinsic reward, nor is it a bribe. It is everlasting life in the presence of absolute goodness, and in the presence of loving community. There is no way that Hitler is going to choose that. No one who had not begun to love such things on earth would choose them for eternity. There is no danger that Hitler will change his mind. God may want him to, Christians may even want him to, but a man like Hitler is not going to want to. Heaven would be the worst place he could imagine being.

Some Protestants are attracted to the postmortem encounter because they are reluctant to place so much weight on decisions made in this life on the basis of general revelation alone. They are reluctant to credit general revelation as adequate for the task given. Stressing the inadequacy of general revelation to mediate a saving knowledge of God, they contend that only an encounter with Jesus Christ would be enough to free sinners from their bondage.[49] How can pagans be said to have had a real opportunity to decide about God only on the basis of general revelation? General revelation lacks fullness and the stimulus for responding to God, something special revelation has, and may not be enough to call forth a decision. A person who would not respond to such weak revelation in this life might respond to stronger revelation in the postmortem encounter. Therefore, they assume an opportunity for the unevangelized after death.[50]

Those who are drawn to the concept of a postmortem encounter are right to think that no one who really wants it will be deprived of salvation. Aquinas grasped an important point when he said that someone facing God's judgment on the last day, were he or she to repent of sin and want to be reconciled, God would pardon that person too.[51] Russell Aldwinkle says that "We are not in a position to say how Socrates will respond when he is face to face with Christ at the end of history."[52] In the postmortem encounter, the problem does not lie with the divine mercy. That is immeasurable. It lies with the decisions people have freely made in this life, and whose eternal destiny depends on those choices. The person who has made firm decisions against God throughout life is not going to be inclined to choose him afterwards. If one has resisted him for a lifetime, one would want to receive him even less when God's nature is revealed more clearly and decisively. Jesus said that only the pure in heart will see God, because only the pure in heart will want to see him. Those who love darkness do not even then come to the light (Jn 3:20).

What about those we call evangelized, those who have been exposed to the message of Jesus only in inadequate ways and have not really heard it? Perhaps they know the name of Jesus but associate it with Zionism (if they are Muslims) or with Auschwitz (if they are Jews), and consequently reject it most vehemently. One can hardly say that they know the Good News and have rejected it. More likely, they are in a position similar to men and women before Jesus came. They are unable to see Jesus as the credible fulfillment of the revelation they have known. There may be many with true faith who do not yet see in Jesus the God whom they seek, owing to some failure in communicating the message properly to them. As a result, they fail to make the connection between the God they know and the Jesus they do not yet know. Can we really know who has truly heard the Gospel? Has the Masai tribesman heard the Gospel just because he was given a tract? And even when the Gospel is well presented, what is said and what is heard may be quite different.

Only God knows the heart and its direction. But we know that God has no pleasure in the death of the wicked, and he is not willing that any should perish. We know he will not cast away those who have had no opportunity to know how good he is. God's enemies will suffer condemnation, but innocent bystanders will not. His judgment falls on those who knowingly and willfully are God's enemies and want to remain so; on "those who do not know God and do not obey the gospel of our Lord Jesus" (2 Th 1:8). Those who will suffer everlasting destruction will not be the unevangelized but those who neither obey the Gospel nor any other form of revelation they have been given. In the last judgment, God's enemies and not the inculpably ignorant are rejected.

It may even be that there is a greater danger for nominal Christians to be condemned rather than those who have not heard of Jesus. Jesus said, "to whom much is given, much will be required" and "the first shall be last." On that basis, Amos wondered why his fellow Israelites were so looking forward to the day of the Lord, when it would almost certainly mean darkness and not light for them (Am 4:12; 5:18–24). And Peter said judgment would begin at the house of the Lord (1 Pe 4:17). Perhaps we should not worry so much about the fate of the heathen before worrying about our own.

RELATED ISSUES

Can an Arminian be sure that a large number will be saved if salvation depends so much on free choice? An optimist of salvation, like Warfield or Shedd, could know this because God can make it happen. But how can one know that the outcome will be large if salvation depends mostly on human decision? What if many people decline God's offer, leaving only a few saved? The standard answer is that God foreknows the large result, and he is able to announce it ahead of time. But what if God does not know free decisions ahead of time? How could one then know that the outcome will be large? It must be because God knows us well, and he knows that what he has done to save us will produce a large result. The delay of the parousia would suggest that God is patiently waiting for more to repent (2 Pe 3:9).

Christians who are serious about holiness might ask, if the outcome of salvation is to be large, does that imply cheap grace? Why should anyone pursue holiness seriously when multitudes gain salvation with such little effort? If (as it seems) a broad way leads to life and not death, then why climb the narrow, more difficult road to heaven? This observation reminds one of the attitude of the prodigal son's elder brother. He had worked hard for years at the father's home and was never given a feast, while his good-for-nothing brother received a feast just for turning up after engaging in a disgusting life (Lk 15:29–32). The elder brother did not value God's mercy. Who are we to judge our brother when we will all have to stand before the judgment seat of God (Ro 14:10)? The thief on the cross had his heart set in the right direction, even though he had no opportunity to pursue it. He was on the road to holiness without having yet been able to take a single step. If eternal life is dynamic, that man will have the opportunity to do so in the New Jerusalem. To pursue holiness is to want to be Christlike. It is to be salt and light in the world as witness to the kingdom and the first fruits of a new humanity. God did not save us because we had cleaned up our lives; he saved us by grace unto holiness.

MOTIVATIONS FOR CHRISTIAN MISSIONS

Access to salvation and the urgency of world missions are in tension. If people have access to salvation wherever they live in time and space, why is it urgent to take the Gospel to them? Where is the motivation for missions if there is universal access to salvation? Many think that the main motivation for missions is the certainty that the unevangelized are doomed unless they believe in Jesus. Is this motivation undercut if universal accessibility is true?

What is the major motivation for missions? Many assume that the major incentive is the hopelessness of non-Christians in the face of eternity. They say that the horror of the prospect of falling under eschatological wrath constitutes the main motive for missions. Anyone questioning this assumption may be accused of jeopardizing world missions, which are thought to be based largely on this motive.[53]

This is not an idle objection. If everyone has access to God, they do not have the absolute need of having the Gospel preached to them. Their need to hear the Gospel would be non-absolute—a need for a clearer message, more stimulating, or perhaps more explicit than anything they had heard before. But is that enough of a reason to preach the Gospel to all nations?

Some who press this motivational objection have no right to do so. Augustinians, for example, have serious problems with motivation themselves. What motive is there for missions if one believes that it has been decided from eternity who will and who will not be saved? Under such a determinist scheme, it is hard to find much motivation for any human action, missionary or otherwise. Is this part of the reason that the Reformers did not support missions to the heathen, whereas Erasmus did?[54] There are also grounds for doubting whether the objectors themselves believe the motivation quite as they state it. Let them ask themselves: if it is absolutely necessary to call on the name of Jesus to be saved, then how was Job saved, how was Abraham saved, how are the babies dying in infancy saved? If any of these are saved (and the objectors grant that they all are), then according to their view it is not absolutely necessary to hear the Gospel and believe on Jesus for salvation. Their objection is at best a muddled one.

But the question of the motivation for missions is an important question. The Christian missionary enterprise is central to what the present age is about, and it must be addressed (Mt 24:14). My suspicion is that we have narrowed the motivation for missions down to this one thing: deliverance from wrath. We have made it the major reason for missions when it is not. I object to the notion that missions is individually oriented, hellfire insurance. Sinners are not in the hands of an angry God. Our mission is not to urge them to turn to Jesus because God hates them and delights in sending them to hell. Jesus did not come to condemn but to save the world (Jn 3:17). No, our mission is to announce the wonderful news of the kingdom of God (Mk 1:14–15). It is not based on the assumption that now there is grace where there was no grace before. Rather, it is news of an event that had not happened before, the news of God reconciling the world to himself in Jesus Christ and the beginning of the age of salvation.

Coming at missions from the perspective of the kingdom explains why everybody without exception needs to hear the Good News, both those who have responded to light and those who have not responded. It does not require any denial of the fact that God is at work in the wider world to feel the obligation to tell the story and issue the invitation. God wants everybody to be part of the kingdom movement. That implies a mission which calls for a multiplicity of activities designed to initiate people into the kingdom—activities like proclamation, church planting, social involvement, Christian presence, and being a catalyst in history.[55] It is a travesty to maintain that the primary motive of missions is to rescue souls from hell. The purpose of the Christian missions is much broader, and its motivation more far reaching. The purpose of the Christian missions involves proclamation and church planting, but it also transcends them. Missions are part of God's strategy for transforming the world and changing history. One goal of missions is quantitative, to baptize and form congregations. The other goal is qualitative, to change life's atmosphere, to infect people with hope, love, and responsibility for the world.[56]

The Gospel proclamation is not an announcement of terror, but news of God's boundless generosity. We are not saying to the world: "Come to Christ, if you want to escape a wrathful judge," as if the idea of missions were to save people from God as though God hated them. On the contrary, he loves sinners and the church proclaims his wonderful deeds to save in the power of the Spirit (Ac 2:11; 1 Pe 2:8–10). We should tell people how good God is, not how frightening he is. The fear of hell is *not* the primary motivation for missions. The deepest motive of all is to see the kingdom come and God's rule established. Like the early Christians, we go in obedience to the Lord's command, with a concern for the glory of God, and in the power of the Holy Spirit.

Since there are some who have responded positively to the light they have received, the motivation for preaching the Good News to them is that they might learn more about the source of that light, have a fuller experience of salvation in the dimension of Pentecost, and be caught up in the kingdom surge. Such people are waiting for this message to arrive. God has already spoken to them, and they are eager to hear and receive this Good News. What a pleasure it will be to meet them, to learn their names, to hear how God has dealt with them, and to share how good God has been to us.

A believer like Job or Melchizedek in the non-Christian world does not need deliverance from eschatological wrath but rather access to the fuller expression of God's grace and power, which is in Jesus. As Peter said, there is messianic salvation in no one else. These people will need to be told about the kingdom and be issued their invitations to the messianic banquet. Those like Cornelius, who have responded to God in pagan contexts will need to turn to Christ to receive what Jesus alone can give them: the Holy Spirit, a portion in the kingdom of God, and the experience of messianic salvation. The fact that persons can give themselves to God on the basis of premessianic revelation does not excuse us from communicating the Gospel to them. Unevangelized believers need a clearer revelation of God's love and forgiveness, and the assurance that goes with love and forgiveness. The fact that people can respond to cosmic revelation does not mean that the word about Jesus need not be proclaimed to them. They need to hear it by way of fulfillment and assurance.

Vatican II put it well: "Though God in ways known to himself can lead those inculpably ignorant of the gospel to that faith without which it is impossible to please him, yet a necessity lies upon the church and at the same time a sacred duty to preach the gospel. Hence missionary activity today as always retains its power and necessity." Later these words are added: "Whatever truth and grace are found among the nations, as a sort of secret presence of God, this missionary activity frees from all taint of evil and restores to Christ its maker, who overthrows the devil's domain and wards off the manifold malice of vice. So whatever good is found to be sown in the hearts and minds of men, or in the rites and cultures peculiar to various peoples, is not lost. More than that, it is healed, ennobled, and perfected for the glory of God, the shame of the demon, and the bliss of men." (*Decree on the Missionary Activity of the Church*, chap. 1)

Premessianic believers, along with many others, need to be challenged to seek God because they have not yet done so. For them the Gospel comes as a stimulus to wake from sleep. God's word has gone out in all the world in general revelation—but it is not of the same high wattage as the light which shines from the face of Jesus Christ. No one at all, whatever his or her spiritual condition, should be denied access to that light.

Is eschatological wrath a factor at all in the motivation for missions? Clearly it is a factor not to be excluded, though it should not dominate the picture. Sin has brought humankind into a situation of guilt and ruin. God's wrath is revealed from heaven against all human ungodliness and unrighteousness, and the day of his wrath is coming (Ro 1:18; 2:5). God gave his Son so that no one would perish. He is unwilling that anyone should (Jn 3:16; 2 Pe 3:9). Christ delivers from the wrath to come (1 Th 1:10).

God's wrath definitely exists, and it is a factor. But how are we to understand it? Luther captured something very important when he said that wrath is the experience of God's love in the state of disobedience. When we are running from God, his presence creates fear in us. Wrath is the frustrated anger of a disappointed lover, not of an unappeased deity or angry judge. Jesus says that God wants his house to be filled with penitent sinners, but that those who refuse the invitation will be excluded (Lk 14:23–24). This is the wrath of the Lamb, kindled against those who choose idols above God. God's love is not sentimental but is roused in opposition to sin and wickedness. Even then, wrath is not purely negative. It strives to conquer what stands in opposition to it. God's wrath is the wrath of love. Although God may sentence a sinner to condemnation, it is the sinner who freely chooses hell. Hell is not the prison from which people are longing to be freed, but a sit-in where sinners have barricaded themselves in to keep God out.[57]

Conclusion

The purpose of this study has been to face boldly the contemporary challenge of religious pluralism in a world that has become smaller, and where relativism looms. The argument pursued has been evangelical in a double sense: first, in its defense of the finality of Jesus Christ and the global mission of the church; and second, in its adherence to the central doctrines of classical theology. My purpose was to stimulate thinking in the Christian community, and particularly to challenge the influence of the restrictivist standpoint among fellow evangelicals. Some of our scholars have remained silent on these issues for fear of criticism. I hope to draw out greater support for the broader outlook from a significant number of these leaders. Perhaps the general direction I have indicated in the book will be the one that our movement can take seriously in the coming years.

Like my writings in general, this book is both conservative and contemporary. It is conservative compared with theological pluralism, but contemporary compared with restrictivism. It resembles the generous spirit of Vatican II, without taking certain steps that have characterized Roman Catholic theology since the Council. My position recognizes God at work among all nations and religions, but it does not fall prey to rosy-eyed optimism about other religions as if they are ways to salvation.

As regards pluralist theology, my book meets the challenge of many religions with a biblically grounded and theologically sound argument. It does not sacrifice any important Christian convictions, and yet it gives some fresh answers and angles of vision. I reject the suggestion that fundamental doctrines like the Trinity or Christology must be surrendered in order to recognize God at work among the people of other faiths. Classical theology is perfectly capable of celebrating this fact and doing so without mutilating itself. On the other hand, I do agree with the pluralists about the necessity of facing up to divergent religious claims and engaging in truth-seeking encounters with people of other faiths.

As regards the debate among evangelicals, the distinctive character of this argument is that it exalts the finality of Jesus Christ as the only Savior of sinners, without falling into an all-too-common pessimism of salvation, or darkly negative thinking about other people's spiritual journeys. If the approach is novel, that is partly because there is so little else in print from evangelicals, and also partly because of its overall conception. Finding an answer to this problem of religious pluralism is rather like working at a crossword puzzle: how to assemble all the pieces in the right configuration? Few pieces I have used are of my own invention. Though admittedly I have drawn upon certain aspects of the Christian tradition that are contested among evangelicals today (and therefore may sound novel to them without being so), rarely have I put forward a really new idea of my own—and then only on the margins of the thesis. All of the pieces I have used for the puzzle have already been defended by respected theologians of the past, as I hope to have shown.

For example, I am hardly alone in criticizing Augustinian thinking when it denies the largeness of salvation, transforms the nature of election, and virtually denies the freedom of the will. Nor am I the first to propose a *logos* Christology or to uphold the value of the Eastern position on the *filioque* controversy. Nor can I apologize for retrieving the neglected "pagan saints" category from the Scriptures just because others choose to ignore it, or for holding to the positive usefulness of general revelation when it seems obvious, or for thinking salvation is possible on the basis of a response to general revelation, or for pondering the meaning of the postmortem encounter with God that all humanity will experience. None of these specific points is novel in the history of church theology.

What may feel novel about the book as an evangelical work is the way I have brought such thoughts together in a total conception. Only J. N. D. Anderson (to my knowledge) has sought to build a similar house using many of the same materials. I applaud him for that. Of course critics will point out that this approach represents only a minority position among evangelicals today, and they will question such a bold departure from restrictivist Protestant traditions. I will respect their opinions. My position does prefer Justin to

Augustine, Erasmus to Luther, Wesley to Calvin, and Anderson to Lindsell on all these questions. Therefore, let my critics speak. Let a dialogue begin. Let those who have remained silent speak up. The evangelical movement is mature enough theologically to take up its responsibility in this area.

In closing, let me say first, how impressed I have again become with the inexhaustibility of the Scriptures in helping us search out answers to the hard questions before us. Though the challenge of religious pluralism is in some ways a new challenge for us, the Bible always proves to have more light to give than church theologians have as yet received. Second, I was inspired by the way this cluster of issues energizes a whole range of theological topics and makes practically everything come alive with fresh relevance and power. What we had mistakenly thought were boring or trivial subjects (like the *filioque* controversy) turn out to be vital and alive. Third, the exercise shows us that much of the work of theology is carting off rubbish to the dump. There are many unnecessary misunderstandings that get in the way of making progress in our thinking and that create needless polarizations. How did we fall into the pernicious fewness doctrine, or suppose that a high Christology entails narrowness, or accept many unsound generalizations about religion, or overlook the distinction between objective and subjective religion, or accept such harsh end-time scenarios? Thank God that our faith is in the living One and not in theological systems.

I have merely sketched in a few ideas with the hope that they will help us move forward in our thinking about some of these matters. It is only a beginning, of course, and there is much yet to do. If I have fallen into errors, may the Lord have mercy, forgive, and shed light on my path. And may God help all of us grasp what Frederick W. Faber (1814–1863) wrote:

> There's a wideness in God's mercy
> Like the wideness of the sea;
> There's a kindness in his justice
> Which is more than liberty.
> There is no place where earth's sorrows
> Are more felt than up in heaven;

There is no place where earth's failings
    Have such kindly judgment given.

There is grace enough for thousands
    Of new worlds as great as this;
There is room for fresh creations
    In that upper home of bliss.
For the love of God is broader
    Than the measure of man's mind;
And the heart of the Eternal
    Is most wonderfully kind.

But we make his love too narrow
    By false limits of our own;
And we magnify his strictness
    With a zeal he will not own.
If our love were but more simple,
    We should take him at his word;
And our lives would be all sunshine
    In the sweetness of our Lord.

Notes

INTRODUCTION

[1]Previously I have faced this issue only in articles: "The Finality of Jesus Christ in a World of Religions" in *Christian Faith and Practice in the Modern World*, edited by Mark A. Noll and David F. Wells (Grand Rapids, Mich.: Eerdmans, 1988), 152–68 and "Toward an Evangelical Theology of Religions," *Journal of the Evangelical Theological Society*, 33 (1990), 359–68.

[2]The literature on religious pluralism is large and includes: Paul F. Knitter, *No Other Name? A Critical Survey of Christian Attitudes Toward World Religions* (Maryknoll, N.Y.: Orbis, 1985); Alan Race, *Christians and Religious Pluralism* (Maryknoll, N.Y.: Orbis, 1982); Gavin D'Costa, *Theology and Religious Pluralism* (Oxford: Blackwell, 1986); G. Richards, *Towards a Theology of Religions* (London: Routledge, 1989); Kenneth Cracknell, *Towards a New Relationship* (London: Epworth, 1986); Arnulf Camps, *Partners in Dialogue: Christianity and Other World Religions* (Maryknoll, N.Y.: Orbis, 1983); Walburt Buhlmann, *God's Chosen Peoples* (Maryknoll, N.Y.: Orbis, 1982).

[3]See Harold Coward, *Pluralism: Challenge to World Religions* (Maryknoll, N.Y.: Orbis, 1985).

[4]Jurgen Moltmann, *The Church in the Power of the Holy Spirit* (London: SCM, 1977), 150–53.

[5]Hans Küng, *On Being A Christian* (London: Collins, 1974), 89.

[6]Hans Küng, *Theology for the Third Millennium: An Ecumenical View* (New York: Doubleday, 1988), 227.

[7]Allan Bloom issued a stirring challenge to relativism in his *The Closing of the American Mind* (New York: Simon and Schuster, 1987).

[8]Reginald W. Bibby discusses this policy in *Mosaic Madness: The Poverty and Potential of Life in Canada* (Toronto: Stoddart, 1990).

[9]Lesslie Newbigin is astute on this as most things: "The Christian Faith and the World Religions," in *Keeping the Faith*, C. Wainwright, editor (Philadelphia: Fortress, 1988), 310–40.

[10]See for example John Hick and Paul F. Knitter, editors, *The Myth of Christian Uniqueness: Toward a Pluralistic Theology of Religions* (Maryknoll, N.Y.: Orbis, 1987).

[11]Don Cupitt, *Radicals and the Future of the Church* (London: SCM, 1989), ch 6.

[12]Paul Knitter discusses the conservative evangelical model in *No Other Name?*, ch 5. J. N. D. Anderson deserves praise in my opinion for consistently challenging evangelical narrow-mindedness over the years. For example, see his *Christianity and World Religions: The Challenge of Pluralism* (Downers Grove, Ill.: InterVarsity, 1984). The whole situation is reviewed by a soon-to-appear manuscript by John Sanders, *No Other Name! A Biblical, Historical, and Theological Investigation into the Destiny of the Unevangelized* (Grand Rapids: Eerdmans, 1992).

[13]Restrictiveness among evangelicals stems from Augustine mediated through Calvin and is very visible in such writers as: James A. Borland, "A Theologian Looks at the Gospel and World Religions," *Journal of the Evangelical Theological Society*, 33 (1990), 3–11; R. C. Sproul, *Reason to Believe* (Grand Rapids: Zondervan, 1982), 47–59; Dick Dowsett, *God, That's Not Fair!* (Singapore: OMF, 1982); Ajith Fernando, *The Christian's Attitude Toward World Religions* (Wheaton, Ill.: Tyndale, 1987).

[14]Vinay Samuel and Chris Sugden call for such a development in "Dialogue with Other Religions—An Evangelical View" in a book they edited entitled *Sharing Jesus in the Two Thirds World* (Grand Rapids: Eerdmans, 1983). Although Colin Chapman gave a challenge at Lausanne II in Manila in the direction of dialogue and greater openness to other faiths, the Manila Manifesto (1989) did not echo it. Chapman's address was printed in *Christianity Today*, May 14, 1990. See also Richard Quebedeaux, "Interreligious Dialogue: Next Step for Conservative Protestant Intellectuals," in Peter Phan, editor, *Christianity and the Wider Ecumenism* (New York: Paragon, 1990), ch 17, and Molly Marshall-Green, "Bernard Ramm and the Challenge of Religious Pluralism," *Perspectives on Theology in the Contemporary World*, Stanley J. Grenz, editor (Macon, Ga.: Mercer Univ. Press, 1990), 79–85.

CHAPTER 1

[1]William G.T. Shedd, *Dogmatic Theology* (Grand Rapids: Zondervan [1899], 1969), II, 712.

[2]John Hick, for example, makes it clear that the root factor which propelled him into pluralist theology was the fewness doctrine he thought orthodoxy required. The idea that the majority of the race might be lost was the first argument he employed in opposition to the Ptolemaic paradigm. See

God and the Universe of Faiths (London: Macmillan, 1973), 122, and Gavin D'Costa, *John Hick's Theology of Religions* (New York: Univ. Press of America, 1987), 41–45, 73–92.

[3]These are the two theses which Rahner promulgates in his own influential and in many ways helpful theology of religions. See the classic essay, "Christianity and the Non-Christian Religions," in *Theological Investigations* (London: Darton, Longman & Todd, 1966), 115–34.

[4]That this has long been a concern is visible in the title of an early book of mine, *Grace Unlimited* (Minneapolis: Bethany, 1975), followed by the sequel *The Grace of God, The Will of Man: A Case for Arminianism* (Grand Rapids: Zondervan, 1989).

[5]See Joachim Jeremias, *New Testament Theology* (New York: Charles Scribner's Sons, 1971), I, 108–21, and I. Howard Marshall, "Universal Grace and Atonement in the Pastoral Epistles," in Clark H. Pinnock, editor *The Grace of God, The Will of Man: A Case for Arminianism*, 51–69.

[6]This is also the burden of Richard H. Drummond's book: *Toward A New Age in Christian Theology* (Maryknoll, N.Y.: Orbis, 1985).

[7]Jewish theology appeals to the covenant with Noah as a way to maintain the election of Israel without leaving the Gentiles outside God's plans; Hans J. Schoeps, *Paul: The Theology of the Apostle in the Light of Jewish Religious History* (London: Lutterworth, 1961), 223.

[8]Karl Barth does not miss it. See *Church Dogmatics*, IV/1 (Edinburgh: T. & T. Clark, 1956), 22–34.

[9]Two recent commentators emphasise the theological importance of the early chapters of Genesis: Gerhard von Rad, *Genesis: A Commentary* (Philadelphia: Westminster, 1972) and Claus Westermann, *Genesis 1–11* (Minneapolis: Augsburg, 1984).

[10]H.H. Rowley established this meaning of election in the Old Testament as a call to service in *The Biblical Doctrine of Election* (London: Lutterworth, 1950). See also Lesslie Newbigin, *The Gospel in a Pluralist Society* (Geneva: WCC, 1989), especially "The Logic of Election" in chap. 7.

[11]Paul K. Jewett, *Election and Predestination* (Grand Rapids: Eerdmans, 1985), or R. C. Sproul, *Chosen By God* (Wheaton, Ill.: Tyndale, 1986).

[12]This is integral to Pannenberg's position in the three-volumed theology now being written; Stanley J. Grenz, *Reason for Hope: The Systematic Theology of Wolfhart Pannenberg* (New York: Oxford, 1990), 173–78.

[13]William W. Klein has established conclusively that the New Testament doctrine of election lines up with the Old Testament doctrine in *The New Chosen People: A Corporate View of Election* (Grand Rapids: Zondervan, 1990), a point made earlier by Robert Shank in *Elect in the Son: A Study of the Doctrine of Election* (Springfield, Mo.: Westcott, 1970).

[14]The other mistake of like magnitude in Western theology came when Anselm cast soteriology in a tightly legal framework forsaking the dramatic "Christus Victor" model of the early church; see Gustaf Aulen, *Christus Victor* (London: SPCK, 1953).

[15]Karl Barth, *Church Dogmatics*, II/2 (Edinburgh: T. & T. Clark, 1957), "The Election of God" chap. 7 and Shirley C. Guthrie, *Christian Doctrine: Teachings of the Christian Church* (Atlanta: John Knox, 1968), chap. 7.

[16]Walburt Buhlmann, *God's Chosen Peoples* (Maryknoll, N.Y.: Orbis, 1982), 124–26.

[17]For a delightful and informative book on these people, see Jean Danielou, *Holy Pagans of the Old Testament* (London: Longmans, Green and Co., 1957).

[18]Kenneth Cracknell has an acute sensitivity to God's work in the wider world: *Towards a New Relationship*, chap. 2–3.

[19]George E. Ladd, *Jesus and the Kingdom* (New York: Harper & Row, 1964); Joachim Jeremias, *New Testament Theology*, 96–121; and, George Beasley-Murray, *Jesus and the Kingdom of God* (Grand Rapids: Eerdmans, 1986).

[20]Joachim Jeremias, *Jesus' Promise to the Nations* (London: SCM, 1958), is an outstanding book developing this theme.

[21]No one better captures Jesus' commitment to God and humanity than Hans Küng in *On Being a Christian* (London: Collins, 1974), 214–77.

[22]On the openness of Luke, see Alan Race, *Christians and Religious Pluralism* (Maryknoll, N. Y.: Orbis, 1982), 38–42.

[23]Richard Lovelace, *Dynamics of Spiritual Life* (Downers Grove, Ill.: InterVarsity, 1979). See comments on "theological integration," 172–84.

[24]G. Aulen, *Christus Victor*, chap. 2, and Henry Bettenson, editor *The Early Christian Fathers* (London: Cambridge Univ. Press, 1956), on Irenaeus in particular.

[25]G.B. Caird, *A Commentary on the Revelation of St. John the Divine* (London: Adam and Charles Black, 1966), 280.

[26]John R. W. Stott and David L. Edwards, *Essentials: A Liberal-Evangelical Dialogue* (London: Hodder & Stoughton, 1988), 327.

[27]Schubert M. Ogden, *The Reality of God* (New York: Harper & Row, 1966), 1–70.

[28]Those whom Rahner calls "anonymous Christians" are precisely the same people, although he has suffered criticism for calling them that: "Anonymous Christians," *Theological Investigations*, VI (London: Darton, Longman & Todd, 1969), 390–98.

[29]For more citations of this kind see, for example, Eugene Hillman, *Many Paths: A Catholic Approach to Religious Pluralism* (Maryknoll, N.Y.: Orbis, 1989), chap. 2.

[30]George Lindbeck, *The Nature of Doctrine: Religion and Theology in a Postliberal Age* (Philadelphia: Westminster, 1984), 58.

[31]Thomas C. Oden and Robert E. Webber are two prominent evangelicals today who recommend going back to the earliest systematic theologians rather than beginning with the Latin theology of the Western church. See, for example, Oden's *After Modernity. . .What?: Agenda for Theology* (Grand Rapids: Zondervan, 1990), and Webber's *Common Roots: A Call to Evangelical Maturity* (Grand Rapids: Zondervan, 1978).

[32]For an introduction to the formula and its meaning, see Hans Küng, *The Church* (New York: Sheed and Ward, 1967), 313–19. A book is expected from Molly Marshall-Green on the use of Cyprian's slogan throughout the history of the church (Macon, Ga.: Mercer Univ. Press, 1991).

[33]Richard H. Drummond explores how theology dropped into these dark paths of reflection in *Toward a New Age in Christian Theology*, chap. 3–4.

[34]Karl Rahner, *Theological Investigations*, 20 (New York: Crossroad, 1981), 99f.

[35]James I. Packer, "Are Non-Christian Faiths Ways of Salvation?," *Bibliotheca Sacra*, 130 (1973), 113.

[36]This letter is translated in *Nicene and Post-Nicene Fathers*, ed. Philip Schaff (Grand Rapids: Eerdmans, 1956), I, 515–20.

[37]B. B. Warfield wrote a major analysis of Augustine's anti-Pelagian writings in the *Nicene and Post-Nicene Fathers*, 5, xiii–lxxi.

[38]Kenneth Cracknell documents this dismal story in *Towards a New Relationship*, chap. 1.

[39]Drummond tells the story more fully how theology has gradually freed itself of pessimism in *Toward a New Age in Christian Theology*, "The Long Way Out and Up" (chap. 5). James D. Hunter documents the same move to greater leniency among the evangelicals: *Evangelicalism: The Coming Generation* (Chicago: Univ. of Chicago Press, 1987), chap. 2.

[40]George H. Williams, "Erasmus and the Reformers on Non-Christian Religions and *Salus Extra Ecclesia*," in Theodore K. Rabb and Jerrold E. Seigel, editors, *Action and Conviction in Early Modern Europe* (Princeton, N.J.: Princeton Univ. Press, 1969), 319–70.

[41]See B. B. Warfield, *The Plan of Salvation* (Grand Rapids: Eerdmans, 1955), 97–104. Also, Lorraine Boettner, *The Reformed Doctrine of Predestination* (Philadelphia: Presbyterian and Reformed, 1965), 130–48.

[42]Gavin D'Costa, *John Hick's Theology of Religions*, 103.

CHAPTER 2

[1]Lesslie Newbigin always emphasizes this theme. See *The Finality of Christ* (Richmond, Va.: John Knox, 1969).

[2]See the discussion by James A. Beverley, *The World Council of Churches' Programme of Dialogue With People of Living Faiths and Ideologies: A Critical Analysis* (Th. M., Toronto School of Theology, 1983, unpublished).

[3]Lucien Richard, *What Are They Saying about Christ and World Religions?* (New York: Paulist, 1981), Introduction.

[4]This is transparently the conviction that drives Paul F. Knitter's research: *No Other Name? A Critical Survey of Christian Attitudes Toward World Religions* (Maryknoll, N. Y.: Orbis, 1985). All the Christian pluralists are driven by it.

[5]Brian Hebblethwaite, *The Incarnation: Collected Essays in Christology* (New York: Cambridge Univ. Press, 1987), chap. 1.

[6]See Daniel I. Block, *The Gods of the Nations: Studies in Ancient Near Eastern National Theology* (Jackson, Miss.: Evangelical Theological Society, 1988).

[7]Walter Eichrodt, *Theology of the Old Testament*, I (London: SCM, 1961), "The Nature of the Covenant God," chap. 5–7.

[8]On God's incomparability, see Adrio Konig, *Here Am I!* (London: Marshall, Morgan and Scott, 1982), chap. 1.

[9]Hendrikus Berkhof, *Christian Faith* (Grand Rapids: Eerdmans, 1979), 19–20.

[10]Walter Kaiser, *Toward an Old Testament Theology* (Grand Rapids: Zondervan, 1978), 244–49.

[11]George R. Beasley-Murray, *Jesus and the Kingdom of God* (Grand Rapids: Eerdmans, 1986), chaps. 4 and 13; Richard N. Longenecker, *The Christology of Early Jewish Christianity* (London: SCM, 1970), 82–93; Richard T. France, *Jesus and the Old Testament* (London: Tyndale, 1971), 144–48.

[12]Larry W. Hurtado sets about to answer the question posed in this form. *One God, One Lord: Early Christian Devotion and Ancient Jewish Monotheism* (Philadelphia: Fortress, 1988).

[13]The apologetic of C. S. Lewis is too crude, though not lacking all force. Jesus did force people to make a decision about himself, if not quite in the way Lewis suggests in *Mere Christianity* (London: Collins, 1952), 52ff.

[14]David F. Wells sees this point in his *The Person of Christ* (Westchester, Ill.: Crossway, 1984), chap. 1–3.

[15]Walter Kasper, *Jesus the Christ* (London: Burns & Oates, 1976), 65–112.

[16]Paul F. Knitter, *No Other Name?*, 174.

[17]Donald A. Hagner, *The Jewish Reclamation of Jesus, An Analysis and Critique of Modern Jewish Study of Jesus* (Grand Rapids: Zondervan, 1984), 257–71, 281–84.

[18]Schlier's article on *amen* in *Theological Dictionary of the New Testament*, edited by Gerhard Kittel (Grand Rapids: Eerdmans, 1964), I, 338.

[19]I. Howard Marshall, *The Origins of New Testament Christology* (Downers Grove, Ill.: InterVarsity, 1976), chap. 7, and James D. G. Dunn, *The Evidence for Jesus* (Philadelphia: Westminster, 1985), chap. 2.

[20]James D. G. Dunn, *The Evidence for Jesus*, 49. Also Martin Hengel, *The Son of God: The Origin of Christology and the History of Jewish-Hellenistic Religion* (Philadelphia: Fortress, 1976).

[21]See Hans Küng, *Christianity and the World Religions: Paths to Dialogue With Islam, Hinduism, and Buddhism* (New York: Doubleday, 1986), 109–32.

[22]Jurgen Moltmann mentions something of this problem in his book *The Way of Jesus* (London: SCM, 1990), 51f, 69f.

[23]Gary R. Habermas and Antony G. N. Flew, *Did Jesus Rise from the Dead?: The Resurrection Debate* (San Francisco: Harper & Row, 1987), 3.

[24]C. F. D. Moule stresses the fact that Christology was present in essence from the beginning; see *Origin of Christology* (New York: Cambridge Univ. Press, 1977).

[25]James D. G. Dunn, *Unity and Diversity in the New Testament* (London: SCM, 1977), 56–59, 227–31, 369f.

[26]James D. G. Dunn, *Christology in the Making: A New Testament Inquiry into the Origins of the Doctrine of the Incarnation* (Philadelphia: Westminster, 1980), chap. 7–8.

[27]George A. Lindbeck, *The Nature of Doctrine: Religion and Theology in a Postliberal Age* (Philadelphia: Westminster, 1984), 63–69.

[28]See Alan Race, *Christians and Religious Pluralism* (Maryknoll, N. Y.: Orbis, 1982), 127–37.

[29]J. A. T. Robinson, *The Human Face of God* (Philadelphia: Westminster, 1973), 209–20.

[30]Edward Schillebeeckx, *Jesus: An Experiment in Christology* (London: Collins, 1979), 658, 669.

[31]Paul F. Knitter, *No Other Name?*, 182.

[32]Ibid.

[33]Ibid., 197–200.

[34]A better guide to what the New Testament writers intended to teach can be found in Murray J. Harris, *From Grave to Glory: Resurrection in the New Testament* (Grand Rapids: Zondervan, 1990).

[35]Knitter returns to this point several times. *No Other Name?*, 31, 36, 143, 200–04.

[36]See, for example, John Hick, "An Inspiration Christology for a Religiously Plural World," in Stephen Davis, ed., *Encountering Jesus: A Debate on Christology* (Atlanta: John Knox, 1988), 5–22. Earlier Hick staked out his position on Christology in *The Myth of God Incarnate* as editor (London: SCM, 1977). A good deal of secondary literature has built up around Hick's work. A book-length study is Gavin D'Costa, *John Hick's Theology of Religions: A Critical Evaluation.*

[37]Martin Hengel, *The Son of God: The Origin of Christology and the History of Jewish-Hellenistic Religion* (Philadelphia: Fortress, 1976).

[38]Besides Brian Hebblethwaite already cited, David Brown, *The Divine Trinity* (Lasalle, Ill.: Open Court, 1985), and Thomas V. Morris, *The Logic of the Incarnation* (Ithaca, N.Y.: Cornell Univ. Press, 1985).

[39]Arnold Toynbee, for one, advocated the view that all religions are essentially the same: *A Historian's Approach to Religion* (New York: Oxford Univ. Press, 1956).

[40]Paul Tillich, *Christianity and the Encounter of the World Religions* (New York: Columbia Univ. Press, 1963), 28f.

[41]David Novak, *Jewish-Christian Dialogue: A Jewish Justification* (New York: Oxford Univ. Press, 1989), 18.

[42]Jay Newman, *Foundations of Religious Tolerance* (Toronto: Univ. of Toronto Press, 1982).

[43]John Hick, *An Interpretation of Religion: Human Responses to the Transcendent* (New Haven: Yale Univ. Press, 1989), 1–15.

[44]Peter Phan, "Are There Other Saviors for Other Peoples? A Discussion of the Problem of the Universal Significance and Uniqueness of Jesus the Christ," in Peter Phan, editor, *Christianity and the Wider Ecumenism*, chap. 12.

[45]David Lochhead, *The Dialogical Imperative: A Christian Reflection on Interfaith Encounter* (Maryknoll, N.Y.: Orbis, 1988), chap. 15.

[46]William J. Abraham, *The Logic of Evangelism* (Grand Rapids: Eerdmans, 1989), 212.

[47]Gerald H. Anderson raises this possibility by way of criticism of the new Catholic position in a book he edited with Thomas F. Stransky, *Christ's Lordship and Religious Pluralism* (Maryknoll, N.Y.: Orbis, 1981), 110–20.

[48]Heinz R. Schlette, *Towards a Theology of Religions* (London: Burns & Oates, 1965).

[49]Miikka Ruokanen, "Catholic Teaching on Non-Christian Religions at the Second Vatican Council," *International Bulletin of Missionary Research*, April 1990, 56–61.

[50]For the Trinity as an open and dynamic model of God, see Jurgen Moltmann, *The Trinity and the Kingdom* (San Francisco: Harper & Row, 1981). On prevenient grace, see H. Ray Dunning, *Grace, Faith and Holiness: A Wesleyan Systematic Theology* (Kansas City: Beacon Hill, 1988).

[51]J. Dupuis, "The Cosmic Christ in the Early Fathers," *Indian Journal of Theology*, 15 (1966), 106–20.

[52]This truth lies behind what Don Richardson shares about the work of God in pagan civilizations in *Eternity in their Hearts* (Ventura, Calif.: Regal, 1984).

[53]Stanley J. Grenz alerts us that a non-filioque doctrine of the Spirit is central to Pannenberg's unfolding systematic theology. *Reason for Hope: The Systematic Theology of Wolfhart Pannenberg* (New York: Oxford Univ. Press, 1990), 51, 110, 215.

[54]Georges Khodr, "Christianity in a Pluralistic World—The Economy of the Holy Spirit," *Ecumenical Review*, 23 (1971), 118–28. David Wells recognizes the presence of the Spirit and of the Trinity itself in the world, but denies God is present to work redemption. David F. Wells, *God the Evangelist* (Grand Rapids: Eerdmans, 1987), 24.

[55]Vatican Two's *Dogmatic Constitution on the Church* places its open and positive attitude on the foundation of a theology of the Trinity, chap. 1.

CHAPTER 3

[1]Martin Luther, *Collected Works* (Weimar), 40, 2, 111.

[2]Few evangelicals have written on other religions. Among them are J. N. D. Anderson, *Christianity and Other Religions*; Robert Brow, *Religion: Origins and Ideas* (Chicago: InterVarsity, 1966); and Ajith Fernando, *The Christian's Attitude Toward World Religions*.

[3]This is the thesis of Paul Kurtz, *The Transcendental Temptation: A Critique of Religion and the Paranormal* (Buffalo, N.Y.: Prometheus, 1986).

[4]I appreciate Hans Küng's great sensitivity in all these matters; *Theology for the Third Millennium: An Ecumenical View* (New York: Doubleday, 1987), 227–56.

[5]Paul Tillich, *Christianity and the Encounter of the World Religions* (New York: Columbia Univ. Press, 1963), 4f.

[6]Evangelicals see the darkness of religions but seldom the positive side. One such is David F. Wells, *God the Evangelist* (Grand Rapids: Eerdmans, 1987), 18–24.

[7]The Council did this in its *Declaration on the Relationship of the Church to Non-Christian Religions.*

[8]See Joseph Blenkinsopp, "Yahweh and Other Deities: Conflict and Accommodation in the Religion of Israel," *Interpretation*, 42 (1988), 354–66. Jack Finnegan, *Myth and Mystery: An Introduction to the Pagan Religions of the Biblical World* (Grand Rapids: Baker, 1989); and John W. Wenham, *The Goodness of God* (Downers Grove, Ill.: InterVarsity, 1974), chap. 8.

[9]An excellent source of information about all these matters is Mircea Eliade, editor, *The Encyclopedia of Religion*, 16 volumes (New York: Macmillan, 1987).

[10]Susanne Heine, *Matriarchs, Goddesses, and Images of God: A Critique of a Feminist Theology* (Minneapolis: Augsburg, 1989).

[11]See Hendrikus Berkhof, "The Way of Israel in the Old Testament," chap. 29, in *Christian Faith* (Grand Rapids: Eerdmans, 1979).

[12]Gregory Baum, "The Ambiguity of Religion: A Biblical Account," chap. 4 in *Religion and Alienation: A Theological Reading of Sociology* (New York: Paulist, 1975).

[13]Robert L. Wilken, "Religious Pluralism and Early Christian Theology," *Interpretation*, 44 (1988), 379–91.

[14]John Hick, *An Interpretation of Religion: Human Responses to the Transcendent* (New Haven: Yale Univ. Press, 1989), 22–29.

[15]Alfred Metraux, *Voodoo in Haiti* (New York: Oxford Univ. Press, 1959).

[16]Lesslie Newbigin, *The Open Secret* (Grand Rapids: Eerdmans, 1978), chap. 10.

[17]Bruce Demarest, *General Revelation* (Grand Rapids: Zondervan, 1982), 244–47.

[18]Michael Green, chap. 6, "Counterfeit Religion," in *I Believe in Satan's Downfall* (Grand Rapids: Eerdmans, 1981).

[19]Jean Danielou cites Gregory in *Holy Pagans of the Old Testament* (London: Longmans, Green, 1957), 4.

[20]Hick, *God Has Many Names*, (London: Macmillan, 1980), 5, and *An Interpretation of Religion*, 300–03.

[21]Jack Finnegan, *Myth and Mystery: An Introduction to the Pagan Religions of the Biblical World*, 37f, 63f, 115ff.

[22] Raymond E. Brown, *The Birth of the Messiah* (New York: Doubleday, 1977), 165–201.

[23]John R. W. Stott acknowledges that this interpretation is possible, but opts for a reduced sense. He takes the term "accepted" to mean only that God prefers righteous behavior to unrighteous, but not that God accepts or

justifies pagans by faith (Stott, *The Spirit, The Church, and The World* [Downers Grove, Ill.: InterVarsity, 1990], 198f.).

[24]Hendrik M. Vroom, "Do All Religious Traditions Worship the Same God?" *Religious Studies*, 26 (1990), 88.

[25]John Hick, chap. 18, "The Ethical Criterion," in *An Interpretation of Religion*.

[26]*Dogmatic Constitution on the Church*, chap. 16.

[27]José Miranda, *Marx and the Bible* (Maryknoll, N.Y.: Orbis, 1974), 44–53.

[28]C. S. Lewis, *Mere Christianity* (London: Collins, 1952). Cf. "tao" in Book 1.

[29]Lewis, *The Last Battle* (London: Penguin, 1956), 149.

[30]Richard H. Drummond, *Gautama the Buddha* (Grand Rapids: Eerdmans, 1974) and Stuart C. Hackett, *Oriental Philosophy* (Madison, Wis.: Univ. of Wisconsin Press, 1979), chap. 3.

[31]Gavin D'Costa refers to these two examples in *Theology and Religious Pluralism* (Oxford: Basil Blackwell, 1986), 62f.

[32]Hans Küng, *Christianity and the World Religions: Paths to Dialogue With Islam, Hinduism, and Buddhism* (New York: Doubleday, 1986), 24–28.

[33]Norman L. Geisler, *Philosophy of Religion* (Grand Rapids: Zondervan, 1974), part 1, and Wolfhart Pannenberg, whose theology is rooted in the religious nature of humankind. See Stanley J. Grenz, *Reason for Hope: The Systematic Theology of Wolfhart Pannenberg* (N.Y.: Oxford Univ. Press, 1990), 12.

[34]Benjamin W. Farley, *The Providence of God* (Grand Rapids: Baker, 1988), 4, 16, 31, 230.

[35]On the Logos doctrine, see Robert D. Young, *Encounter With World Religions* (Philadelphia: Westminster, 1970).

[36] Carl E. Braaten and Robert W. Jenson, editors *Christian Dogmatics* II (Philadelphia: Fortress, 1984), on the cosmic work of the Spirit, 165–78, and also Walter Kasper, *The God of Jesus Christ* (New York: Crossroad, 1986), 227–29.

[37]See Bruce A. Demarest, *General Revelation: Historical Views and Contemporary Issues* (Grand Rapids: Zondervan, 1982).

[38]Dale Moody, *The World of Truth* (Grand Rapids: Eerdmans, 1981), 59.

[39]Charles Ryrie, *Dispensationalism Today* (Chicago: Moody, 1965), 123.

[40]Karl Barth, *Church Dogmatics*, I/2, chap. 17, and Karl Rahner, *Theological Investigations*, 5, chap. 6.

[41]Michael Green, *Evangelism Through the Local Church* (London: Hodder & Stoughton, 1990), chap. 3.

[42]Richard J. Plantinga, *The Relationship Between Christianity and Non-Christian Religions in the Thought of Hendrik Kraemer* (M. A. thesis McMaster University, 1985), and Richard H. Drummond, *Toward A New Age in Christian Theology* (Maryknoll, N. Y.: Orbis, 1985), 114–18.

[43]On the Roman Catholic positions, see Lucien Richard, *What Are They Saying About Christ and World Religions?* (New York: Paulist, 1981), chap. 2.

[44]What else can be said about Paul Knitter when he jettisons the classical consensus on Christology? *No Other Name?* (Maryknoll, N. Y.: Orbis, 1985), chap. 9.

[45]James D. G. Dunn, *Jesus and the Spirit* (London: SCM, 1975), 291–300.

[46]W. C. Smith, *The Meaning and End of Religion* (New York: Macmillan, 1962).

[47]Smith's background in Methodism may be showing here in the distinction between heart religion and the institution. Cracknell, *Towards a New Relationship* (London: Epworth, 1986), 56f.

[48]Compare Schubert M. Ogden, *Christ Without Myth* (New York: Harper & Row, 1961), 153.

CHAPTER 4

[1]Gavin D'Costa discusses this feature of Kraemer's theology in *Theology and Religious Pluralism* (Oxford: Blackwell, 1986), 60–64.

[2]This emphasis is central to the work of Wolfhart Pannenberg; see his *Theology and the Kingdom of God* (Philadelphia: Westminster, 1969).

[3]Thomas Finger, *Christian Theology: An Eschatological Approach* II (Scottdale, Pa.: Herald, 1989), chap. 12, "Mission Amid Other Religions and Worldview."

[4]In Wayne C. Booth's unusual terminology this makes me a monist in the area of truth; *Critical Understanding: The Powers and Limits of Pluralism* (Chicago: Univ. of Chicago, 1979), 12–17. A monist, in his classification, is one who believes in objective truth, that views of God and reality will eventually be confirmed or falsified.

[5]Brian Hebblethwaite, *The Ocean of Truth: A Defense of Objective Theism* (Cambridge: Cambridge Univ., 1988), chap. 8, "Religions—Theistic and Non-Theistic."

[6]Wolfhart Pannenberg, *Basic Questions in Theology*, II (Philadelphia: Fortress, 1971), 113.

[7]G. R. Beasley-Murray, *Jesus and the Kingdom of God* (Grand Rapids: Eerdmans, 1986) and Anthony A. Hoekema, *The Bible and the Future* (Grand Rapids: Eerdmans, 1979).

[8]John R. W. Stott, *Our Guilty Silence* (Downers Grove, Ill.: InterVarsity, 1967).

[9]Oscar Cullmann, *Christ and Time: The Primitive Christian Conception of Time and History* (London: SCM, 1951), 157.

[10]Since this is a time when people in the West generally discount the demonic, I should refer the reader to two authors who do not: the books of Jeffery B. Russell, *The Devil: Perceptions of Evil from Antiquity to Primitive Christianity* (Ithaca: Cornell Univ., 1977); *Satan: The Early Christian Tradition* (Ithaca: Cornell Univ., 1981); *Lucifer: The Devil in the Middle Ages* (Ithaca: Cornell Univ., 1984); *Mephistopheles: The Devil in the Modern World* (Ithaca: Cornell Univ., 1986); *The Prince of Darkness: Radical Evil and the Power of Good in History* (Ithaca: Cornell Univ., 1988); and the trilogy of Walter Wink, *Naming the Powers* (Philadelphia: Fortress, 1984), *Unmasking the Powers* (Philadelphia: Fortress, 1986), and *Engaging the Powers* (Philadelphia: Fortress, 1989).

[11]Calvin R. Schoonhoven, *The Wrath of Heaven* (Grand Rapids: Eerdmans, 1966), chap. 2, "Heaven and the Power of Evil."

[12]Robert Webber, *The Church in the World: Opposition, Tension, or Transformation* (Grand Rapids: Zondervan, 1986).

[13]The best book remains Hendrikus Berkhof, *Christ and the Powers* (Scottdale, Pa.: Herald, 1962).

[14]Walter Wink sees the potential when he includes a chapter "The Gods" in *Unmasking the Powers*, 108–207.

[15]The first Christian systematic theology was the Christus Victor motif of the early Greek fathers, as pointed to by Gustaf Aulen, *Christus Victor* (London: SPCK, 1953).

[16]Paul G. Hiebert, *Anthropological Insights for Missionaries* (Grand Rapids: Baker, 1985), chap. 5.

[17]Hendrik M. Vroom, *Religions and the Truth* (Grand Rapids: Eerdmans, 1989), 379f.

[18]Eugene Hillman, *Many Paths: A Catholic Approach to Religious Pluralism* (Maryknoll, N. Y.: Orbis, 1989), chap. 1, "Religion, a Component of Culture."

[19]Vroom, *Religions and the Truth*, 103–45.

[20]Ibid., 146–84.

[21]Finger, *Christian Theology: An Eschatological Approach*, II, 315.

[22]Mark Heim, *Is Christ the Only Way?* (Valley Forge: Judson, 1985), 42–50.

[23]Daniel Isaac Block, *The Gods of the Nations: Studies in Ancient Near Eastern National Theology* (Jackson, Miss.: Evangelical Theological Society, 1988).

[24]John T. Seamands, *Tell It Well: Communicating the Gospel Across Cultures* (Kansas City: Beacon Hill, 1981), 22f.

[25]Peter L. Berger, *The Capitalist Revolution* (New York: Basic, 1986), 215.

[26]Hendrikus Berkhof handles these matters well; *Christian Faith* (Grand Rapids: Eerdmans, 1979), chap. 52–55.

[27]What gives process theism credibility is its view that the deity faces opposition and struggles against resistance to bring good out of evil. The Bible agrees that God is not at present effectively sovereign, but handles the issue from the standpoint of spiritual warfare and not cosmological dualism. David R. Griffin, *God, Power and Evil: A Process Theodicy* (Philadelphia: Westminster, 1976), chap. 18.

[28]Jay Newman, *Competition in Religious Life* (Waterloo, Ont.: Wildrid Laurier Univ., 1989).

[29]Ibid., 212f.

[30]Ibid., 214.

[31]Kurt Koch, *Between Christ and Satan* (Grand Rapids: Kregel, 1966), and John W. Montgomery, editor, *Demon Possession: A Medical, Historical, Anthropological and Theological Symposium* (Minneapolis: Bethany, 1976).

[32]John Wimber calls this "power evangelism" in his book entitled *Powr Evangelism: Signs and Wonders Today* (London: Hodder & Stoughton, 1985). Its practice in the context of folk Islam is discussed by Vivienne Stacey, "Practice of Exorcism and Healing," in J. Dudley Woodberry, editor, *Muslims and Christians on the Emmaus Road* (Monrovia, Calif.: MARC, 1989), 291–303.

[33]In case it escaped notice, this book is highly competitive in an area in which major differences of opinion exist. I make no apology for that—it is as it should be.

[34]An indispensable book in mission and its activities is William J. Abraham, *The Logic of Evangelism* (Grand Rapids: Eerdmans, 1989).

[35]John R. W. Stott, *Christian Mission in the Modern World* (Downers Grove, Ill.: InterVarsity, 1975), and Donald C. Posterski, *Reinventing Evangelism* (Downers Grove, Ill.: InterVarsity, 1989).

[36]F. F. Bruce, *Commentary on the Epistle to the Colossians* (London: Marshall, Morgan & Scott, 1957), 171.

[37]On this philosophy of ministry, see Richard N. Longenecker, *Paul Apostle of Liberty* (New York: Harper & Row, 1964), chap. 10.

[38]On the nature of dialogue, William C. Placher, *Unapologetic Theology: A Christian Voice in a Pluralistic Conversation* (Louisville, Ky.: Westminster/John Knox, 1989), 143–49.

[39]On the dialogue of worldviews, see Norman L. Geisler, *Christian Apologetics* (Grand Rapids: Baker, 1976).

[40]D. Martyn Lloyd-Jones, *Preaching and Preachers* (London: Hodder & Stoughton, 1971), 46f.

[41]James Beverley calls attention to such problems with dialogue in his Th. M. thesis, *The World Council of Churches' Programme of Dialogue with People of Living Faiths and Ideologies: A Critical Analysis* (Univ. of Toronto, 1983).

[42]Peter L. Berger, *The Heretical Imperative: Contemporary Possibilities of Religious Affirmation* (London: Collins, 1980), chap. 6.

[43]Hans Küng, *Christianity and the World Religions* (New York: Doubleday, 1986), xviii.

[44]On relativism and dialogue, see Wolfhart Pannenberg, *Theology and the Philosophy of Science* (Philadelphia: Westminster, 1976), chap. 4–5; David K. Clark and Norman L. Geisler, *Apologetics in the New Age: A Christian Critique of Pantheism* (Grand Rapids: Baker, 1990), 198–202; and Arnulf Camps, *Partners in Dialogue: Christianity and Other World Religions* (Maryknoll, N.Y.: Orbis, 1983), 27–30.

[45]John Hick, *Faith and Knowledge* (Ithaca, N.Y.: Cornell Univ., 1957).

[46]John Hick, *Evil and the God of Love* (New York: Harper & Row, 1966), chap. 17.

[47]Brian Hebblethwaite, *Ocean of Truth*, 120–22.

[48]I see that hope in *Death and Eternal Life* (London: Collins, 1976), chap. 22. Joseph Campbell holds a fully Eastern concept of deity, beyond personality, beyond good and evil.

[49]Hans Küng, *Theology for the Third Millennium: An Ecumenical View* (New York: Doubleday, 1988), 234f.

[50]Jay Newman, *Foundations of Religious Tolerance* (Toronto: Univ. of Toronto, 1982), chap. 3.

[51]On fideism, see William J. Abraham, *An Introduction to the Philosophy of Religion* (Englewood Cliffs, N.J.: Prentice-Hall, 1985), chap. 7–8.

[52]The data is rehearsed in the debate between Antony Flew and Gary Habermas, *Did Jesus Rise From the Dead?: The Resurrection Debate* (San Francisco: Harper and Row, 1987).

[53]Compare Stott's cautious remarks, *Christian Mission in the Modern World*, 60, and M. Darrol Brant, editor, *Pluralism, Tolerance and Dialogue: Six Studies* (Waterloo, Ont.: Univ. of Waterloo, 1989).

[54]William A. Christian, *Oppositions of Religious Doctrines: A Study in the Logic of Dialogue Among Religions* (New York: Herder and Herder, 1972).

[55]For comparison, Robert B. Sheard, *Interreligious Dialogue in the Catholic Church Since Vatican II: A Historical and Theological Study* (Lewiston/Queenston: Edwin Mellen, 1987).

[56]Richard J. Mouw, *When the Kings Come Marching In: Isaiah and the New Jerusalem* (Grand Rapids: Eerdmans, 1983), 19.

[57]George Lindbeck, *The Nature of Doctrine* (Philadelphia: Westminster Press, 1984), 61.

[58]Stuart C. Hackett, *The Reconstruction of the Christian Revelation Claim* (Grand Rapids: Baker, 1984), 249f, and *Oriental Philosophy: A Westerner's Guide to Eastern Thought* (Madison: Univ. of Wisconsin, 1979).

[59]Paul Kurtz, for example, *The Transcendental Temptation: A Critique of Religion and the Paranormal* (Buffalo, N. Y.: Prometheus, 1986).

[60]Herman E. Daly and John B. Cobb, *For the Common Good: Redirecting the Economy Toward Community, The Environment, and A Sustainable Future* (Boston: Beacon, 1989), chap. 20. This is the concern of others also such as Richard J. Neuhaus, *The Naked Public Square: Religion and Democracy in America* (Grand Rapids: Eerdmans, 1984).

[61]Arnulf Camps, *Partners in Dialogue: Christianity and Other World Religions* (Maryknoll, N. Y.: Orbis, 1983), chap. 13, "The Renewing Force of a Dialogic Approach."

[62]Richard F. Lovelace, *Dynamics of Spiritual Life: An Evangelical Theology of Renewal* (Downers Grove, Ill.: InterVarsity, 1979) on theological integration, 172–84. And Gavin D'Costa, *Theology and Religious Pluralism*, 121–25.

[63]From the Foreword to John V. Taylor, *The Primal Vision: Christians Amid African Religion* (Philadelphia: Fortress, 1963), 10f.

[64]For an example of what can be done, Paul V. Martinson, *A Theology of World Religions: Interpreting God, Self, and World in Semitic, Indian, and Chinese Thought* (Minneapolis: Augsburg, 1987).

[65]David Novak, *Jewish-Christian Dialogue: A Jewish Justification* (New York: Oxford Univ. Press, 1989), 140f.

[66]Allan Brockway, editor, *The Theology of the Churches and the Jewish People: Statements by the World Council of Churches and Its Member Churches* (Geneva: World Council of Churches, 1988).

[67]Donald A. Hagner, *The Jewish Reclamation of Jesus* (Grand Rapids: Zondervan, 1984), chap. 7.

[68]Pinchas Lapide, *The Resurrection of Jesus: A Jewish Perspective* (Minneapolis: Augsburg, 1983).

[69]Kenneth A. Myers, "Adjusting Theology in the Shadow of Auschwitz," *Christianity Today*, Oct. 8, 1990, 41–43.

[70]Stuart E. Brown, *The Nearest in Affection: Towards A Christian Understanding of Islam* (Geneva: World Council of Churches, 1990).

⁷¹J. Dudley Woodberry, editor, *Muslims and Christians on the Emmaus Road*, chap. 6–10.

⁷²W. Montgomery Watt, *Islam and Christianity: A Contribution to Dialogue* (London: Routledge & Kegan Paul, 1983).

⁷³Hans Küng, "Christianity and World Religions, Dialogue with Islam," in Leonard Swidler, editor, *Toward a Universal Theology of Religion* (Maryknoll, N.Y.: Orbis, 1987), 192–209.

⁷⁴Harold Coward, editor, *Hindu-Christian Dialogue: Perspectives and Encounters* (Maryknoll, N.Y.: Orbis, 1990). Roger H. Hooker, *Themes in Hinduism and Christianity: A Comparative Study* (New York: Peter Lang, 1989).

⁷⁵Richard H. Drummond, *Gautama the Buddha: An Essay in Religious Understanding* (Grand Rapids: Eerdmans, 1974).

⁷⁶Such questions are posed by Hans Küng in *On Being A Christian* (London: Collins, 1977), 106–09.

⁷⁷Hans Küng, *The Church* (New York: Sheed and Ward, 1967), 79–104.

CHAPTER 5

¹John Gerstner, "Heathen, Fate of" in *Baker's Dictionary of Theology* (Grand Rapids: Baker, 1960), 263f.

²It is not a problem for Augustinians, who do not believe God is obliged to treat people fairly with respect to the opportunity of salvation.

³Catholic concern is expressed by Riccardo Lombardi, *The Salvation of the Unbeliever* (London: Burns & Oates, 1956), and evangelical concern is expressed by William V. Crockett and James G. Sigountos, *Through No Fault of Their Own* (Grand Rapids: Baker, 1991) and John Sanders, *No Other Name! A Biblical, Historical, and Theological Investigation into the Destiny of the Unevangelized* (Grand Rapids: Eerdmans, 1992).

⁴Quoted by Augustine in a letter to Deogratias; Philip Schaff, editor, *Nicene and Post-Nicene Fathers*, series 1, vol. I, 416.

⁵Elton Trueblood, *Philosophy of Religion* (New York: Harper & Row, 1957), 221f.

⁶David L. Edwards and John R. W. Stott, *Essentials: A Liberal-Evangelical Dialogue* (London: Hodder & Stoughton, 1988), 327f.

⁷Paul E. Sigmund, *Liberation Theology at the Crossroads: Democracy or Revolution?* (New York: Oxford Univ. Press, 1990).

⁸Wolfhart Pannenberg, "Can Christianity Do Without Eschatology?" in G. B. Caird, *The Christian Hope* (London: SPCK, 1970), 31.

⁹There are notable exceptions, though. For example, Abraham Kuyper, *Lectures on Calvinism* (Grand Rapids: Eerdmans, 1953), 59f.

[10]Lesslie Newbigin, *The Finality of Christ* (London: SCM, 1969), 61f, and *The Open Secret* (Grand Rapids: Eerdmans, 1978), 88, 195f.

[11]Joachim Jeremias, *Jesus' Promise to the Nations* (London: SCM, 1958), 57–73.

[12]J. N. D. Anderson, *Christianity and World Religions: The Challenge of Pluralism* (Downers Grove, Ill.: InterVarsity, 1984), 162–69.

[13]Tasker, *The Gospel According to the St. Matthew* (London: Tyndale, 1961), 69.

[14]John A. T. Robinson, *In the End, God* (London: James Clarke, 1950), chap. 9.

[15]Jacques Ellul, *What I Believe* (Grand Rapids: Eerdmans, 1989), 192. It is common to draw upon coercive thinking in a pinch. Baptists do it at the point of eternal security, if not ordinarily.

[16]J. I. Packer, "The Problems of Universalism," *Bibliotheca Sacra*, 130, (1973), 3–11, and Robert A. Morey, *Death and the Afterlife* (Minneapolis: Bethany, 1984), chap. 9.

[17]Stephen Travis, *I Believe in the Second Coming of Christ*, (Grand Rapids: Eerdmans, 1982), 194–96.

[18]David Edwards and John Stott, *Essentials: A Liberal-Evangelical Dialogue*, 313–20. For other references, see Pinnock, "The Destruction of the Finally Impenitent," *Criswell Theological Review*, 4 (1990), 243–59.

[19]E. G. Selwyn, *The First Epistle of Peter* (London: Macmillan, 1961), 358. The best defense of this view is Edward Fudge, *The Fire That Consumes: A Biblical and Historical Study of Final Punishment* (Houston: Providential Press, 1982).

[20]Geoffrey W. Bromiley, editor, *Zwingli and Bullinger*, in the *Library of Christian Classics* (Philadelphia: Westminster, 1953), 275f.

[21]John Wesley, *The Works of John Wesley* (Peabody, Mass.: Hendricksen, 1986), vol. VI, 286, and vol. VII, 196–99, 258, 353.

[22]A. H. Strong, *Systematic Theology* (Philadelphia: Judson, 11th edition, 1947), 842.

[23]Stuart C. Hackett, *The Reconstruction of the Christian Revelation Claim* (Grand Rapids: Baker, 1984), 244.

[24]Among many other evangelicals who agree, let me refer to John E. Sanders, "Is Belief in Christ Necessary for Salvation?" *Evangelical Quarterly*, 60 (1988): 241–59; Joseph M. Ferrante, "The Final Destiny of Those Who Have Not Heard the Gospel," *Trinity Studies*, 2 (1980): 55–62; Evert D. Osburn, "Those Who Have Never Heard: Have They No Hope?" *Journal of the Evangelical Theological Society*, 32 (1989): 367–72.

[25]Charles H. Kraft, on those who are pre-Christian in their understanding, *Christianity in Culture* (Maryknoll, N.Y.: Orbis Books, 1979), 253–57.

[26]So Richard Swinburne, *Responsibility and Atonement* (Oxford: Clarendon Press, 1989), 190–92.

[27]William L. Craig supports the idea of middle knowledge and applies it to this case in Pinnock, editor, *The Grace of God, The Will of Man* (Grand Rapids: Zondervan, 1989), 141–64.

[28]Charles C. Ryrie, *Dispensationalism Today* (Chicago: Moody Press, 1965), 123.

[29]Bruce A. Demarest, *General Revelation* (Grand Rapids, Zondervan, 1982), 260.

[30]J. I. Packer, *Evangelical Affirmations*, edited by Carl F. H. Henry and Kenneth S. Kantzer (Grand Rapids: Zondervan, 1990), 123.

[31]Millard Erickson, *Christian Theology* (Grand Rapids: Baker, 1983), 173.

[32]J. N. D. Anderson, *Christianity and World Religions*, 144.

[33]I used to take this view, following T. W. Manson, *The Sayings of Jesus* (London: SCM, 1949), 249–51, and George E. Ladd, *Jesus and the Kingdom* (New York: Harper and Row, 1964), 313.

[34]Robert H. Gundry, *Matthew: A Commentary on His Literary and Theological Art* (Grand Rapids: Eerdmans, 1982), 511–16.

[35]George R. Beasley-Murray cites several such parallels in Jewish and even Egyptian texts; *Jesus and the Kingdom of God* (Grand Rapids: Eerdmans, 1986), 308f.

[36]Joachim Jeremias, *Jesus' Promise to the Nations*, 47f.

[37]This is Beasley-Murray's view in *Jesus and the Kingdom of God*, 310f.

[38]Matthew Henry, *Commentary on the Whole Bible* (New York: Fleming H. Revell, n.d.), VI, 133.

[39]John R. W. Stott, *The Spirit, The Church, and The World* (Downers Grove, Ill.: InterVarsity Press, 1990), 198f. Calvin appears though to regard Cornelius as a true believer illumined by the Spirit as a non-Christian. See his *Institutes*, bk. 3, chap. 17, par. 4.

[40]Robertson McQuilken, *The Great Omission* (Grand Rapids: Baker, 1984).

[41]Karl Rahner, editor, *Sacramentum Mundi* (New York: Herder and Herder, 1966), I, "Baptism of Desire," 144–46.

[42]B. B. Warfield, "The Development of the Doctrine of Infant Salvation" in *Studies in Theology* (New York: Oxford Univ. Press, 1932). See also Robert P. Lightner, *Heaven for Those Who Can't Believe* (Schaumberg, Ill.: Regular Baptist Press, 1977). Unfortunately, Lightner limits "those who can't believe" to infants.

[43]Karl Rahner, *Theological Investigations*, V, 120.

[44]J. A. MacCullough, *The Harrowing of Hell* (Edinburgh: T. & T. Clark, 1930), chap. 15.

[45]C. E. B. Cranfield thinks so, "The Interpretation of 1 Peter 3:19 and 4:6," *Expository Times* 69 (1958): 369–72.

[46]Wolfhart Pannenberg, *The Apostles' Creed in the Light of Today's Questions* (Philadelphia: Westminster, 1972), 95.

[47]George R. Beasley-Murray, *Baptism in the New Testament* (Grand Rapids: Eerdmans, 1962), 258. Hans Küng doubts whether the descent into hell means that. See his *Eternal Life?* (New York: Doubleday, 1984), 124–29.

[48]Cranfield, "The Interpretation of 1 Peter 3:19 and 4:6," 378.

[49]Donald G. Bloesch, *The Future of Evangelical Christianity, A Call for Unity Amid Diversity* (Garden City, N.Y.: Doubleday, 1983), 121; and, Carl E. Braaten, "Lutheran Theology and Religious Pluralism," *Lutheran World Federation* 23–24 (1988): 109–24.

[50]George Lindbeck, *The Nature of Doctrine* (Philadelphia: Westminster, 1984), 55–63.

[51]"There would be no everlasting punishment of the souls of the damned if they were able to change their will for a better will." (*Contra Gentiles* 4.93.2.) Aquinas did not think they would do so, but the point is right. They are rejected for their choices, not God's.

[52]Russell F. Adlwinkle, *Jesus—A Savior or The Savior?* (Macon, Ga.: Mercer Univ. Press, 1982), 211.

[53]This is practically a defining characteristic of conservative-evangelical theology. See, for example, Lorraine Boettner, *The Reformed Doctrine of Predestination*, (Philadelphia: Presbyterian and Reformed, 1965), 119; Dick Dowsett, *God, That's Not Fair!* (Toronto: OMF, 1982), 39; Ajith Fernando, *The Christian's Attitude Toward World Religions* (Wheaton, Ill.: Tyndale House, 1987), 132; Dick Hillis, *Are the Heathen Really Lost?* (Chicago: Moody Press, 1961), chap. 8; and Robert H. Gundry, "Salvation According to Scripture: No Middle Ground," *Christianity Today*, Dec. 9, 1977.

[54]E. C. Dewick, *The Christian Attitude to Other Religions* (London: Cambridge Univ. Press, 1953), 125.

[55]William J. Abraham, in *The Logic of Evangelism* (Grand Rapids: Eerdmans, 1989), discusses these various activities of mission.

[56]Jurgen Moltmann, *The Church in the Power of the Holy Spirit* (London: SCM, 1977), 152.

[57]Gustaf Aulen, *The Faith of the Christian Church* (Philadelphia: Muhlenberg Press, 1948). See "The Wrath of Love," 139–41.

Index of Subjects

Index of Scripture

215